THIS *SPECIES* OF *PROPERTY*

THIS *SPECIES* OF *PROPERTY*

Slave Life and Culture in the Old South

Leslie Howard Owens

OXFORD UNIVERSITY PRESS

Oxford New York

Copyright © 1976 by Oxford University Press, Inc.
First published by Oxford University Press,
New York, 1976
First issued as an Oxford University Press
paperback, 1977
printing, last digit: 20 19 18 17 16 15 14 13 12 11

Library of Congress Cataloging in Publication Data

Owens, Leslie Howard.
This species of property.

Includes bibliographical references and index.
1. Slavery in the United States—Condition of slaves.
2. Slavery in the United States—Southern States.
3. Southern States—Social conditions. I. Title.
E443.09 1977   301.44'93'0973   77-2741
ISBN 0-19-502245-9 pbk.

Printed in the United States of America

For my Mother, Father and Family

Preface

The black experience in slavery is one of the most poignant in American and world history. And anyone who sets out to investigate that experience quickly sees that there is a great deal to learn about the human behavior of slavery's participants and also about himself or herself. The task, though certainly never dull, is often frustrating and perplexing. The available evidence, even in its most varied forms, is at best fragmentary and often difficult to utilize. Slaves have left us with few written records, though the results of their labors and cultural creations are very helpful in understanding their side of bondage's story.

The question any non-participant in slavery would like to answer is, how did it feel to be a slave? In truth, we can never know this even when we try to see bondage from the slave's viewpoint. My hope has been to try to get inside the slave's experience as much as possible, to convey a mood as well as offer an analysis of slave life. I hope that for most of my readers mood and analysis are inseparable as they began to be for me after a time. For the slave one mood, arising from the sense of his existence as property, seemed to dominate all others, and I have tried to capture this both in the title of my study and the pages that follow. The ex-slave Solomon Northup expressed it like this: "He [a slaveholder] looked upon a colored man, not as a human being, responsible to his Creator for the small talent entrusted to him, but as a 'chattel personal,' as mere live property, no better, except in value, then his mule or dog." There were exceptions to this observation, but for the slave his status as property was a dominating consideration.

I would like to offer what for some have become the traditional thanks for assistance or advice given in the preparation of one's study. Traditional recognition is not my intent here, and the people that I mention will understand this. Professor Hal Bridges listened to my early thoughts in his office with that narrow window. Occasionally the sun shone there. The "Dean" helped too even when he didn't know it, and Ron N. and Mark W. at least didn't discourage me. Gary H. was a help too. I am grateful to all of them. My engaging wife, Irma, knows how many thanks I owe her. In the final stages of publication two people at Oxford were most gracious: Stephanie Golden and Susan Rabiner. I fully appreciate their assistance. In a larger sense, too, I owe a great deal of thanks to those black historians and researchers whose earlier efforts continue to reveal their importance as the years pass.

Ann Arbor, Michigan   L. H. O.

Contents

Were it not then that I am principled against selling negroes, as you would do cattle at a market, I would not in twelve months hence, be possessed of a single one as a slave. I shall be happily mistaken if they are not found to be a very trouble some species of property ere many years have passed over our heads (but this by the bye)—. . . .

George Washington to General Alex.
Spotswood, November 23, 1794

THIS *SPECIES* OF *PROPERTY*

Introduction
".. . The Necessity of Bondage"

In the winter of 1845, John C. Calhoun penned a letter as secretary of state to J. W. Jones, speaker of the House of Representatives, in which he reflected back to the Census of 1840, the first to have surveyed the state of mental health in the nation. Calhoun wrote with particular reference to the higher level of insanity reported "among . . . free blacks" in northern states as compared with slaves in the Old South. His argument was direct. Freedom for the "negro or African race . . . would be, indeed, to them a curse instead of a blessing." It would cause an alarming rise in the number of black mental cases, and thereby inconvenience society at large, as well as the black community.[1]

Calhoun was merely confirming in this letter a stand he had taken several years earlier when the survey first appeared. Its findings had struck him even then as most noteworthy: "Here is proof of the necessity of bondage. The African is incapable of self-care and sinks into lunacy under the burden of freedom. It is a mercy to him to give him the guardianship and protection from mental death."[2] Relying heavily on the Census Bureau's findings, Calhoun concluded that the slave's mental development, even as an adult, was as delicately balanced as a child's and needed constant

3

guidance to prevent it from self-injury. Although some of his contemporaries argued that their own detailed examinations of the survey's data showed these conclusions to be unproved, Calhoun, little inclined toward a critical approach on matters relating to slavery, answered that errors in the survey, "if they exist," did not substantively affect the "correctness of the general result. . . ."[3] So influential a force in southern and national society was Calhoun as a result of his powerful advocacy of the state of South Carolina's rights against the federal government he now served that these arguments, based on a discredited census survey, gave even some antagonists of slavery cause for reflection.

As both heir to and perpetuator of those southern racial myths that have a familiar ring even today, Calhoun helped entrench the vocabulary of Southern bigotry. Others, however, picked up the torch he passed on, many in the name of scholarship. Nearly one hundred years later, for instance, the well-known historian James G. Randall, although no advocate of bondage, reinforced the long-held southern position that the black man was somehow especially suited to a life of enforced toil. In 1937 Randall wrote, "In contrast to other races, the Negro adapted himself to bondage with a minimum of resistance, doing cheerfully the manual work of the South and loyally serving those who held him in chains."[4] Still another historian, Stanley M. Elkins, focusing twenty-two years later on the racial stereotype "Sambo," indicated that this Sambo, with his childlike mannerisms was an adequate and justifiable characterization of the bondsman. The harsh slave system, he argued, fundamentally altered personality, producing a slave type.[5] Subsequent research has discredited many of the earlier and harsher interpretations of the slave mentality, those who advanced them having been charged with permitting racial biases to distort their judgment. But the ostensibly kinder portrayal of blacks as Sambos proves to be more difficult to combat. Partially sustained by a popular lore that fed on its delightful images, this conception of the slave has, in fact, gained too wide a following in historical and non-historical literature to be easily knocked down, despite the fact that hypothesizing a bondage that

4

would produce such Sambo figures requires the purposeful omission of many other conclusions drawn from solid analyses of slave conditions.

If the bondsman, then, was neither a Sambo figure nor a loyal and cheerful slave, what was he really like? Surprisingly, in the long history of writings on slavery, few scholars have critically examined the slave himself in any detail.[6] As a consequence, the bondsman remains largely an enigma down to our day. Was his behavior unavoidably marked by "infantile silliness and his talk inflated with childish exaggeration,"[7] and did he merely act the clown "in order to win the maximum rewards within the system"?[8] Unless one first familiarizes oneself with all the information that has come out in the often acrimonious debate on the slave's makeup, a truer picture of the slave and new insights into a variety of other important slavery issues are not possible.[9]

A reading of slave sources suggests interpretations of the slave that differ markedly from the venerable Sambo. In fact, the Sambo figure as the typical representative of southern slavery would seem to be a major distortion unacceptable even to slaveholders. This stereotype is seldom described in source material—the diaries, letters, and notebooks of those planters in close contact with bondsmen. When talking to friends about slaves they knew personally, owners were prone to describe them as persons whom fate had frowned upon. When they applied stereotypes at all, planters usually directed them at slaves other than their own; slaves close at hand were apt to appear fully dimensional. On many plantations and farms the relationship of master and bondsman involved a mutual reliance that led many slaveholders to feel that they too had their bondage. As one plantation mistress said following a dispute with a slave, she "exercises dominion over me —or tries to do it—one would have thought to see her in the fury she was in yesterday that I was the Servant, she the mistress. . . ."[10]

This incident and others like it give some indication of the twists and turns, not always sudden or unexpected, that master-slave relationships frequently took. Slaveholders continually described bondsmen as far more complex people than the stereotypes that subsequently were substituted. Yet these stereotypes stubbornly survived. Partly responsible is the researcher's tendency simply to mirror popular clichés about slaves rather than to base his interpretations on hard evidence that exposes misconceptions.

My investigation will focus on the personality and behavior of the slave within the context of what it meant to be a slave. Most of the primary sources useful in getting inside the slave's experience were written between the years 1770 and 1865 and include a vast variety of plantation records, diaries, slave narratives, travelers' accounts, and other items bearing on the slave's experiences in his relationships to slaveholders. Even today the rich material in these sources has not been adequately explored.

When I have thought it important to do so, I have made refences to the bondsman's African past in the text and footnotes. Some of my own explorations into the patterns of thought and behavior linking black Africans and black Americans suggest that until both experiences are better understood statements made about the connection must be advanced with care. Yet, to be sure, the African influence on American slaves was profound and deserves full-scale treatment from a number of approaches.

Though slavery is gone one of the most apparent vestiges of its American history, the dark complexion, remains an echoing reminder of the past. Throughout the years of bondage and after, American society labored long and hard to make this badge of servitude virtually synonymous with inferiority, carefully refining the rationale its guilt required.[11] The fact that the process of justifying the color line is still ongoing is very important to understanding the history of black people in the United States.

1
Drawing the Color Line

The Old South, a region of great geographic diversity,[1] may well be understood best when viewed as a society of masters and slaves. Yet in 1619, when a Dutch ship loaded with a cargo of twenty Africans arrived in Jamestown, Virginia, it hardly suggested the extent of slavery's future development in North America during the next 250 years. Scholars have written, in fact, that the social and economic characteristics of what subsequently became the Old South differed little from those of the North down to the time of the American Revolution.[2] In the early years of the American colonial period there was every indication that the South, like the North, would have an agrarian economy worked by yeoman farmers rather than by hundreds, thousands, and then millions of slaves.[3] But the emerging Old South was to fix a place in history in its own way, a way that would become defined by the white South's relationship to a growing number of black slaves on its plantations and farms.

Slavery existed legally in the North, in New Jersey, until 1846. But by comparison with the Old South the number of northern bondsmen in nineteenth-century America was not large. In 1830 the North had 3,568 slaves, two-thirds of these living in New Jersey,

7

while the Old South had 2,005,475.[4] A survey of the U.S. census returns illustrates slavery's hold. In 1790, the time of the first national census, more than 600,000 of the 697,624 slaves in what has become the continental United States resided in the southern states. By 1820 slave numbers had increased to 1,538,022, with only a small fraction of these either residing in or even visiting the northern states. The Census of 1850 reported 3,204,313 slaves, and by 1860 there were nearly 4,000,000, all but a small number living within the political boundaries of the southern slavery system.*

One may obtain an even clearer picture of the population density of slaves in this period by selecting random figures of their numbers in specific areas. In 1790, their lowest level in any southern region, slaves made up 9.6 per cent of the inhabitants of Tennessee. In Virginia, slaves comprised 39.1 per cent of the population in 1790, 39.9 per cent in 1820, and 33.3 per cent in 1850. In South Carolina by 1850, 57.6 per cent of the total population was slave. By the same date in Georgia, 55 per cent was slave and in Mississippi 51 per cent. Throughout the antebellum years slaves comprised roughly one-fourth to one-third of the entire southern population. And from 1820 down to the time of the Civil War nearly one out of every two people in the Black Belt— Alabama, Georgia, Mississippi, Louisiana—was a slave. For slave-holding Southerners, being surrrounded by black faces was a constant, if occasionally discomforting, fact of life.[6]

In the seventy-year span covered by the census, rural as opposed to urban slaves accounted for more than 95 per cent of the black population. This was a consequence of requirements of slaveholders. The bulk of slaves worked in the cultivation of cotton, sugar cane, tobacco, and rice. A much smaller number produced such products as hemp and turpentine. Less than 5 per cent were employed in industry. From colonial times most bonded blacks lived on plantations whose masters' holdings counted more than twenty slaves. This was particularly true of the Black Belt in

* Interestingly, in 1860, New Jersey still permitted the enslavement of eighteen blacks within its borders despite its abolition law.[5]

8

the nineteenth century. By 1860, one-tenth of the planter community of 385,000 slaveholders held half of the existing human property.

The population figures of slavery reveal not only that a relatively small number of planters controlled most of the investment in slave property but that this same group was able to shape, far out of proportion to its size, much of the social development and many of the attitudes of a region and to a great extent a nation. Only 3000 individuals throughout the period owned 100 or more —sometimes many more—bondsmen. And only 10,000 owned 50 or more slaves. It is perhaps worth noting in contrast that 72 per cent of the estimated 385,000 slaveholders in 1860 owned 10 slaves or less, although 25,000 persons identifiable as planters owned nearly 50 per cent of all bondsmen in holdings of 20 or more, while one quarter of all slaves worked on plantations having 50 or more laborers.

At their highest numbers in 1860, masters and their relatives made up no more than a quarter of the southern white population, which totaled a little more than 12 million.[7] Yet nonslaveholders acquiesced in slavery's subjugation of the black man. Indeed, this was one of those matters about which southern society had little difficulty in agreeing.[8]

The relatively large gatherings of slaves in the Old South had a direct impact on both white and black behavior. Try though they might, Southerners—or, more accurately, Americans—could not shake loose from the notion that the color of the slave's skin, as well as the swelling ranks of these captive people, seemed a most fitting reminder of black inferiority and, therefore, of white superiority. Blacks' degradation was somehow appropriate; but why?

Thomas Jefferson, priding himself on being a careful observer of the characteristics distinguishing races, wrote in his *Notes on the State of Virginia* (1781) that the "first difference which strikes us is that of color."[9] "This unfortunate difference of color and perhaps of faculty," he further noted, "is a powerful obstacle to emancipation of these people. . . ."[10] Benjamin Banneker, the most noted black scientist and intellectual of the day, sent a biting letter to the Virginia Sage in which he ridiculed Jefferson's racial theories while holding himself and his accomplishments up as proof contrary to the "prepossession which is so prevalent in the world against those of my complexion."[11]

Though latent with ambiguity, as Winthrop Jordan has shown, Jefferson's racial attitudes were in many respects quite typical of eighteenth-century white feelings about blacks. Jefferson and his contemporaries, as heirs to a long-established colonial fascination with Africans, were curious about the meaning of the African's color. It had a "powerful impact" on their senses and system of values.[12] In addition, recognition of this color contrast at the visual and, subsequently, social and moral levels was a fundamental lesson of Bible study. In Amos 9:7 the Lord expressed his anger to the Israelites by comparing them to the darker-skinned Ethiopians and admonishing, "You are no more to Me than these Cushites. . . ."[13] In the book of Lamentations, while suffering from the wrath of God and from famine, the princes of Jerusalem, whose complexions "were purer than snow" and "whiter than milk," undergo a transformation, after which they appear physically as "blacker than darkness; they are not recognized in the streets."[14] Thus, in some of the earliest biblical literature wrongdoing is brushed in strokes of black.

The devil played a prominent role in these attitudes too. Some of the great colonial ministers—Thomas Hooker, George Whitefield, and Jonathan Edwards—sermonized at length on his habits, sprinkling their jeremiads with the color of sin—black. Churchgoing colonists, like American society in general, were thus amply indoctrinated with physical descriptions of the color of evil.[15] A minister could draw upon centuries of Western tradition. A flashback to a first century A.D. account of the devil (Satan) gives us a graphic picture of him and his misdeeds:

> . . . the Way of the Black One is crooked and full of cursing, for it is the way of death eternal with punishment, and in it are the things that destroy their soul: idolatry, forwardness, arro-

gance of power, hypocrisy, double-heartedness, adultery, murder, robbery, pride, transgression, fraud, malice, self-sufficiency, enchantments magic, covetousness. . . .[16]

In eleventh-century France, authorities accused ten formerly devout Christians of heresy. At their trial, the prosecutor charged them with adoring the "devil, who appeared to them first as an Ethiopian. . . ."[17]

Still, there was another aspect of the color question in the European experience that ran alongside suspicions about blackness. Its antecedents are not clear, but it received careful expression in the twelfth-century sermons of St. Bernard of Clairvaux entitled "On the Blackness and the Beauty of the Bride Groom and the Bride." St. Bernard, a Frenchman, reminded his communicants that "colour, such as blackness, belongs only to the superficies." He added, "Countless are the times, which, looking to their colour alone you would pronounce [some persons] unprepossessing, but which appear really beautiful in form."[18] In an effort to explain further what he meant, St. Bernard pointed out that sometimes circumstances of penitence altered one in complexion and aspect, as in the case of St. Paul, who became a darkish color from fasting. The color change, he insisted, should not be scorned but admired. Yet, though he defended some features of blackness, his need to devote two celebrated sermons to the issue in part demonstrates the extent to which the problem penetrated the white man's psyche.[19]

In the late eighteenth century, the African Olaudah Equiano (Gustavus Vassa) seems to have captured the meaning of St. Bernard's sermons. In an African twist of the color phenomenon he wrote,

. . . in regard to complexion, ideas of beauty are wholly relative. I remember while in Africa to have seen three negro children who were tawny, and another quite white, who were universally regarded by myself and the natives in general, as far as related to their complexions, as deformed.[20]

11

Equiano spent only a short time as a slave in the plantation South, but black slaves there skillfully pursued and expanded his argument. An ex-slave commented in 1863 that she knew "what whas [sic] white folks was like, and what white folks wanted, if she had got a black skin."[21] Other bondsmen made comments on what whites were like in their folklore. In some of these accounts the Devil is depicted as a silk-hatted white gentleman with wavy hair, an image easily fashioned from the myths and realities of the southern scene.

With regard to masters and slaves in the Old South, the fundamental distinction between whites and blacks from which others appeared to flow was physical appearance. Black was the slave's mark, at all times burdensome and, from necessity, internalized in his consciousness. Commenting on the widespread attention paid to complexion the poet James Russell Lowell once wrote, "There is nothing more sadly and pitiably ludicrous in the motley face of our social system than the prejudice of color." In the United States, he believed, "color is made the most prominent feature."[22] Novelist James Fenimore Cooper made a similar observation in the 1820's by drawing a comparison between the vulgarity associated with a black face in the United States and the gentlemanly status associated with rank, stars, and ribbons in Europe.[23] In 1839 the writer and jurist Beverly Tucker of Virginia suggested the effects that color distinction might have on the average white man's ego: "It is certainly well calculated to inspire the humblest white man with a high sense of his own comparative dignity and importance, to see a whole class below him in the scale of society."[24]

The Northerner Frederick Law Olmsted, traveling through the South in the 1850's, observed a curious bend in the color line in New Orleans, where he noticed that some mulatto slaves received special treatment. The law prohibited them, even after they were legally freed, from marrying whites, but planters "frequently sent" mulatto females "to Paris to be educated."[25] These slaves were light-complexioned and possessed physical appearances often belying their African ancestry. Many times they were the planter's illicit children.

The preoccupation with color determined the Old South's race relations. Color provided an easy and practical way to protect the legal distinction between slave and master and enforced the conveniently contrived differences between them as humans. Among southern whites, a contemporary explained, "materials have been in great demand by some, for improving the complexion, so as to render it if possible, the very opposite of black."[26] Slaveholders, backed by southern medical opinion, said that the healthiest slaves were also the blackest.[27] The mulatto bondsman became the subject of many misleading rumors, with some masters saying that though he was more intelligent by virtue of his white blood, he had less stamina for physical labor and was the parent of weaker offspring. In some quarters it was an occasional practice, as corollary to the above, to darken slaves' skins with the pigmentation agent aquafortis (nitric acid) before showing them to a prospective buyer.[28]

But slaveholders who otherwise "felt no scruples about black negro slavery" on occasion admitted that "these yellow people [mulattoes] ought to have their freedom, on account of their superior intelligence, compared with the genuine negro—."[29] From another viewpoint, Francis Fedric, a mulatto slave, wrote that "slavery is bad enough for the black" but mulattoes had it much harder because they "know it is their own fathers who are treating them as brutes. . . ."[30]

For both slave and freedman, blackness was a catchall. In testimony taken from a co-conspirator of the insurrectionist Denmark Vesey in 1822, Vesey, a freedman, was said to have "read frequently in a Book about the complexion of people" and to have remarked that "it was the climate of Africa made them Black but [they] were not inferior to whites on that account."[31] The statement of the abolitionist sympathizer Fanny Kemble that "the faintest admixture of white blood" in slaves "appears at once, by common consent of their own race, to raise them in the scale of humanity" stands in curious contrast to Vesey's beliefs,[32] though it finds support in the observation of the slave William Wells Brown that the "nearer the negro or mulatto approaches to white, the more he seems to feel the superiority over those of darker hue."[33] To be sure, Fanny Kemble's was the accepted interpretation among whites; when held by blacks, it is more the logical extension of the slaveholder's bias than an opinion that grew out of the experiences of most slaves in their daily lives.

Needless to say, the problem of color created countless difficulties impeding a broader perception of slaves by their masters. One planter, perhaps trying to transcend his biases, noted that "some of the whitest souls I have ever known dwelt in the blackest of skins! . . . certainly, if color, as well as servitude, was a part of the curse denounced upon Canaan for the sin of Ham, it will be changed."[34] Another master engraved this hope on the tombstone of a deceased slave:[35]

> Here lies the best of slaves,
> Now turning into dust.
> Cesar, the Ethiopian, craves
> A place among the just.
> His faithful soul is fled
> To realms of heavenly light,
> And, by the blood, that Jesus shed,
> Is changed from black to white.
> January 15, he quitted the stage
> In the 77 years of his age.

Nonetheless, not all comments were so innocent-sounding. A Georgia physician raged at his sister: "We must now stand by our 'Color.' We can out-think and out-work the black. The poor Devil! . . . He is himself but a monument of the white man's power, and is now the most helpless of all God's creatures face to face with the most aggressive animal that ever rivalled or shocked Omnipotence."[36]

The black-white racial divisions of the Old South fixed what one meant in speaking of slave character. When someone had a black face his behavior took on meaning from that fact. Southern law did much to refine this definition. A petition presented before the Mississippi General Assembly requesting the release of William Johnson of Natchez from bondage in 1820 recognized the dilemma. It requested that the Assembly "extend the hand of humanity to a rational Creature, on whom unfortunately Complexion, Custom and even Law in This Land of freedom, has conspired to rivet the fetters of Slavery."[37] In June 1847 the state court of North Carolina ruled that "in this state a black person is presumed to be a slave."[38] The decision adjudged the selling of liquor to a freedman, not known to be free at the time of sale, to be an illegal act since the freedman had not provided proof of his status before the transaction and thus should have been "presumed" a slave.

In each southern state blackness was accompanied by a score of legal restrictions (black codes). In 1838 the North Carolina legislature passed a law forbidding "marriage between colored and white persons. . . ."[39] Five years later a North Carolina court, presumably acting under that law, dissolved the marriage of a free black man to a white woman. The court did "admit that the defendant's grand-father was white, and the grand-mother only half African—of which last there is no evidence," but held that "still the defendant would have been within the degree prohibited from contracting marriage with a white woman. . . ."[40]

Southerners with black ancestors in their backgrounds kept this a secret and passed for white, a practice well known to continue down to the present. The reasons for their doing so are obvious. Louis A. Bringier of Virginia suspected a "colonel"—anyone might use the title—of passing. In a reply to a friend he wrote, with a trace of amusement, "How was the Virginia Colonel Come on! If you watch him you will discover some 'lard jumping' He is one of them; merely look at his nose. There can be no mistake about it. . . . All the dark gals must rejoice at his advent. 'I want it all for massa' will be the song again."[41]

Who, then, did southern authorities consider officially black? An answer was forthcoming. To keep the master class as pure as possible was a foremost concern of institutional slavery. Any person who had any or as much or as little—depending on one's perspective—as one sixty-fourth proportion of known Negro blood flowing in his veins was classified black.[42]

Other laws, using skin color as "evidence of incompetency,"[43] sought to modify the concept of personality in its application to bondsmen. Bondage's designation of slaves as both men and property was always perplexing. John C. Hurd, a publicist and judicial expert, accurately recorded much of the confusion. In his compilation of slave laws he wrote, in a frequently cited passage, that in "slavery . . . the supreme power of the state, in ignoring the personality of the slave, ignores his capacity for moral action. . . ." This was but one side of the law as he saw it; as he concluded, "So far as it may hold the master and slave, as individuals, morally responsible to the state in their mutual relation, it so far recognizes the personality of the slave, and changes the property into a relation between persons."[44] Various interpretations of these principles were worked out by masters as the occasion arose. The process was not easy, and debate over whether slaves were more men or more property continued throughout the antebellum years. Some masters did not bother with debate, however. One observed that slaves "are as much, his right and property as the teeth in his mouth or the fingers on his hands. . . ."[45] Many other slaveholders, a little more wordy but hardly less direct, discussed slave property in casual business terms to relatives and friends. In 1818 James Steer of Louisiana gave this advice. "For a young man, just commencing life," he wrote to an uncle, "the best stock, in which he can invest Capital, is, I think, negro Stock.—while cotton can command from 20 to 30 cts pr lb: negroes will yield a much larger income than any Bank dividend."[46]

So simple could slavery seem in the Old South, "where people grow up with notions of associating everything that is low and degraded with persons of a dark complexion."[47] But in 1846 a North Carolina state court showed how easily this simplicity could be undermined. It recognized the slave's mental powers and the immortal nature of his soul and suggested that these "constitute him equal to his owner, but for the accidental position in which fortune has placed him. . . ."[48]

Yet slaveholders were less concerned than southern politicians and later historians have been with understanding precisely worded legal manifestos. For them, bondsmen possessed the identities of the ones they owned. In a sense, the comments of George Washington to an acquaintance are a good example of how many thought. His letter reflects the slaveholder's ability to cut through an excess of thinking about bondsmen. "With respect to the other species of property [slaves]," he wrote, "I shall frankly declare to you that I do not like even to think, much less talk, of it."[49]

But masters did, quite naturally, talk about slaves; they also kept some detailed records. From these sources it is apparent that none of the burdens attached to color were as weighty for slaves as the chores they performed and the lives they led in their working hours. Since the rules regulating the form of adult slave labors were usually strict, obedience to the master's authority became an acute concern. He set down the guidelines for his plantation's operations. And it was in the fields on each and every plantation that the meaning of being black was brought forcefully home.

The bondsman's work routine had aspects common throughout the Old South. Often, just before sunrise, the overseer sounded a horn or bell, signaling slaves to awaken and rise.[50] He would sound it again in a short while, but in the meantime slaves had approximately thirty minutes to get dressed. Most had the routine down to a trot. "It was the rule for the slaves to rise and be ready for their tasks by sun-rise . . . and woe be to the unfortunate, who was not in the field at the time appointed."[51] Many had fallen asleep in their work clothes, helping to wear those garments out at an alarming rate. Often their only other clothes were those lively colored "Sunday best," which they had carefully tucked away. Once dressed, the slave's thoughts might turn to food. Some had saved a few bites of the previous night's dinner; they gulped these down on the way to their work gang. Others went without food till midday or maybe took a few sips of hard cider before stepping out the doors of their cabins. A usual practice, however, had bondsmen work until eight or eight-thirty when the horn sounded to summon them to the "morning's bit," perhaps no more than bread brought out to the fields.

This work equation was an easy one, though it sometimes balanced more towards work than rest: twelve hours or more of work a day and the remaining hours at rest, five or six days a week. At noon the overseer blew the horn again. In the summer slaves normally received the two-hour lunch break they needed to recover partially from the intense humidity and heat. During the remainder of the year they received one hour. In spite of this, J. R. Brock, an Alabama overseer, observed in June of 1840 that ". . . the sun appears to have a peculiar effect on many of the old hands." It made their feet swell and "3 of the women complain of violent pains in the breast since they first come. . . ."[52] The work schedule was demanding on physical and emotional energies. Few but the slave understood the extent of his exhaustion after just an average day's labor in the southern climate. But this was what being a black slave meant.

The American South is a perplexing region, and its complicated past tempts interpreters to overstate or oversimplify particular events and those particular meanings these events seem partially to conceal. With added emphasis, this observation holds true for slavery and the color line it helped draw so indelibly. It appears that the possessor of a black face was netted in the age's negative symbolism and could not shake loose. Seeing him but not his netting, many contemporaries and later scholars, sometimes without realizing it, made no distinctions between blackness, circumstance, and slave behavior. Nor could they have done so with any ease. Since whites legally could never become slaves themselves, they did not need to grapple with some of the problems slavery posed.[53]

2
Into the Fields—
Life, Disease, and Labor
in the Old South

In the Old South they had a saying, almost a slogan. They said
that slaveholders lived life to the fullest on the spacious plantations of the southern terrain. Travelers below the Mason-Dixon
line frequently endorsed this claim and told how they too had
shared in the hospitality that accompanied the full life. An observer wrote, not without regard to exceptions, that "a comfortable living can be found here by the most indolent."[1] But these
travelers also noted that disease, death, and sorrow were prominent features of southern existence, and that things would have
been even better if masters could only control the sicknesses that
so plagued them and their slave labor forces. One slaveholder remarked in disgust about conditions near the Red River in Louisiana that ". . . the Doctors reap the largest portion of the profits
in the above mentioned places."[2]

Many farm journals kept by plantation owners or their overseers carefully chronicled the number of slave workers in the
fields each day or week and the number sick. Planters paid close
attention to the time lost by the bondsman because of illness, and
occasionally even commented on a change in a particular slave's
current and potential worth to the labor force. Diary entries also re-

19

corded the illnesses of masters and their families. Though they may have enjoyed many of the better things in life, planters, it seems, often rivaled slaves in the amount of time spent on sick lists.

The vast majority of bondsmen spent most of their lives outdoors at work in the soil. On plantations and farms, slaves roamed the fields in work gangs whose size varied with the job assignment at hand. Many chores required the joint efforts of gangs ranging from a handful to twenty or twenty-five slaves. Sugar cane gangs were frequently composed of more than fifty bondsmen, and on occasion, regardless of the crop involved, neighboring plantations might pool their work gangs to accomplish certain duties. Indeed, slaves and the southern environment had a complex and intimate relationship, each acting upon the other. Unfortunately for the bondsman, this intimacy was often fatal.

For instance, bad weather did not always discourage a planter or overseer from calling bondsmen to their chores. Masters, on occasion, forced their bondsmen to labor in rain or even snow. Slaves shook snow off tobacco, corn, and cotton plants in attempts to save portions of the crops. They drained water from the fields, and on colder days kept themselves warm as best they could by running to and from nearby bonfires set in or near the fields.[3] Frederick Douglass, writing of his bondage while a slave under a Maryland master, recalled: "We worked all weathers. . . . It was never too hot, or too cold; it could never rain, blow, snow or hail too hard for us to work in the field."[4] Some slaveholders, however, did curtail work in inclement weather. In February 1772 a planter entered in his diary a description of a period of "rain in the night and now a prodigious moist fog which is dangerous even to well people in a house because the walls are running down with the moisture brought in by the fog."[5] On this plantation the weather prohibited slaves from working for many days.

Other slaveholders curtailed slave labor in inclement weather in order to protect the human species of property. Charles Manigault of South Carolina advised his son Louis to permit his bondsmen to do ditch and mud work only "as long as it is prudent—*But No Longer*," since the day was damp. He took into consideration that "Negroes are to[o] valuable now to run any risk to their health & pneumonia is awful."[6] But too frequently the demands of plantation life outweighed such considerations, to the detriment of the bondsman.

The efficiency with which bondsmen labored was most directly related to the length of their work day in the field and the type of work performed, though it is easy for the researcher to miss this relationship as he glances back over the record. For this reason, it is important to examine the working patterns and conditions of laborers used in the cultivation of the Old South's largest crops.

As a mass crop, rice was grown mostly in the coastal areas of the Carolinas and Georgia. Planted in March and April, it required year-round care by slave work gangs. Its planting was simple, but cultivation sometimes required the slave to stand knee-deep in water for several hours each day. Foot rot and chills were common. A Georgia physician told Captain Basil Hall, an English traveler visiting the Old South in the 1820's, that in the cultivation of rice "pulmonary [lung] complaints are those which prove most fatal to the negroes. . . ," He also mentioned a "friend of his who lost 40 out of 300 slaves last year."[7] Another Southerner further commented, "No white person could remain on the plantation without danger of the most virulent fever, always spoken of as 'country fever' afflicting him during the summer months in the rice country."[8]

Even in the cultivation of other crops, such as cotton, which could be produced on any scale, the ground might become saturated with water from a storm, making labor hazardous and difficult. On the Haller Nutt estate in Madison Parish, Louisiana, slaves picked cotton "in water up to their knees . . . ," and some of the most able hands "have the chills every time they get their feet wet."[9]

The working of sugar cane was also especially hard on the

thousands of men and women who labored in the semi-tropical fields by 1860. Sugar cane requires constant cultivation and weeding. Strenuous physical effort was necessary to care properly for the sugar cane stalks, to clear the fields, to dodge an occasional snake, and to load and carry the stalks to the pressing mills when the time arrived. The cane fields gave rise to an intricate pattern of work and social life all their own.[10]

But there were a score of difficulties associated with this life. Each summer the oppressive heat created its own problems. "The weather is extremely hot and we have to be very careful with hands and teams."[11] Occasionally, adequate judgment was not used, and slaves and some of the animals died from heat exhaustion. W. P. Gordon, an overseer, wrote to his employer about the precautions he was taking: "I stay very close to the hands and when tha [they] complain I send them to the shade."[12] In most instances, overseers expected slaves to complain a lot to make the work load in the fields more bearable. In a manner, these complaints allowed the bondsman one of his few opportunities to help shape plantation operations. Though some feigned exhaustion from the heat, many requested rest time only when they needed it. An overseer's or master's proper handling of slaves in these circumstances could win for him their partial respect.

At work or at play, slaves wore virtually the same negro clothes, as everyone called them. "They consisted of jeans, linseys, kerseys, and osnaburgs for men and calico and homespun for the women."[13] But many children were dressed only in smocks or wore no clothes at all during warmer periods of the year. Adult slaves' garments sometimes became so torn from wear that they too went nearly unclad. Normally, planters gave bondsmen two suits of clothes each year—one for warm weather, the other for cold—and one pair of shoes. However, a writer in *De Bow's Review*, the influential planter's journal, argued that three suits, not two, were barely enough to keep his bondsmen decent and that boys between the ages of ten and sixteen required at least four suits of clothes per year.[14] A South Carolina physician, Dr. R. W.

Gibbes, added that "where pneumonia . . . is apt to prevail, flannel shirts are frequently distributed, and woolen stockings to the females."[15]

In some cases, masters on large plantations gave the few nice clothes purchased to their house slaves, hoping to put the family's best foot forward when company appeared. Field slaves, on the other hand, seldom allotted enough to keep them protected from the weather, often ran from visitors to hide their unclad figures. A repeated complaint of overseers ran: ". . . in regard to the negroes clothing and shoes. They are very much in need of both. . . ."[16] The allotment, in part, was supplemented by the labors of slave women, sewing in the evening hours. One may suppose that these women received many thanks from other bondsmen for services rendered.

Masters knew, the Reverend Charles C. Jones believed, that "increased attention to the temporal comfort of servants would improve their *health*," but nonetheless they did not rigorously act upon this knowledge. Had their response been wholehearted, much of "the expense of lost labor by sickness, and of physicians' bills would be saved."[17] Slaves needed better clothing and more than just a place to lay their heads in the evening, but many had little but that. The construction of slave huts clearly demonstrated the lack of concern shown by some planters in providing protection for bondsmen against weather conditions in the colder months of the year. A bondsman gives some indication of the extent of the neglect: "In the winter time," he said, "we had to stop up the cracks in the wall [of the cabin] and in the floor with old rags and pieces of paper. This kept the wind out."[18] Nor were most planters unaware of these conditions. A North Carolina slaveholder remarked one summer that "all our negroes seem to be dissatisfied here, Such Shantees as they have will not do in the winter—The Mosquitoes torment them almost to death in the night time. . . ." In the same state another planter made a quite different statement about his slave huts: "I will have 4 framed houses with good brick chimneys for negroes to live in and after I build a store house next summer The present store house will make a fifth negor house framed. . . ."[19] In Louisiana a slaveholder ordered floors put in his slaves' huts and a two-hour rest period during the summer at midday in order to curb "sickness owing to working all day without rest and then sleeping in crowded dirty apartments."[20] These comments typify the diversity that existed.

There were, admittedly, those plantations where a master could "brag" about the facilities he provided for his hands. James Henry Hammond, a United States Senator from South Carolina in the 1850's, wrote in a letter to abolitionist Lewis Tappan that his slaves occupied nearly thirty well-structured, shingled huts. One family shared rooms with another family, each set of two rooms having a brick fireplace.[21] But more typical than this description was the one advanced by a Louisiana planter. He observed to a relative, ". . . my Negro cabins are to be completed all the present ones affording scarcely a shelter. . . ."[22]

Although planters recognized that "one of the most prolific sources of disease among negroes, is the condition of their houses and the manner in which they live,"[23] often they did nothing about these conditions because they themselves lived little better, suffering along with bondsmen from the impact of the environment and from illness. But it was most frequently the slave who absorbed the worst the Old South had to give and, consequently, who endured both major and minor attacks of disease caused by unsatisfactory living conditions. The number of sick varied from one to five on most plantations at any given time, but climbed markedly during the winter and summer months. A judicious master, while calculating his labor schedules, figured in the number of days slaves might be away from work sick, but many others apparently failed to do so. Bondsmen, again and again, came down with colds, flu, pneumonia, and diarrhea. Each of these ailments could reach epidemic proportions; pneumonia accounted for a significant share of slave deaths. "During the winter we have suffered greatly from pneumonia which has been epidemic in many places," read a letter to Dr. William N. Mercer of Louisiana about his slaves.[24] But most feared by bondsmen and slaveholders alike were the dreaded malarial fevers—typhoid, yellow, and scarlet. Thomas Affleck, author of a series of printed plantation journals widely used in the Old South after 1840, advised slaveholders to protect their bondsmen by engaging in preventive medicinal practices. He reminded them in an article that *"the principal causes of sickness* upon plantations, are the use of spring, well, creek or bayou water—." He warned that "it is a *fixed fact,* that cistern or rain water alone is healthy. . . ."[25] The remark of a frustrated Tennessee planter indicates that he, or rather his slaves, learned this lesson the hard way. He commented to a friend, ". . . I have been disappointed in having cisterns made at my River place" and "my people suffered very much last year for the want of it. . . ."[26] The health threats that particularly menaced the field hand thus took on seemingly endless forms.

It was natural then that concerned slaveowners search for methods and schemes to safeguard their investment in slave property. Underwriting the value of bondsmen by insurance seemed an inevitable development considering the situation.[27] The practice does not appear to have been widespread, but in an effort to secure part, or all, of his possible financial loss, some masters insured some of their bondsmen or, as in the case of a misused hired slave, sued persons responsible to recover damages. In 1847 an agent of the Nautilus Mutual Life Insurance Company of New York insured ten Louisiana bondsmen, ages 17 to 39, for a low of $500 to a high of $600. The insurance did not cover the total market value of the slaves. The policy premiums cost from eight dollars and seventy-five cents to thirteen dollars and twelve cents annually.[28] A master, if he wished, could also insure himself against slave loss through specific diseases, injury, unnatural death, and running away.

Slaves used in public projects were frequently insured, although it is difficult to know how often this was done. In one instance, the planters near Drerrysville, Virginia, were reluctant to loan slaves to the Buford Company for use on a public road. One of the Buford agents wrote:

> They are unwilling, they say to put their hands on any Publick work unless There is a Gurantee for the value of The slave in case he should come to his death by being on such work . . . it is true there has been several valuable servants work and few escapes [runaways] in adjoining sections.[29]

Another Buford agent commented to John Buford that a competitor, the Richmond Company, "will insure negro fellows [railroad hands] from 18 to 50 years of age to the amount of $600—."[30] Still another insurance company, though it would "not pay Medical Examinations of slaves" as it did for "every white person" prior to insuring them, was nonetheless willing to take applications "on all sound and healthy slaves" for insurance up to two-thirds of the bondsman's value.[31]

The practice of insuring slaves was, one need little doubt, fraught with countless latent opportunities for slave abuse, deliberate or otherwise. Dr. J. C. Nott, a well-known and respected southern physician and pro-slavery advocate of the 1850's, noted that the practice of insuring bondsmen posed "strong temptations to be feared." He was quick to enumerate what these were:

> As long as the negro is sound, and worth more than the amount insured, self-interest will prompt the owner to preserve the life of the slave; but, if the slave become unsound, and there is little prospect of perfect recovery, the underwriters cannot expect fair play—the insurance money is worth more than the slave. . . . though their slaves, as a general rule, meet with more kindness than any laboring class in the world, yet when it ceases to be the interest of the owner to preserve the life of the slave, he will in many instances cease to be careful of it. Any man who will drive a horse cruelly will drive a negro or operative to death, if he can gain anything by so doing.[32]

Nott's comment is a sad indictment of race relations under bondage, but nonetheless one sensitive to the variety of problems facing slave field hands at every turn.

In the midst of a bad year of illness, a South Carolina planter agonized that ". . . out of about fifty souls, white and black on the plantation not one escaped the fever, and I lost my lovely . . . daughter Thirza. . . ."[33] While it was unusual for an entire work force to be sidetracked with disease, it was not at all uncommon for one-half to two-thirds to be afflicted. The field hand's health was constantly a factor in his work, and though he might pretend to be ill on occasion to escape labor, he knew there would be other times when though actually sick he would be ordered by his master to the fields.[34] In Virginia in 1771 the slaveholder Landon Carter surveyed both his crop prospects for the coming year and his slaves' health, and then scribbled in his diary, ". . . this year I fear the people have been made so weak and lazy with the fevers and agues that I shall not do much."[35]

These health problems were devastating intruders into slaves' private lives. A manager of the Quitman plantations in Mississippi wrote General Quitman, the Mississippi filibusterer, "We still have a good many on this place sick with the Scarlet fever but they are mostly children and their loss of time—in the field is not so much felt."[36] One may suppose that slaves were not so openminded about the ill health in their ranks. When their children were sick, parents naturally worried about them. Some adults even jeopardized their own health by rushing through work-task assignments in order to return to the bedside. It was difficult for a master to set aside their concerns without calling his motives and humanity into further question among his slaves, for there are some indications that bondsmen throughout the South saw masters' and overseers' neglect of their health needs at certain times as deliberately leading to undue suffering and death in their ranks. And this, as we will see, could lead to serious management problems.[37]

Bondsmen and slave managers alike, however, often neglected

to pay adequate attention to the first signs of diseases. Diarrhea in particular portended many ailments, including cholera and scarlet fever, and could by itself slow down or cripple the work pace. Planters mentioned it repeatedly in their farm journals. "Wm & Levy have just recovered from a severe attack of diarrhea," remarked one. "All the Negroes have been affected with it."[38] Another master noted that a close personal friend "had been confined to her bed 3 or 4 days" suffering from a very severe case.[39] Some slaves suffered in the same way but were not afforded the luxury of a bed. Nevertheless, they required frequent work breaks during the day to allow them to attend to their bodily functions. Plantation rules had to be flexible at such times for any work to be done. It appears, therefore, that to say that slaves worked either badly or efficiently, and to leave it at that, is a careless generalization about the forces that shaped patterns of slave labor and plantation life.[40]

It was not unusual on many plantations and farms to find at least some slaves recuperating from some sickness at all times of the year. Farm animals became ill, too, many dying from exhaustion; and slaves continued to work some sick animals in the fields, sometimes taking out personal vengeance on a master by destroying his property or perhaps working the animals at the behest of an overseer trying to get a last plot of land plowed. Work performed under these conditions was most often done inefficiently, and usually the blame is placed on the slave when actually a great variety of motivations and circumstances are in need of further examination. In relatively healthy times, complaints about the poor quality of field labor dwindled, taking a back seat to more honest assessments of slaves' contributions. "I finished cutting my rye yesterday," commented a slaveowner, "and can assure you that I never felt the heat more sensibly than I did yesterday morning. My hands I thought would have given out several times, but the poor fellows stuck to it manfully. . . ."[41]

Disease likewise had a profound impact on work patterns in southern cities. During summer months many urban areas were considerably depopulated as their inhabitants fled to the security of selected regions of the countryside. Most of the great epidemics of the antebellum period started in coastal cities and spread inland, taking enormous tolls in white and black life. The practice of literally fleeing the onslaught of disease was common in rural and urban settings as the slave regime ran in search of safety.

> I removed the negroes from their houses and camped them in woods for three weeks. I continued part of the day with the white family [his own] the balance of the day and night I stayed in the camps with the negroes, I removed the negros supposing there might be some local cause for the diseases, after their removal there was no case of cholera among them.[42]

Serious diseases brought unimaginable horrors to the inhabitants of plantations and cities. With the appearance of cholera the slave's work often came to a halt, and crops were neglected. In one area in Louisiana a planter reported that cholera had felled "8 negroes out of 12" belonging to a neighbor "and after taking off one or two hundred from St. Martins to Franklin Parishes has entirely ceased." Its victims "were principally poor, half nakid, starved French Negroes. . . ."[43] wrote Margaret Brashear to her daughter, not without a note of scorn for the French. During cholera's first appearance in the United States in 1832—it occurred irregularly thereafter—planters observed that "it seems particularly fatal amongst the blacks—."[44] In an epidemic, food of all kinds became contaminated and scarce. Some individuals rightly believed that fruits and vegetables were favorite haunts of disease germs. But slaves and masters both nevertheless ate what was available and endangered their lives. In 1855 the Mississippi slaveowner Lucian Polk lost "27 negroes by Cholera, produced it was supposed, by eating soured meat and corn . . . ," which comprised their rations of food for the week.[45]

Yellow fever was another major disease that visited the Old South, but unlike cholera it made yearly appearances after 1820. It was an affliction common to all southern and northern states but was particularly widespread in the Deep South. Scarlet fever often accompanied it, and together these two diseases enfeebled many bondsmen. A Louisiana overseer expressed his concern for the slaves under his care one summer, writing that "the Negroes that have had scarlet fever has done no work yet thay air most all well. But the weather is so bad that I am a fraid to put them out, for if tha[y] get wet or catch cold thay will be apt to die."[46] These fevers struck southern cities especially hard. In New Orleans, nicknamed "the graveyard of the Southwest," the slaveholder John Mc Donogh observed that in a short period during 1822 yellow fever had killed 1500 people. He wrote that "it was however entirely con-fined to strangers or those who had been here a year or two. . . ."[47] But this was little consolation for the victims. Slaveholders also knew that slaves who suffered from fevers in summer months "had a great tendency to relapse too frequently during the fall and winter" and that a "certainty of relapses and sometimes frequent relapses" could usually be expected "so as not to be subdued until warm weather in the spring."[48]

In the meantime, how were affected bondsmen treated? Here we may reach a guarded conclusion. Slaveholders and overseers usually returned them to work, sometimes at lighter tasks, telling them to work the best they could. And, to be sure, these slaves not only worked falteringly but also very likely appeared especially slow moving or lazy to an outside observer like a traveler. It seems an error to say simply that they were.

We know now that mosquitoes can transmit yellow fever and other fever viruses to humans,[49] but that this was the mode of transmission was a fact not known to inhabitants of the Old South and elsewhere. They posited a variety of explanations for its cause, the most common attributing it to a noxious vapor, a swamp miasma.[50] Aside from their disease-bearing properties, mosquitoes were a serious nuisance to slaves and whites. During the humid summer months they drove planters off their plantations and urban dwellers out of cities. They were incredibly numerous in rice-growing areas along the Atlantic coast; their larvae bred in the large bodies of water needed for cultivation.[51] They swarmed in the early evening hours and massed their assault upon human victims, biting bondsmen into mounds of bumps. Scores of slaves spent restless and sleepless nights trying to escape these winged tormentors. Evening activities slowed to a crawl. Mosquitoes also attacked farm animals, and if the modern livestock industry is any indication, they could be responsible for keeping cattle as much as fifty pounds under their normal weight. Slaves tried a variety of methods to control the itching that resulted from their bites. They scratched and rubbed ointments, pork grease, and plant juices on their skins—all to little avail. Their labors during the day were notably affected by these distractions.

Many bondsmen probably suffered needlessly at times because some of them, and even more of their managers, overemphasized slaves' partial immunity to certain diseases—various strains of malaria, yellow, and scarlet fevers—and this immunity occasionally led to carelessness in safeguarding personal health. Slaves were also the natural prey of pneumonia viruses. Children did not try to conceal the dizzying feeling brought on by diarrhea or other early signs of pneumonia but adults sometimes did, mistaking their nausea and coughing for a cold. Many simply believed that it was better to endure the side effects of an affliction than to take the bad-tasting medicine or submit to the misguided treatment often administered to them on such occasions. A Mississippi planter noted to his mother with questionable regret in a time of sickness that "the negroes unfortunately for Themselves and Equally so for us had no confidence in our treatment—they Said it was certain death to take our medicine and we were compelled to stand by and See them die—."[52]

According to Dr. R. W. Gibbes of South Carolina, "No one doubted that pneumonia was the most fatal of all illnesses to the Negro."[53] Dr. Samuel Cartwright, however, was quick to attach an odd behavioral explanation to its occurrence. A particular type of pneumonia, which he called Scorbutic, was common among "bad, vicious, ungoverable negroes . . . ," he said. This part of his hypothesis, perhaps, did not persuade many southern physicians, but he also pointed out more knowingly that apparently because of their type of work slaves were very liable to "Typhoid fevers, Rheumatism and hepatic [liver] derangements. . . ."[54]

A closer look by Cartwright would have uncovered further behavioral information of value. Where disease reached into the slave quarters it transformed them into somewhat nightmarish settings. After work some slaves would not return to their cabins because they wanted to avoid contact with the sick. But there were few other places they could go to rest. Physicians encouraged the lighting of bonfires to dry the air, believing this lessened susceptibility to germs. The great fires presented quite a dazzling spectacle but did not conceal the loud crying and moaning, which often carried on long into or through the night.

Planters did, of course, take many concerted steps against disease. Haller Nutt of Louisiana placed high priority on treatment of the sick, noting that the "first consideration is to *feel* the importance of attending to the sick. To *feel* that it is above all other duties of the plantation."[55] Still, masters seldom took adequate precautions to lessen the effects of the seasonal visits of pneumonia, serious colds, and other ailments.

"Humanitarian and economic considerations combined to guarantee slaves at least minimum protection and attention," writes Eugene D. Genovese.[56] But even the most careful planters nonetheless felt that because of plantation economics they usually could not avoid sending their slaves to the damp fields, for example, after a rain, if only to perform some light tasks. In Virginia a master wrote in his diary, ". . . indeed we can't go out on the ground at all without being wet over our shoes in mud, mire, and water. . . ."[57] Poor judgment, despite economic and humanitarian concerns, brought about continual abandonment of health guidelines as they applied to slave work gangs.

Attempts to control disease thus posed a multitude of problems. Another illustration of this point is the fact that smallpox—despite the availability since the early eighteenth century of an easy preventative—flared up occasionally among slaves and planters. A mistress wrote to a friend about an acquaintance in Washington, D.C., that ". . . his little boy is dreadfully disfigured with the smallpox, all the children had it but so slightly they will not be marked. . . ."[58] Following such an occurrence, planters winced a bit and usually vowed anew to have every member of their household, black and white, vaccinated, but they rarely did. Some physicians indulged a hope that "the smallpox would ultimately be exterminated by universal inoculation," but others expressed the opinion that such a possibility was unlikely.[59]

What planters did try to do was stop the slaves' night wanderings, which were often cited as the cause of the spread of disease. These nightly visits occurred in all seasons despite personal hazard and slaveowners' orders not to leave the plantation. Masters devised some ingenious schemes to prevent them. Some were disciplinary in nature: a slave who wandered about without permission during the sickly season might be whipped in front of other bondsmen. Yet at other times, the wandering might go unnoticed.

The slave's vacillating response to personal illness was perplexing to many whites. "So perverse and stubbornly foolish are these people," wrote a dumbfounded master, "they are either running into the hospital without cause or braving such a disease as the cholera, by concealing the symptoms."[60] Perhaps a reason for "braving disease" was that in most areas of the South a doctor would not be summoned unless a final effort was deemed necessary to snatch the slave from the hands of death. One planter put it this way: "I have so far applied to no physician partly because I tho't they could do but little more than I could do myself. . . ."[61] We do not know if any of his slaves fell victim to this practice. Doctors were indeed scarce throughout the Old South, and most slaves had to make do without them. One account informs us that to "send for the doctor was, in plantation belief, to give up the case; and the doctor's patients recovered only by a special miracle. . . ."[62] The bondsman Josiah Henson, adding a certain colloquial touch, noted too that a "nigger will get well anyway, was a fixed principle of faith, and facts seemed to justify it."[63] He was in error in the last portion of his statement; sickness lingered. Partial recoveries were the norm.

Medical quackery is still a serious concern in the United States today, and southern doctors in the antebellum period believed it to be a major cause of death among both slaves and masters, but particularly slaves. Medical care administered at bedside with the aid of a home medical guide was too often the slaveholder's habit. And plantation managers sometimes gave out "such medicine as is most easily given, without regard to symptoms."[64] This was the practice of South Carolina senator James Henry Hammond, who advised a friend to "treat every case systematically ignoring the name of the disease." He continued, "I have not taken of or given in all my family white or black any Doctor's Stupf for over seven years. The statistical result is wonderful."[65] Hammond's distrust of physicians' remedies ran deep, to the point where he actually considered some of their medicines poisonous to humans.[66]

Because of a scarcity of doctors, planters relied increasingly on themselves and on any number of medically oriented bondsmen. The slave Sam in New Orleans engaged in ". . . bleeding, pulling teeth, and administering medicine to slaves."[67] One master trained the bondsman Louis Hughes to be the plantation medical man. According to Louis, "he always showed me each medicine named and had me smell and carefully examine it that I might know it when seen again."[68] When masters were unable to effect a cure by their own methods they might send for a black "doctor," maybe a conjuror skilled in folk medicine. This was necessary because some sick slaves often showed a complete lack of confidence in a master's or white physician's ability to cure them, while they might place themselves willingly in the care of another slave.

Many of these black "doctors" displayed great confidence in their ability to cure the sick. This bothered those white practitioners who found their skills on the short end of a comparison. A few, such as Henry Clay Lewis, the Louisiana Swamp Doctor, adopted some of the slave methods, and others followed, stimulated by warnings that their fees depended on positive results.[69] Black physicians held their posts proudly, some administering to white families as well as slaves. In Virginia the slave Michael suggested to his master that to cure the slave Suckey, who was "greatly afflicted with Fits," he send for "black Hannah," who lived on the estate of Bennett Real of Charles County, for "she has been great distances fm home to visit sick people. . . ."[70] Another planter obtained a cure for his slave Jack by remanding him to the care of "Old Man Doctor Lewis," a slave, for more than a month. Doc' Lewis treated Jack for poisoning, and though Jack "went over to him the 5th of June I believe almost blind his sight seems as good as ever. . . ."[71] This slaveholder, Robert Carter, made regular use of Doc' Lewis' services for a number of years.

The visit of a slave doctor to a plantation brought the local slaves out in mass and remained a topic of conversation for weeks. It demonstrated to slaves the slaveholder's dependence upon them in some things and, no doubt, inflated their pride. One may gather that bondsmen identified with the "doctor," for they asked him countless questions about his cures, which he, quite naturally, seldom answered. Parents perhaps imagined one of their children rising to a similar rank some day. But most important was the fact that the arrival of the slave doctor on the plantation gave field slaves a chance to observe the way in which traditional master-slave roles interconnected.

Usually one or more of a plantation's bondsmen gained expertise in treating the sick and handled most cases of illness, even the most serious. Much of their effectiveness stemmed from the psychological comfort they provided an afflicted bondsman, especially when he had determined that his time had arrived, "and if it be 'come' they expect to die; and, if not, they will get well without medicine."[72] During all their sufferings, physical and mental, slaves largely treated slaves. The heroic master or mistress who stayed by the bedside of a bondsman until he died or saw him through emotional difficulties was rare. The slave more readily looked to his fellows. Children of eight to thirteen often nursed infant brothers and sisters while their parents were away in the fields.[73] On General Pinckney's plantation in South Carolina the traveler Adam Hodgson observed that the medical care of slaves was given over to a "nurse and doctor, both Negroes I believe. . . ."[74] The pattern was the same throughout the Old South. Slave women frequently vaccinated children when vaccination was done at all, and slave midwives—not always as ignorant as some scholars have led us to believe—delivered many babies.[75] These midwives were, to be sure, responsible for a share of infant deaths. Thomas Affleck claimed that they "do not know how to take care of the navel—that is how to tie it off in order to prevent infection."[76]

Some of the midwives were talented folk doctors "who brewed medicines for every ailment." These folk remedies were legion throughout the plantation and urban South and took on many variations form region to region. A Florida ex-slave remembered that colds were treated with horehound tea, pinetop tea, and lightwood drippings on sugar; the many fevers might be treated with a tea prepared from pomegranate seeds and crushed mints; and spasms were treated with garlic or "burning a garment next to the skin of the patient having the fit."[77]

All of this is relevant to an important question: with whom did slaves primarily identify at such times?[78] By analyzing some of the issues related to this question we should come to a fuller understanding of where bondsmen looked for role models—in the master class or among themselves. The bondsman lying in a sickbed respected the care given him by a slave nurse. The same was true for the expectant mother, the safe arrival of whose offspring depended on the care of the midwife. Most slaves shared in these experiences and were mindful of the talents possessed by those of their fellows who, by virtue of these special gifts, had obtained additional freedoms, often no more than time away from field duties. A slave could easily appraise himself in relationship to these talented others, whether he liked them or not.

Slave doctors and nurses naturally made mistakes in their care of bondsmen stemming from a lack of proper medical knowledge.

But overseers and masters saddled with similar responsibilities showed the same lack. Haller Nutt reprimanded his overseer for "improper treatment of the sick—puking and purging too much merely for colds. . . ."[79] The overseer had "10 or 12 on the sick list all the time."

The percentage of the plantation's budget spent on medical needs fluctuated widely depending on the diseases prevalent during the year. Normally expenses ran much less than a dollar per slave. In 1845 the bill of one slaveowner amounted to fifty dollars for roughly fifty persons. He wrote, "It has been a very sickly year; but no verry bad cases."[80] There were, occasionally, major expenses, such as for amputation, but the average plantation was not budgeted to absorb many large or even many small medical bills. For instance, one physician charged, a master thought, the exorbitant fee of twenty dollars for treating a slave with syphilis. Syphilitic bondsmen were not uncommon, but most went unattended because of the prohibitive cost.

From the slaveholder's viewpoint, field hands' health problems defied solution; they were an endless stream, inseparable from conceptions of the slave's personality. Travelers in the Old South commented on happy slaves who were slow moving and, they had heard, slow thinking. Comparing American bondsmen with European peasants was a favorite pastime of Southerners and foreigners. On a trip in Europe in 1832 Dr. Samuel Cartwright noted that peasant "field laborers are also very slow motioned." But he wrote, in partial defense of slavery, "They do not plough half as fast as negroes with lazy mules." Furthermore, "the only active persons I have seen are the waiters and servants about Hotels."[81] In near agreement, the English geologist Sir Charles Lyell found slaves generally better off than English peasants. Masters and visitors bantered the relative differences back and forth, and the former prided themselves on the favorable way their bondsmen compared on the scale of civilization. These observations, however, tended to obscure more than they illumined.

Planters spoke constantly of acclimation to the southern climate, placing heavy stress upon the weather's influence on health and behavior. Slaves' death certificates frequently mentioned that they had resided in a community for less than a year, and slaveholders usually predicted that bondsmen moved from other states or neighborhoods to their own would have health problems shortly following their arrival that would interfere with their work and might even sideline them for awhile. Slaveholders also applied such comments to field gangs working in areas of a plantation that had not been brought previously under cultivation. The breaking of new ground not infrequently raised the specter of ill health. When slave women became pregnant within a couple of years' residence in a new area, it surprised no one if they miscarried. These circumstances consequently increased the anxiety most slaves had about being moved and added to fears of never seeing loved ones again. One planter commented, following the removal of some of his bondsmen to Natchez, Mississippi, that the "people here say, that this is a very healthy section of the country but that we may calculate upon loosing some of them in becoming acclimated."[82]

But, as they did in other situations, many slaves took advantage of the effects of acclimation to lighten their daily chores, perhaps continually complaining of faintness shortly after arrival in a new region. This does not rule out the fact that many were whipped. Some bondsmen also clung to the sickbed as long as possible to avoid returning to their duties. The slave Nora was apparently one of these. Her overseer observed that she "won't mind me at all, unless I watch her, and she knows, that I wont whip her because she is sick and weak." He later gave her what he called fifteen or twenty swats for not taking her medicine. "She took it then and afterwards," he wrote, "but swore, that she'd run away—that she had done swore so when you whipped her before. . . ." And then he appended a character note: "She is the most insufferable liar and quarrels with every body."[83] Still budget-conscious masters watched these factors carefully; some, especially in the Deep South, aware of accusations that they worked slaves to death within six years after arrival.[84] It appears that the acclimation factor joined to harsh work loads goes far toward explaining the rise of these claims.

Yet following sickly seasons many planters pursued a dangerous course in slave management. They placed the health of their slaves second to the success of their harvest. The profit motivation of slaveholders is a deceptive element in evaluating the care given bondsmen, since a "profit" often meant just breaking even. "Indeed," observed a Southerner who criticized Louisiana planters while himself determining to become one, "I am of the opinion that one of the leading characteristics of the Louisiana planters is an apparent determination to be always in debt; notwithstanding the sufficiency of their ordinary incomes to support them in ease and affluence."[85] Balancing the financial records was tricky business, however. Many masters realized that slave property was their most valuable asset, but others were unsure, seeing the fruits of slave labor above and beyond the upkeep as the chief objective of slave management. Bondsmen could be much misused when this latter conception operated at full throttle, as it often did.

Among field hands, women were often most acutely menaced by health problems. Slaveholders constantly meshed women's duties with those of male slaves, sometimes rationalizing that "men being so hard to obtain it is necessary to learn to get along with women."[86] A standard claim was that "women can do plowing very well & full well with the hoes and equal to men at picking."[87] In the raising of tobacco, cotton, and rice they occupied key positions. Their labors frequently included the strictly routine assignments of weeding to prevent crop strangulation or caring for vacant land to keep it in condition. However, no task was too large or too small for them, despite disclaimers from masters who still continually gave them heavy duties. In Mississippi the traveler Frederick Law Olmsted observed that "plowing, both with single and double mule teams, was generally performed by women. . . ."[88] The slave Solomon Northup confirms Olmsted's observation and adds that "some planters, owning large cotton and sugar plantations, have none other than the labor of the slave woman."[89] Constant and heavy tasks, such as clearing land of "trees, logs, and stumps," went on continually, and "some of the more able bodied women slaves sometimes lent a hand in this sort of work."[90]

Hard labor in the fields increased the hazards of such experiences as childbirth. Movements necessary for picking and hoeing increased in difficulty as women became swollen by pregnancy. Slaveholders widely applied the rule that "pregnant women should not plough or lift but must be kept at moderate work until the last hour if possible."[91] Infections and hernias were common. Historians have generally set the time at which slave women were sent back to work after childbirth at three weeks.[92] But a more general rule applied to many of the sick suggests what could have happened to a slave after childbirth: "make her do something, for as long as she hugs that sick house, sh'll never get well. . . ."[93]

The slave, it appears, seldom spent her three weeks off for birth and recovery in repose. She often had to do her own cooking and cleaning due to the misconception of some slave managers "that negro women needed very little care at such times, which may partly account for the high rate of infant mortality."[94] Thomas Affleck observed in this regard that of "those born, one half die under one year; of the other half, say one-tenth die under five years. . . ."[95] It appears that contributing to this practice of neglect was the frequently held belief that some females deliberately got themselves in a family way to avoid work. We have no way of knowing the truth. Yet amidst this confusion of opinions is the solid evidence that the female slave suffered much. And even when a master allowed a three-week period for postpregnancy recovery he might expect the slave to reassume her full chores shortly after returning to the fields. The impact was telling. Women complained of backaches; their work lagged. Germs often attacked the uterus. A physician in Alexandria, Louisiana, reported "fevers of a highly bilious type combined in some cases with disentery. . . . Attacking pregnant women, it generally produced abortion. It affected the uterus even in those not pregnant."[96] Such infections help to explain widespread sterility among slaves. Further, a slave belonging to Landon Carter of Virginia suffered also ". . . by her miscarriage . . . worms in her womb," a not infrequent malady.[97] The myth of the slave amazon, the female field hand of unusual strength, is hard to comprehend, since at such times, work efficiency radically declined.

The lack of real consideration of childbearing slaves carried over to their infants, with many growing "puny and sickly for want of proper care." A repeated complaint was that "because the milk the mother nursed to them was heated by her constant and excessive labors [in the field] as to be unwholesome" infants obtained improper nourishment.[98] Henry Bibb, a slave, explained that "mothers have not time to take care of them—and they are often found dead . . . for want of care of their mothers."[99] It was among slave children in West Feliciana Parish, Louisiana, that the world's first epidemic of poliomyelitis occurred in 1841. The disease, which attacked children ages one and two who were teething, was contracted while their saliva was in an infectious state during a critical period of several days.[100]

Many masters seemed to expect and accept the death of slave children without special alarm; this general attitude applied also to some nonslave children in both the North and South during the disease-ridden eighteenth and nineteenth centuries. This near-fatalistic outlook extended, in fact, to the slaveholder's own children on occasion. After losing an eleven-month old son, Ebenezer Pettigrew of North Carolina wrote, "Our bereavement was great, but I have brought myself to view these evils with much more composure than formerly, knowing that all things which we see and have are transitory."[101] Bondsmen had an outlook on death akin to Pettigrew's, but often there was a noticeable difference. The slave Charles Ball wrote that a woman "told me she was rejoiced that her child was dead, and out of a world in which slavery and wretchedness must have been its only portion."[102] Yet the loss of many youngsters drove some parents into frenzied desperation. Mourning was more apt to be the typical response.

Child neglect, either deliberate or otherwise, was inseparable from slavery and its work demands. "I begin very much to fear that the children are neglected at the plantation," wrote Sophia Watson to her husband Henry. "Peggy complains that she has nothing that they can eat when they are sick." Conditions were not atypical on the Watsons' estate, but indeed reflected specific deficiencies elsewhere. The Watson plantation was, in financial terms, very successful, and the fact that it too incurred difficulty in the area of child care indicates how severe the situation could be on other plantations in the Old South. Sophia Watson added that few of the children "will eat rice—Molasses is not good for them—and they have no milk—I think you will have to keep a cow down there to furnish them with milk—."[103] For those children who survived the early years, life was still a trial. The slave Francis Fedric ridiculed the so-called child care features of slavery and commented that on one of the plantations ". . . children feed like pigs out of troughs, and being supplied sparingly, invariably fight and quarrel with one another over their meals."[104]

Thus at every stage of his life from birth to death the bondsman's lot was a difficult one. And if these physical aspects of health directly affected a field hand's behavior, so also did the slave's beliefs about the origins of sickness. It was not really surprising, because of the widespread character of ill health, that some mystique should come to cloak it. Slaves expected short sicknesses, but extended illness might take on an aura of bewitchment.[105] Many masters, though deeply superstitious themselves, attached the label "lazy" to the slave's behavior at such times. Their judgment was somewhat hasty.

During personal sickness many slaves believed that an enemy of theirs had somehow managed to project a physical object into their bodies. It usually took the form of a snake-like creature, wiggling just beneath the surface of the skin. A slave's behavior might undergo considerable modification while his body remained the host of mysterious forces. Some refused to work until cured, labored badly, or ran off. Others hid the ailment as long as they could control the accompanying physical and mental discomfort in an effort to fight back against the evil force. In any case, they usually experienced noticeable anxiety until the source of irritation was somehow removed.

That bondsmen should fix so often upon snakes or wormlike creatures to explain their discomfort was not strange. There was probably a close connection between this belief, the importance of snakes in the slave's African past, their extensive existence in the southern terrain, and bondsmen's frequent infestation with maggots, an affliction sometimes concealed out of fears of the occult. For example, "Matilda, John's wife, was taken about five weeks ago with swelling of the face," wrote a Mississippi overseer. "I applied a poultice, when lo! there droped out of her nose three of the largest maggots I ever saw in my life. . . ."[106] Matilda mentioned feeling worms moving inside her head in the vicinity of her ears, but though a reported fifty later made their way out of her system there is no record that she died. Two male slaves on the same plantation had maggots, and among slave children generally the problem was often a serious one. In other cases, when a bondsman became sidelined by so-called imagined afflictions there was little anyone could do to shake his belief—even severe punishment often failed to move him. Thus a planter, after observing the behavior of one of his sick slaves, wrote briefly: "The Negroes believe in this Species of Witchcraft, his left leg is very Sore & painful he says . . . Adam also in bed with a pain in his head and back. . . ."[107]

In a published letter to Dr. Samuel Cartwright, Dr. W. S Forwood of Maryland observed that among slaves "rheumatic and neuralgic pains are very frequently attributed to the evil designs of the witches. . . ."[108] And Dr. Cartwright himself, in a moment of real insight, advised the readers of *De Bow's Review* that one had better "throw medicine to the dogs" than give it to a bondsman convinced that he had "been in some other way tricked or conjured."[109] These influences, when combined with ordinary matters of health, make slaves' behavior, even that behavior attributable to sickness, appear very complex.

On occasion, tired slaves said that a witch had ridden their backs during the evening's rest, wearing them out for the next day's labors. This manner of belief still lingers in a few areas of both the black and white, urban and rural, North and South. Bondsmen also said they conjured masters and overseers in the same way. This could be a reasonably safe and ego-building kind of conjuration, which nature and deficient medical knowledge supported. At any rate, there was always enough disease and death among members of slaveholders' families for a perceptive bondsman to take credit for some of these misfortunes if he carefully assessed the situation and was able to conceal his own identity, if need be, from emotionally distraught masters who might find his claim momentarily upsetting and, from their viewpoint, inconsiderate.

Although nearly every kind of disease afflicted bondsmen, proponents of slavery and later scholars have been adamant in the near exclusion of one—mental illness. Indeed, many believed— and the Census of 1840, so brilliantly propagandized by Calhoun, seemed momentarily to demonstrate—that independence, not slavery, opened the Negro's mind to derangement. However, the research of William Dosite Postell suggests that mental disorders among slaves occurred more "frequently . . . than physicians were aware."[110] Unbalanced bondsmen, he notes, learned simple work routines and thus could be gainfully employed by masters. A few years following Postell's statements, Clement Eaton perceived anew, nonetheless, that "insanity seems to have been rare among the slaves."[111] But what does the evidence indicate? Briefly, manuscript references such as ". . . Negro Betty, about 17, one of the people of the plantation just mentioned is thought to be a Lunatic"[112] are not unusual.

The difficulty encountered by a North Carolina master illustrates the problems slaveholders faced when they determined a slave to be mentally disturbed. William Pettigrew wrote his sister asking her to find out about an asylum near Raleigh. "I make the inquiry as my man Bob is deranged, & has been since last Oct.," he said. "The cost and trouble of taking care of the poor fellow is no little. . . ."[113] In her answer, his sister informed William that there was no place in Raleigh to accommodate black mental patients, but she had obtained the counsel of a physician who recommended that William send Bob to Williamsburg, Virginia. In another letter to his sister, William Pettigrew noted, "I regret no provision has, as yet, been made for persons of that description in our State. . . ." He considered such a facility for slaves necessary, and privately chastened the state's legislators, who "whilst making provision for the white man should not be unmindful of the sons of Africa who sojourn among us."[114] His later communications with a Doctor Fisher at the Williamsburg Eastern Lunatic Asylum were no more helpful, however, the doctor informing him that the asylum there was for white patients only.

The standard treatment for mental disorders among slaves seems to have been neglect; but there is evidence that slaveowners placed some of the seriously ill in "jails and strong rooms of poorhouses when deemed dangerous. . . ."[115] The number of mentally ill bondsmen during any given period in any part of the South is impossible to estimate, but rolls of slaves on larger estates might include two or three beside whose names the planter or overseer placed the notation "insane."[116] Also, references to insanity or other forms of mental ill health occur sporadically in manuscript sources, yet frequently enough to indicate that masters were fully aware of the problem. In an interesting contrast to the difficulties William Pettigrew had with his slave Bob, a year later the planter Hill Carter of Virginia received from the Eastern Lunatic Asylum at Williamsburg a bill concerning his slave Celia, who was apparently a patient there; the "amount of the account in full, including board, clothing, and expenses home, was $47.50."[117] Carter boarded Celia at the asylum for more than thirty weeks at a cost of $1.50 a week. Why the keepers accepted Celia as a patient and did not receive the slave Bob is unclear, unless it was because she was from Virginia; but acceptance of a slave was not a normal practice. At any rate, the cost of housing a bondsman thus was too high for most planters.

Historical estimates of the incidence of mental illness among field slaves are clearly in need of an upward revision. The findings of social researcher Marc Fried have much validity for the antebellum period. "The evidence," he writes, "is unambiguous and powerful that the lowest social classes have the highest rates of severe psychiatric disorder in our society."[118] But in the Old South the attention paid to mental health was negligible at any level. Planters who were fond of parading the easy-going features of southern life were loath to discuss its negative aspects. On most occasions it was the slaves in the quarters in regular contact with the disturbed person who had the burdensome responsibility of dealing with the situation. Sometimes a neglected slave's mental agitation was so pronounced that his peculiar behavior attracted the attention of the judicial authorities, but most times it seemingly did not. A Virginia court order of 1832 directed a planter to bring his female bondsman forward. Personal observation had apparently convinced the judge himself that "Alcie a negro slave the property of Chas. Hill is a person of insane or disordered mind and is going at large in this county to the great danger of the citizens of the commonwealth."[119]

Slaves and masters suffered extensively from lesser emotional disorders as well. A cheerful frame of mind was a suggested remedy, and a writer in the *New Orleans Medical and Surgical Journal* recommended diverting the mind "from old into new channels; to give it healthful exercise. . . ." A "judicious system of reading," he suggested, might accomplish this end.[120] Illiterate slave field hands and a great many white Southerners, however, obviously could not take advantage of this advice.

The strictures imposed by health problems were therefore everywhere apparent in slave society. Still, field slaves worked as efficiently as whites engaged in similar occupations. The same can be said of the more skilled slaves who manned southern industry. Bondsmen did all this while living largely at a subsistence level, as did whites similarly employed.[121] In the mining industry, owners considered slaves to be very efficient laborers. In the coal mines twelve miles outside Richmond, a master noted that slaves in shifts worked "night and day by turn."[122] White workers had similar hours, but during times of severe disease they sometimes elected to leave the premises. In the salt mines near Richmond in 1833, "more than half of the Salt furnaces were Stopped" during part of the summer "on Account of White labourers leaving her[e] for the fear of Disease [cholera] . . . ," wrote John Cabell to a friend.[123] He was unable to obtain more hired bonded help because local slave owners feared the loss of their property. At no time did he differentiate between the skill of blacks and of whites.

In her study of Virginia manufacturing in the antebellum years, Kathleen Bruce writes, with reference to the Tredegar Iron Works, that slaves' "power to labor sustainedly through summer heat, which was apt to reduce the capacity of white mechanics engaged at the puddling furnaces" was "their genius."[124] Under the circumstances, a talent of this sort was indeed a dubious one, as slaves so employed found out.

With the approach of old age the field hand's effective work days slipped away, and the character of his active life changed: "Jacque's labours, as is customary with aged slaves had been gradually suspended. . . ."[125] Masters assigned some of the aged light duties taking care of children. But it seems, nevertheless, that many slaveholders viewed the presence of some of the old ones as a tax on plantation resources.[126] A lifetime of vigorous labors had exhausted much of their physical reserves, making them of little use in a culture in which physical labor defined one's existence.

Assuredly, elderly slaves could get in the way on a plantation, moderately disrupting operations by their slow labors and need for additional rest time. Planters often classified them as half hands (most slaves were full hands) or as the equivalent to no hand when they were unable to work, and cut the rations they received. Occasionally, even when seriously hampered by blindness, they were set aside in the woods to fend for themselves. The assistance of their relatives was therefore essential. The slave Moses Grandy remembered:

When my mother became old, she was sent to live in a little lonely log-hut in the woods. Aged and worn out slaves are commonly so treated. . . . Their children or other near relations, if living in the neighborhood, take it by turns to go at night, with a supply saved out of their own scanty allowance of food, as well as to cut wood and fetch water for them: this is done entirely through the good feelings of the slaves and not through the masters' taking care that it is done.[127]

A similar fate sometimes befell the infirm. One slave was abandoned by her master to live alone in a room in Alexandria, Virginia. A concerned citizen wrote the following letter to the mayor of that city in 1813:

> I am impelled by feelings of humanity to call upon you . . . in behalf of a poor sufferer, the greatest object of misery I ever beheld. . . . She is the property of on[e] Posten in whose service she was burnt almost to death before Easter, & has ever since remained in the most shocking situation, she is now loathsome to every beholder, without a change of clothing, or one single necessary of life, or comfort. Can you not compel the savage creature who owns her to do something for her?[128]

If this is not a usual story, it certainly has enough evidential support from elsewhere to alert us to its not being exceptional. A planter who had previously shown concern for his slaves wrote from Baltimore to a friend making a more typical admission. "As to the Old woman," he said, "I assure you I did not mean to impose upon your goodness in taking care of her—I really had lost sight of her as much as I never had heard of her, not that her uselessness induced this for I really have others of value which I have not recalled until mentioned."[129]

Yet the lot of old slaves was not always so bleak. Many planters cared for them till the end of their lives, although the close attention and loving care given to the aged stressed by some historians applies mostly to a small number of domestics or favored slaves who were linked to slaveholders by strong mutual bonds of affection.[130] One such slave belonged to William Pettigrew of North Carolina. At this slave's death, Pettigrew confided to his brother Charles that it "is irreparble to me. . . . The death of this faithful old friend & servant cast over me a feeling of solitude & disolation."[131]

The approach of old age brought unexpected freedom to a few slaves. Masters emancipated some as a reward for a lifetime of faithful service, but other planters intended many of these seeming generosities simply as part of a larger scheme to set themselves and their relatives free of responsibility for care of the old persons. The aged slaves sometimes drifted aimlessly, winding up in cities where urbanites thought them burdensome additions to the population. Cunning slaveholders doctored the appearance of numbers of the old to make them appear a few years younger, rested them, and then sold them to anyone who paid a respectable price.[132] In all, the aged slave could not look forward to leisurely final years with certainty. There was no way to assure that a master's humanitarian outlook would ease his slave's circumstances. On the larger estates, moreover, a planter might be unfamiliar with the care and food rations actually given to the old ones by an overseer. If they moped about, he assumed it was because of age and little else.

At every stage of the field hand's life, his health played a near-central role, more so than with individuals whose activities are sedentary. The slave did, in fact, develop part of his judgment of self from the vigor of his active existence. And a planter's complaints of lost work days in the fields usually blamed disease rather than laziness or deficient slave character. What was more, he spoke of slave labor in connection not only with disease but also with dietary needs, an important element in our discussion of the slave's behavior. Yet all too frequently, later interpreters of the slave experience have bypassed the connection between disease and behavior (which planters observed and understood), thereby distorting the historical picture of the slave's bondage and personality in important ways.

3
Blackstrap Molasses and Cornbread—Diet and Its Impact on Behavior

Of central importance to the numerous problems involved in the maintenance of slaves was the relationship between diet and health. How did bondsmen keep up their stamina through long hours of work? One learns immediately from existing primary and secondary sources that only a handful of slaveholders raised enough varieties of vegetables, fruits, and meats to satisfy the nutritional needs of their families and slaves.[1] Yet frequently, both families and slaves lived solely on the food crops cultivated on the plantation and the livestock and poultry fattened there. All things considered, it is doubtful that the slave's diet bestowed upon him even the appearance, if little else, of good health, though several historians have written that it did.[2] We have not paid as much attention to the details of nutrition during slavery as perhaps we should. The slave's diet reveals a great deal about the quality of his life, his endurance at certain labors, and his general conduct and mannerisms.

Throughout the Old South masters held to similar standards in their definitions of appropriate basic diets for slaves. They rationed out a peck of cornmeal and two to four pounds of bacon (salt pork) a week to each full hand. On numerous Atlantic coastal plantations, slaveowners substituted rice for corn. Corn and rice cooked into various dishes were the mainstays of planters' diets too. The instructions in one farm journal stipulated that "allowances are given out once a week" and that "no distinction is made among work-hands, whether they are full hands or under field hands or adjuncts about the yard, stable & c."[3] Exceptions were made to this rule, however, as the occasion arose. "Each ditcher who does full work without occasioning annoyance for a week, received an extra pound of meat on Wednesday night."[4] Ditching was very hard labor, and the reference to annoying conduct serves as a reminder of the master's ever-present concern with dissident slave behavior.

Small slaveholders especially were sometimes unable to guarantee stable amounts of food for their bondsmen's diet. They purchased some food items from large plantation holders. We do not know the extent of this inter-plantation trade, but further investigation could move us closer to a fuller understanding not only of matters of diet but of the extent and quality of slaves' and masters' community life and cooperation. Perhaps as a partial consequence of these arrangements, one farmer believed that "four pounds of clear meat is too much. I have negroes here that have had only a half pound each week for twenty years. . . ."[5] Food rations also underwent changes with the season, particularly in warmer months when many slaveholders thought it best to cut allowances of meat.[6]

Paralleling matters of diet, and in fact shaping them in part, was a problem that has perpetually challenged men's ingenuity— the preservation of food over extended periods. In the Old South the following was a frequent farm journal entry: "Hung up bacon in smoke house & found a good many shoulders & some hams of 2^d spoiled owing to hot weather I suppose."[7] Unfortunately, masters often did not notice spoiled meat until those slaves who had eaten it became ill or even died.

To preserve meat it was necessary to cure it in salt and place it in the open air for a period of days. Though ages old, the process sometimes failed to take hold even when meticulously controlled;

and the slave benefited little from his one peck of corn and four pounds of bacon if something was wrong with these supplies. During the winter of 1829 one master wrote in a letter to a friend, "There is more spoiled meat in Georgia, than good by a wide difference—."[8] "The worms were very bad in the bacon," recalled another planter about a time twenty years earlier, "and are the same this year [1862] but have it more plentiful this than that year. . . ."[9] These remarks underscore the potential for widespread specific food shortages among the general population.

In one instance, officials of a railroad company knowingly or unknowingly fed spoiled goods to hired slaves. Upon discovering what had happened the bondsmen's owner "kicked up a dust about feeding the negroes with Spiled meal—."[10] In this instance, the fact that many bondsmen in the neighborhood were already sick apparently did not encourage the railroad officials to take special precautions. The slaves probably ate the spoiled items because they were the only food available, not a rare occurrence. But such lack of caution was not limited to isolated instances. Certain kinds of neglect often reached incredible levels in the feeding of imprisoned slaves. Henry Bibb, housed in a slave pen in New Orleans for three months as punishment for attempted escape, wrote, "I have often seen the meat spoiled when brought to us, covered with flies . . . and even worms . . . when we were compelled to eat it, or go without any at all."[11]

Adversity, slavery's constant companion, persistently cut into the slave's food provisions. For him and for those white Southerners who labored daily in the fields, the effects were telling. They accomplished less work because of an inadequate caloric intake. If the labor schedule continued unabated the slave wore himself down, increasing his vulnerability to disease. A lethargy set in that became difficult to reverse under a load of unending labor and poor diet. It is not surprising, considering these circumstances, that many times bondsmen displayed little energy for work. To casual observers, they often appeared inefficient or worse. But if they worked badly—which many did not—if they complained of feeling faint, it may be attributed partly to the imbalance in their diet.

There were ways for the slave to add to the amount and variety of his diet, however, such as by planting a garden, picking wild fruit, and hunting small animals. But these supplementary methods sound somewhat easier than in reality they were. A great many planters who permitted their slaves to cultivate gardens or plant portions of the fields for their own use might deduct from the services and goods they then allotted to the selected bondsmen. Some slaveholders cut the yearly or seasonal allowances of clothes. Bondsmen now had to purchase their clothes out of earnings made from the sale of portions of their crops.[12] A master might also cut down on the amount of food rations given such slaves during times when their gardens and crops had matured.

Slaves also had numerous discouraging encounters with nature as well. Gardens require regular, though not daily, cultivation and irrigation. This was not always possible if water for such purposes had to be transported in large quantities and carried from long distances. Rain did assure that some vegetables and fruits grew wild in the forests, but there were other forms of animal life, as well as insect life, competing for these foods, and rain was not predictable. Certain kinds of greens could be raised all year but had to be eaten quickly, once picked. This could deplete the slave's supply in one to three weeks. Sweet potatoes were occasionally stored in cool, dark places for preservation as were dried beans, but both items then had to be protected from numerous rodents. Of course, the essential growth variable in all of this was always water, and in the Old South uncontaminated water was often in short supply, even for drinking.[13]

Still, many slaves had vegetable patches strewn about the slave quarters or planted in special grounds designated by the planter. "I know plantations," wrote the Reverend Charles C. Jones, "upon which industrious men [slaves] improving their opportunities, sell during the year poultry, stock, and produce of their own raising to the amount of thirty, fifty and a hundred dollars."[14]

Some bondsmen were persistent in this regard, getting the maximum profit from their private labors even when selling to their masters. There can be no doubt that these endeavors bolstered their self-esteem. In a letter to General John A. Quitman, a friend reported with annoyance in the 1840's that ". . . chickens are scarce at this time—the negroes sell all they have to the boats . . ." where their bargains were better.[15]

The first black frost of autumn, when "all the potato vines and all the other delicate plants had been killed so completely that the leaves were black,"[16] destroyed many of these small crops, leaving bondsmen with just a few days' or weeks' supply of greens for the winter months. The appearance of this frost was also a signal to planters, who had absented themselves from plantation life to escape summer diseases, that it was now safe to return. Under these conditions, only when masters grew vegetables in large quantities could they hope to have some in store for family and slaves.

All this partially explains why corn was the dietary mainstay of most Southerners. It endured, as did rice, most changes in the weather, and planters could store it for many weeks and months, as well as grind it into meal for a wide range of dishes. The same cannot be said for Irish potatoes, for example, which could begin to rot with the first blush of summer weather. A North Carolina slaveowner wrote, forcefully but with a touch of sarcasm, "We are all blessed with uninterrupted vigorous health altho we have scarce anything to live on but cornbread, bacon and molasses. We eat heartily. . . ."[17] A traveler in the South in the 1850's made a similar observation: "The sole food of the majority is corn, at every meal, from day to day, and week to week."[18]

Physicians in the Old South and in our day have delineated with considerable detail the connection between diet and behavior. Historians, too, have noted the relationship, but have not yet pursued its implications as fully as they should. Eugene D. Genovese writes that "the diet to which the slaves were subjected must be judged immensely damaging, despite assurances from contempories and later historians that the slave was well fed."[19] And a cursory glance at the bondsman's diet reveals that it was greatly deficient in foods rich in protein and elements of the vitamin B complex series essential to bodily functions, growth, and mental activity.[20]

Though certain food items were regularly consumed by slaves, there remained some doubt among contemporaries as to the relative nutritional value each possessed. Perhaps a discussion of pork is a good place to begin our examination. A great many slaveholders claimed that bondsmen preferred fat pork to lean. In a magazine article, Solon Robinson, a northern agricultural authority, confirmed this observation and added that slaves "want nothing more delicate than pork, fat pork."[21] When a writer in *De Bow's Review* argued rightly that for the sake of nutrition slaves should be fed lean meat, one slaveholder took issue with him and insisted instead that "it is . . . a well known fact, that the more exhausting the labor the fatter the meat which the negro's appetite *craves*. . . ."[22] But caution is required in generalizing about the diet rationed to slaves. Even on plantations in the same neighborhood the amount of food given to bondsmen could vary significantly. "Talking 'bout victuals," said an ex-slave, "our eating was good. Can't says the same for all places. Some of the plantations half-starved their niggers and 'lowanced out their eating till they wasn't fitting to work."[23]

Fanny Kemble, who lived on a Georgia plantation for a while, understood part of the subtle connection between diet and behavior manifestations. She made the important observation that the "low diet" of bondsmen was probably responsible for "some want of stamina in them." She added, "it is astonishing how much less power of resistance to disease they seem to possess than we do."[24] Actually there was little need for surprise considering the sizeable deficiencies in the slave's diet both in vitamins and often in quantity.

Slaves and masters complained periodically of the conditions modifying the quality and amount of the foods they ate. Many times cooks prepared bondsmen's food too hurriedly. Several planters remarked that the cooking was miserable. This might frequently be the case on plantations where one cook fixed most slaves' meals in a central kitchen. A farmer explained why he followed this practice. "I do not regard it as good economy," he wrote, "to say nothing of any feeling, to require negroes to do any cooking after their day's labor is over."[25] But this did not remove the difficulties. "Very often," remembered a bondsman, "so little care had been taken to cure and preserve the bacon, that, when it came to us . . . it was still more alive than dead."[26] Other bondsmen pointed out that they received an allowance of rations for only two meals per day, which was not enough to sustain their work efforts. Many of them exhausted their rations midway through the week in an effort to satisfy ravenous appetites.[27]

The hardiness of the slave's appetite gives us some suggestive leads about the importance of nourishing foods in his diet. The caloric value of these foods—the amount of energy produced for body uses—is of particular importance. Three substances found in foods (proteins, carbohydrates—including sugars and starches—and fats) supply the body with energy. Fats furnish 255 calories to the ounce, as compared to 115 for carbohydrates and proteins.[28] But fat calories can be difficult for the system to break down when consumed on a regular basis. Possible byproducts are boils, eczema, pimples, and an imbalanced system, all of which slaves suffered from extensively. Furthermore, slaves usually cooked their meals in large amounts of pork grease. Observers thought that by doing so they made them virtually inedible, corn fritters dripping with grease not being their idea of an enticing meal. But grease is rich in the calories (energy) needed to help see slaves through plantation labors. The same was true of the cornmeal they consumed. It possessed the equivalent of more than 100 calories per ounce.

Though it would be difficult to estimate on the average how many calories slaves needed to sustain them at their labors, some guidelines can be followed. At the peak of the slaves' work years, between the ages 16 and 26, modern estimates place an individual's daily needs at anywhere from 20 to 25 calories per pound of body weight, so that a slave weighing 130 pounds would need approximately 2600 to 3250 calories per day.[29] But this estimate is based upon age with no particular reference to occupation. During one's working years, caloric requirements are as much influenced by occupation as by age. It seems that an upward revision is called for because of the slave's strenuous outdoor labors that repeatedly ended in physical exhaustion. For adolescents and children the caloric situation is even more acute, since just by virtue of growing they burn more energy proportionally than do adults.

The protein needs of slaves should also be considered. From most indications slaves suffered from dangerously insufficient levels of protein consumption. Yet protein is essential for building and repairing the body's tissues.[30] Modern estimates place the protein needs of adults at roughly two calories of protein per pound of body weight. For children the rate is double or more. Pork could not have supplied the necessary quantity since it was mostly fat.[31] When broken down into their chemical components, proteins are composed of a number of amino acids, but only eighteen of more than forty known amino acids can be utilized for building body tissues. Proteins that contain all eighteen of these building blocks are called complete proteins and are needed by the body for growth and repair. Animals are the main source of such proteins, for few vegetables contain complete protein units; thus a diet consisting mainly of vegetables has to be carefully monitored to keep the body healthy or, especially in children, to sustain growth.[32]

Bondsmen's diets showed significant imbalances in other ways. Dr. Cartwright wrote of slaves, "They do not consume much sugar but are occasionally supplied with molasses."[33] Lean meats, poultry, eggs, milk, and grain products other than corn—foods needed to help the system produce antibodies to fight off infections[34]—were only sporadically seen on most slaves' plates. The consequences of these deficiences were severe.

Sight impairment in various degrees was the burden of many slaves, and this was usually not the consequence of natural blindness. Serious cases of cracked lips were also common; and both these defects may have resulted from a shortage of vitamin A and vitamin B$_2$ (Riboflavin) in the slave's diet. Green and yellow vegetables, sweet potatoes, and collards were not present in sufficient amounts throughout most of the Old South to supply this need. This is not to say, for instance, that sweet potatoes were not eaten by many Southerners. They sometimes formed a share of an otherwise routine diet in parts of Georgia, Kentucky, and elsewhere, but we are unable at present to document their extensive growth and consumption by slaves. Dr. Daniel Drake estimated that in the Upper South around 1800 the "diet of the field slaves was generally little else than rice or unground Indian corn, with such fish as they might happen to catch."[35] He hastened to add that in 1851 this was no longer the case, but about the same time Thomas Affleck was warning slaveholders that "not nearly enough vegetables are grown and fed to negroes."[36] Masters and slaves persistently suffered from sore eyes. Writing to his brother about the birth of a son, a North Carolina planter observed that "he is to all appearance, as promising a child as any we have had, except, that he has been afflicted with sore eyes, almost from his birth. . . ."[37] A relative of the same family subsequently noted her own inability to finish a letter to her mother because "one of my eyes has been so sore as to deprive me of that pleasure."[38] The account left by a Louisiana planter describes what happened to one slave whose vision went uncared for. The planter wrote to John Mc Donogh demanding a refund of his money for a bondsman he had purchased. He claimed, "It was only when I was in a position to use him on my work that I noticed that this negro had . . . lost his sight, to such a degree that when he was weeding the crops, he could not distinguish the grass from the plant—. . . ."[39]

When they occurred, sore eyes made working uncomfortable and less than precise, and doctors were rarely called to treat them. The stinging eyes of which so many diarists and correspondents wrote did not go away for days or weeks, if then. One may imagine that slaves rubbed their eyelids to relieve the itching, but thereby merely accentuated it; and the distraction further affected their labor. Sore eyes led to headaches and heightened emotional irritability. It is worthwhile to stress here that eye troubles were a widespread concern, and their occurrence added to the discomforts of constant physical movement, which was the slave's waking state. Bondsmen lived with this inconvenience, though some were let off work for days because of it.

Planters who suffered from the effects of sore eyes could also be laid up for days, their affliction greatly curtailing even their minor chores.[40] But slaves who complained of eye problems might be accused of laziness or trying to get out of work, although those planters and overseers who were careful observers of plantation life were slow to make this charge. They encouraged the slave to do his tasks as best he could, some providing eye ointment, which helped but little. Others used force, realizing that such difficulties were ever with them—come what may.

Complaints of skin irritations were legion in the slaves' ranks too. The mildest forms appeared as scaly patches on legs and arms that caused some itching but seemed to interfere little with work. Slaves were also "very liable to colics, cramps, convulsions, worms, glandular and nervous affections, sores, biles, warts and other diseases of the skin," wrote a southern doctor.[41] Among the ailments that compelled a purchaser to send a slave back to his former owner were the "running sores on his legs. . . ."[42] Moses Liddell of Louisiana witnessed on his own estate that "we still have a number of our people laid up with sore fingers, hands & biles and a few as usual with head Aches, pain in breast and sides. . . ."[43]

Bondsmen also came down with white swelling, maladies of the spine and hip joints, and rickets. It is interesting that rickets, though largely a disease of childhood, was frequently reported in adults. Its symptoms include softening of the bones. The appearance of rickets is related to insufficient vitamin D, which the body needs to build strong bones and teeth; this deficiency meant also that slaves had often to accustom themselves to working with the pain of nagging toothaches. Sunshine is necessary for the synthesis of vitamin D by the body, and slaves spent much time outdoors, but their dietary insufficiency was still sometimes so great as to cause rickets. Responsible for the onset of rickets as well are insufficient consumption of calcium and phosphorus, both of which vitamin D helps to synthesize, and the generally poor quality of one's diet. Eggs, butter, and fish-liver oils are a ready source of all three nutrients and would have reduced incidences of rickets, but even these food products were not always in ready supply.

Cornmeal, as we have seen, led the list of foodstuffs consumed by slaves. "You must know," wrote a Mississippi planter to his New York cousin, "that corn in this country is truly the staff of life . . . it is almost the whole food of Thousand[s] of Negroes . . . there is perhaps a greater consumption of that necessary grain, made her[e] than in any other place on the globe, in proportion to the number of people."[44] One may suppose that this heavy consumption of cornmeal led occasionally to the dietary deficiency disease pellagra, which was common in the South in the early part of the twentieth century. Pellagra, according to one medical authority, "occurred where diets consisted mainly of cornmeal, salt pork, and molasses"[45]—precisely the slave's diet. Although it can end in death when left untreated and allowed to run its course, a leading medical authority on pellagra has written that "pellagra must be charged with causing" a "great amount of sickness and debility, much of it vague and ill-defined and thus frequently unrecognized. . . ."[46] Dermatitis, diarrhea, and dementia, the symptoms by which it is diagnosed, as well as its side effects—dizziness and vertigo, frequently referred to in the Old South as "Bling staggers"—are traceable among bondsmen; plantation records are replete with accounts of both men and animals who experienced these effects. Slaveholders' diaries, farm journals, and letters all leave a trail of evidence, without attaching a name to the sickness, pointing to the existence of a great deal of pellegra among slaves. Masters considered it primarily a skin disease, which is perfectly understandable since in a scientific sense we have not known much about the causes of pellagra until this century.[47]

Also very serious was pellagra's last symptom—dementia. Large numbers of slaves complained of an inability to concentrate on work assignments over extended periods of time; and an indeterminate number were victims of occasional hallucinations—both possible signs of the effects of dementia. Many more bondsmen than one would expect displayed restlessness and hypersensitivity in what might be considered normal situations for them. Southern physicians observed these symptoms with interest. At least one, however, Dr. Samuel Cartwright, ignored their relationship to diet. He contended instead that most of the slave's physical and mental sluggishness was an unavoidable by-product of insufficient air getting to the brain. This, he wrote, resulted in a "hebetude [blunting] of mind and body. . . ."[48] That the slave's physique might be equal or superior to the white's Cartwright conceded, but he still believed bondsmen had a smaller lung capacity which cut down the amount of air reaching the brain, thereby decreasing its ability to function. It is difficult to tell if Cartwright's medical views were taken seriously by other southern physicians. Although many of these views came under considerable criticism in the 1850's, Cartwright, even so, remained a very influential spokesman.[49]

The focus of dietary concern in the Atlantic coastal communities was rice, the mainstay of the slave's diet there. In a number of cases on several Savannah River plantations of Georgia, bondsmen "would suddenly swell in every part of the body, and in five or six days the case would invariably prove fatal."[50] The disease, though not identified in this slaveholder's account, exhibited the symptoms of beriberi, a dietary deficiency disease not uncommon to other rice-eating societies in the Far East. In this example, the "disease was supposed to have been caused by the continual eating of rice (it being almost impossible to procure corn)." The slaveowner, understandably distraught, angrily and unfairly blamed the slaves in question for "eating rice not sufficiently cooked, knowing the lazy character of the Negro, and with little or no salt."[51] But his anger served no constructive purpose; the slaves were dead.

We may conjecture that beriberi began to make regular appearances in the Old South in the early nineteenth century when rice mills, to please the tastes of a clientele more palate-conscious than formerly, began polishing away the outer cover of the rice grain, which is rich in thiamine. Thiamine (vitamin B_1) is a beri-beri preventative, but it works its way out of the system quickly and must be replenished often.[52] The first symptoms of beriberi can appear within a few days after the body's supply is gone. On the coastal rice plantations of Georgia, South Carolina, and lower North Carolina, rice graced most slaves' tables, and unbalanced diets were common. There, beriberi's most noticeable sign was a general loss of strength accompanied by weakness in the limbs. Even when the disease did not develop full-blown, it is possible that slaves experienced some of its weakening effects and an accompanying impact on their work. As an observer in the Old South noted, slaves in rice regions "complain more of being faint, when fed on rice and potatoes, than when fed corn."[53] Of course, ailing slaves could not put down the hoe or plow to rest whenever they felt somewhat dizzy and uncomfortable.

By far the great majority of masters possessed minimal knowledge about the formulation of a balanced diet, and apparently even less about the slave's increased dietary needs resulting from his hard physical labors. Taking into account William Dosite Postell's warning that "it must not be assumed that the antebellum planter was entirely lacking in knowledge or appreciation of the importance of providing a balanced diet,"[54] we must still conclude that the bondsman's meals lacked flexibility and variety. A slaveowner might accuse a slave of gluttony if he found him eating the range of foods that often graced some masters' tables or was offered in the name of southern hospitality to satisfy plantation visitors' appetites. For some slave managers, sadly, carelessly filling bondsmen's stomachs with any sort of food frequently seemed all right. Noticing the exhausted condition of both his overseer and his field hands one summer, one planter searched his conscience and then questioned whether he "did not err in giving them i[n]different whiskey in considerable quantities and herrings for breakfast."[55] Providing liquor for bondsmen in warm weather was nonetheless a frequent practice, for it palliated some of their desires and made them sweat more freely. No doubt some slaves drank too much, numbing themselves into readiness for their monotonous chores. A partially inebriated bondsman who performed his scheduled duties was, we might suppose, more useful at certain times than a troublesome sober one. "I question," continued the same planter, "but they would enjoy better health in harvest without the regular allowance of spirits if they did not do as much work."[56]

In dietary practices a number of larger and smaller estates were exceptions to the general rule, and in this respect the Pettigrew wheat plantations of North Carolina stand out. The Pettigrews provided their slaves with probably the most balanced diet that any bondsmen received in the Old South.[57] The list of foods included, among others, fruits, vegetables, chickens, and geese. In the Deep South, Dr. James G. Carson's Canebrake plantation in Louisiana is also noteworthy. He owned more than 150 slaves in 1858 and raised large quantities of corn, potatoes, and peas, which his bondsmen tended during the course of the day. Yet despite Canebrake Plantation's dietary benefits, the slave "children had to do without shoes and headgear . . ." when they needed them.[58] Usually a plantation was not able to raise everything that it required, and small slaveholders were therefore, to some degree, dependent on large planters from whom they purchased foodstuffs that they could not raise themselves. When they were unable to obtain certain goods in this way, they merely went without, and their slaves made do—a well-established custom in bondage.

Often slaveholders refused to grow fruit because of its rumored germ-harboring properties. But fruits were a source of vitamin C, a substance dangerously lacking in most of the food slaves ate. Many came down with scurvy, a disease common at the time among sailors away from shore for lengthy periods. A supply of fruits on board ship furnished the necessary vitamin and solved the problem. One physician had a somewhat misplaced opinion about it all, but one which again hits directly upon the issue of the difficulties in evaluating slave behavior. "A scurvy set of negroes," he wrote, "means the same thing, in the south, as a disorderly, worthless set."[59] It seems that if one important item was not missing from the slave's diet another was.

The dietary deficiencies that plagued the adult slave population naturally affected their children, almost without exception. Left to fend for themselves on some plantations, young slaves developed some fatal habits, perhaps the most peculiar being the practice of eating dirt. Many children even today experiment with it, but in bondage it was "the dread of every planter, this frightful malady, noticed all over the South. . . ."[60] A master in South Carolina remarked with reference to his infant bondsmen that ". . . one of the Boys about 3 years old died this Morning (from Eating Dirt as Stated by the Doctor.)."[61] Adults, too, frequently fell into this practice. There was considerable speculation as to its causes; but the most commonly held interpretation of the time was that dirt-eating was a by-product of poor diet.[62] Dr. James B. Duncan of St. Mary's Parish, Louisiana, argued for nutriment deficiency. "The diet of negroes on most plantations being salt pro, [pork], corn bread and molasses—rarely eating fresh meat and vegetables," he wrote, "a condition of the system is thus produced closely allied to scurvy."[63] There were also some psychological implications, as suggested by a New Orleans physician. Focusing on the manner in which planters treated their slaves of all ages, he proposed that harsh treatment gave rise to "depressing emotions and a sense of degradation,"[64] which could lead to dirt-eating, among other things.

When the slave first started to eat dirt, he appeared normal but acted somewhat idle. He dragged about sluggishly, according to planters and doctors (who often detected the habit too late), and it was easy to attribute his affliction to just ordinary laziness or, at least, some vague quality of slow movement hereditary among Africans. The precise cause of dirt-eating is not known, and the start of the practice in adults, sometimes the aged, is not easy to explain.[65] Many southern physicians thought that dirt-eating caused much of the widespread consumptive problems found among bondsmen. And pregnant women often took up the habit to satisfy a "depraved appetite."[66] Interestingly, slaves themselves considered the practice juvenile, and hid it when possible from relatives, even when they knew that if they did not receive medical treatment death might result. Eventually, however, they "were betrayed by their full, swollen shiny skin, puffy eyelids, pale palms and soles."[67]

Planters did take a few preventive steps to guard against dirt consumption. Chewing tobacco not only served as a luxury item for adult bondsmen, but hopefully distracted them from the temptation for that first mouthful. Adults, in turn, whipped children repeatedly to discourage them from playing in dirt; and some planters and parents went so far as to place muzzles on them so that when they were at play they might put nothing in their mouths.[68]

Perhaps because of their diet the majority of slaves were rarely in adequate physical shape to keep them immunized from most common, to say nothing of severe, diseases. "The approach of the summer, therefore, brought dreaded intestinal diseases of all types, just as the approach of winter brought respiratory diseases."[69] Under this constant onslaught, the inadequacies of plantation food preparations became all too obvious. When bondsmen needed varieties of food most, food itself was scarce. Also, it was a standing rule on many plantations that when a work hand was not performing his full duties, for whatever reason, his rations were often diminished. This was an unfortunate practice designed, in part, to encourage fakers to return to work. But it failed to take into account the fact that during illness energy exerted by the body to repair itself is akin to labor. Knowing that this was a widespread practice, some slaves worked till they nearly dropped from over-exertion rather than submit to a circumstance in which they would be furnished with fewer rations than they ordinarily received. Reduced food supplies were often enforced as a discipline for disobedience too. But a master's rash judgment could be costly if his slave became ill and died from such a reduction or even if he just needed medical care.[70]

There were ways to supplement the flawed or inadequate food

rations given to slaves, and bondsmen helped to fill this need themselves. As we have seen, slaves planted gardens and raised livestock and poultry to supply their own tables. The keeper of one plantation journal recorded on a Wednesday: "Greater part of today negroes planting their own crop."[71] Another journal pointed out: "this day had to break Negroes up in raising chickens. . . ."[72] Looking after these interests sometimes extended the slave's workday into the mid and late evening hours, but there were few complaints by slaves on this account. One plantation manager wrote to his employer that one of his bondsmen "called for provisions of which he says he is destitute & gives as a reason for not working for it, that he is attending his garden—. Please inform me if I shall supply him with it."[73] Other slaves turned to less honest means. In Louisiana, planter J. Maynard told a neighbor, "I beg to express my regrets that two of my men have been found guilty of killing one of your calves. . . . It is one of those occurrances that occasionally happen with all who have to deal with these people."[74]

Sometimes both adults and children stole items of food to satisfy their appetites: "Whipping couldn't stop us."[75] To add further to the hardships of bondage, famines of varying durations swept through southern states down to 1850. The Valley of Mississippi was especially hard hit. Keeping this in mind, it seems likely that many acts of theft were committed by "famished negroes."[76] In an instance perhaps representative of many, some North Carolina masters caught several bondsmen in the process of skinning a stolen steer.[77] Another slave ran away to escape punishment after refusing to tell his owner what he had done with a half-dozen chickens.[78] These planters were fortunate, compared to some others. One year South Carolina's James Henry Hammond accused his slaves of taking more than a hundred hogs from his estate.[79] Stealing on this scale surely required the cooperation of many of the plantation's bondsmen, yet Hammond makes no mention of any widescale plot or the apprehension of the offenders.

On their own livestock and poultry bondsmen sometimes per-

formed strange identifying mutilations. They chopped off chickens'
toes in varying lengths, and tied odd-colored pieces of string to
animals' legs. Each slave tried to develop a distinctive brand. Yet
despite great pride in ownership most were quick to share their
fortunes with fellows in periods of special hardship.

Some bondsmen turned their livestock and the rewards of
hunting into various culinary delights. They cooked stews and
broths, mixing meat, spices, white potatoes, and other vegetables
when they were available. Some slaves mastered and advanced
the art of pastry cooking which they put to good use both for
masters and themselves. When there was a variety of foods
around, bondsmen could be sure that talented slave cooks would
make it into something tasty. The Christmas season was especially known for this. The familiar opossum played a spicy role,
and even snake meat was eaten by a few slaves although most
were put off by the taboos surrounding snakes in general. Sweet
potatoes used as the filling for pies or baked on the hearth, cornbread and pieces of pork blended with it and pot liquor to make
crackling bread, found their way onto the slave's table in happier
times. A glass of syrup water might provide the beverage. When
they were available spices and herbs were liberally used by slave
gourmets. Many vegetable and meat dishes were generously laced
with red pepper, not only because it added to the taste of much
of the slave's monotonous diet but for conjuring purposes too.
Pork and beef were roasted, barbecued, and seasoned with red
pepper and vinegar. Many of the recipes bondsmen created or
contributed to come down to us today in such dishes as jumbolia
and southern fried chicken. The juices and drippings from these
dishes were often saved and used in the preparation of less fanci-
ful creations.

For slaves who hunted, coons, squirrels, opossums, and turtles
were favorite catches. Following these forays participating bondsmen often came down sick from eating unripe fruits or vegetables
which they found growing wild in the woods. They also drank
unsafe water and waded in waters polluted by a wide range of
disease-bearing organisms. They were wise if they rinsed off with

clean water when they came back from these hunts, but most times water could not be used for such purposes and it was seldom thought that it should be so used. A Louisiana master showed concern for a runaway slave because of these potential dangers. He wrote, "I am not otherwise uneasy about him but that he may eat green corn, melons or whenever he may find them, which will be seen to make him sick & if not taken in time may operate fatally."[80]

Fishing, if a stream, lake, or river was close by, was also popular with slaves. Bondsmen on the South Carolina sea islands often fished for crabs and oysters, according to Solon Robinson.[81] But on these same islands traveler Basil Hall wrote that masters give slaves "salt fish, as well as salt beef occasionally, but only as a favour, and it can never be claimed as a right."[82] Fish is a valuable source of protein. In a few places in the Old South there were "fine facilities . . . for procuring fresh fish, clams & oysters, at almost all times of the year."[83] But usually slaves got fish only rarely, when the plantation's supply of pork ran out. One diarist noted, "Meat gave out a week ago bought 8 barrels of Herrings and began to serve them out."[84] Still another commented that luckless slaves living near Charleston received only "one peck of corn per week, unless they perform their task and redeem time to go fishing."[85] Many bondsmen everywhere did just that. It should be understood that the slave's private labors were not merely of supplementary benefit to the diet. They were often a vital part of his upkeep.

A necessary accompaniment of such private efforts was the accumulation of goods that slaves sold or traded. Their bargainings spilled over into towns on Sundays, eliciting widespread complaints from whites about "nigger tradesmen." Rachel O'Connor of Louisiana complained to her brother David Weeks that after giving her overseer orders about paying slaves "for the amount of there crops of corn & Pumpkins . . . he only pays them a little & then keeps them runing to Town every Sunday for what they get. . . ."[86]

The dietary deficiencies that plagued slaves take on another dimension when briefly compared to health conditions in our century. In the 1930's, studies of diet indicated that black families living in the Yazoo–Mississippi Delta area were subsisting on diets which were 10 per cent or more deficient in protein, calcium, phosphorus, and iron. Many suffered a lack of vitality as a consequence. Dietary experts have also made the connection between diet and general disposition, while pointing to thousands of people in the United States who are presently undernourished. This is not to say that you are what you eat, but simply to underline the interrelationship between diet, disease, and behavior.[87] Without doubt, nutritional factors too little considered have played an unsuspected but significant role in those behavioral manifestations that have contributed to the confusion about the personality of the slave—chiefly, that is, attributions of laziness and docility. We need now to give much additional weight to diet and disease in slave profiles, for such forces greatly modify static conceptions of behavior and add to our appreciation of the complexity of the slave scene.

4
The Logic of Resistance

The patterns of resistance and non-resistance that characterized the slave's adjustment to bondage have been more disputed by scholars than almost any other issue relating to slaves. Yet such disputes have frequently been rather narrowly focused, treating bondsmen as members of an oppressed group who accommodated to their fortunes as best they could, manifesting a high level of docility and lack of initiative. In this view, slaveholders are of primary importance because they held the reins of authority and thus could greatly influence behavior. But how much influence could they exert? Mrs. Isaac H. Hilliard of Arkansas had some ideas. "I believe it . . . to be my duty," she wrote, "so long as I own slaves, to keep them in proper subjection and well employed."[1] The bondsman Henry Bibb was to observe later that this meant the frequent use of that well-known enforcer, the lash, which was intended "to degrade and keep me in subordination."[2] His observation had much to back it up, and, as a contemporary sociologist points out, "the use of violence (or what is known as 'power')"—by masters, in this case—"is an indispensable condition for attaining the condition of accommodation. . . ."[3]

Slave society tried to dictate those actions by slaves that were appropriate and those that were not. But this, after all, is a cardinal rule of subjugation. With reference to his bondsmen, a North Carolina planter reminded his father that "a feeling of independence alters the relations of individuals marvelously."[4] To deprive the slave of that feeling seemed often the slaveholder's main purpose—to impose upon him, in part at least, what the slave system held to be the proper habits and conduct of slaves.[5] Bondsman James L. Smith recognized this early, and without relinquishing his identity "strove," he said, "by my prudence and correctness of demeanor to avoid exciting his [master's] evil passions."[6] This, he believed, was simply a careful reading of his predicament, not capitulation to it.

Past analyses of slave resistance have regularly recognized only a few possible responses to the condition of bondage. If the slave was not a Nat Turner, they appear to say, then he was submissive—a typical slave type (Sambo). But if we want a fuller explanation of slave behavior we must reach it by raising more questions about bondsmen's motivations. For instance, why did slaves conduct themselves as they did when resisting the laws of slavery? And what roles did they play in shaping the nature of their own enslavement?

The circumstances prompting masters' attempts to regulate slaves' movements were complex. Most feared that bondsmen would seize the most innocent opportunity to revolt.[7] There is a great deal of evidence supportive of the notion that the planter class felt a general unrest about their own physical safety in the presence of so many slaves, despite assertions then and later that a white man could control a score of blacks.[8] To assist them in coping with these feelings of unrest slaveholders relied on various helpers. Chief among these was the plantation overseer, whose primary duties were to supervise bondsmen's work and to police their behavior.[9]

Slaves, in turn, closely watched the behavior of their managers, obtaining a fund of useful information about the peculiarities of a master's character. They pieced their conception of him together from such diverse sources as the bragging of haughty house slaves about idiosyncracies they had witnessed in the Big House and the pointed-finger warnings of old slaves. Slaves "found the 'management of whites' as complex a matter as their masters found the 'management of Negroes,' " writes Kenneth Stampp.[10] The difficulties multiplied since masters, even on the same plantation, did not treat slaves uniformly. Charles Ball was a favorite slave of one of his masters, though he was greatly abused by his mistress.[11] Other slaves never gained favor. Sometimes, if a master suspected them of possible troublemaking, he locked them in a work house before they could act. One small slaveholding farmer, however, relied less on anticipation than on discipline after the fact to prevent misdeeds. "The first negro that steals," he wrote, "or runs away, or fights, or who is hard to manage in order to get a day's work, must be locked up every night as soon as he comes in from work, and turned out next morning; kept up every Sunday."[12] Southern politician John C. Calhoun followed a similar course. He had one of his slaves disciplined by lodging him "in Jail for one wee[k], to be fed on bread and water" and to have administered "30 lashes well laid on. . . ." Why such severe measures? In this case Calhoun interpreted the slave's offenses—running off and an inflated ego—as a threat to his handling of other bondsmen in his plantation's labor force.[13]

Calhoun's remedy for unwanted behavior calls to mind the analogies scholars have made between slavery's plantation system and what are today known as total institutions: prisons and concentration camps are the two favorite examples.[14] Because of his disciplinary techniques it is easy to view Calhoun as a jailer or prison guard, keeping unwanted outside influences away from his slaves while physically restraining their movements within the plantation's "walls." Yet the plantation actually bore little real resemblance to today's total institutions. On the contrary, it possessed qualities that permitted many slaves enough leeway within the setting of bondage to work out a variety of personally beneficial responses to the demands of their existences.[15] At times, perhaps, some masters probably wished they did have adequate facilities to restrain all their bondsmen. One slaveholder raged under a heavy burden of irritation, "I am nearly worried to death with them [my slaves] if I had a jail I should lock them up every night."[16]

Southern jails were in fact filled with slaves who struck out against bondage. Some had killed their masters or inflicted bodily injuries on whites or fellow blacks. Others had been convicted of lesser crimes; but still others were jailed briefly by slaveholders who sought merely to control their disobedience. The frequency of this kind of discipline is not known, but even in jails slaves' survival methods are revealing. One story is of special interest. It comes to us from a bondsman who was imprisoned in a New Orleans jail for ten months. He wrote,

> I soon demonstrated that a man with a plan always had the advantage. . . . There were certain positions which were blind spots to my [jail] captors. If I occupied one of these blind spots, if I timed my next movement correctly I could do anything up to murder without my victim knowing of my presence. It became a sort of a play with me, which I enjoyed, because I made the white man helpless against me.[17]

Masters kept the behavior of their slaves under close watch when they could, relying on southern society at large to help keep bondsmen in their place. But the heart of the official network of surveillance was the patrol system. Sometimes financed by a small tax on slaves above the age of twelve, and sometimes voluntary, it was an obvious way for whites to guard against slave resistance while making sure that slaves remained careful of their moves.[18] During periods of special alarm, slaveholders also formed groups of concerned citizens (vigilantes). The bondsman John Parker recalled that "the woods were patroled nightly by constables and any man black or white had to give a good accant of himself, especially if he was a stranger. . . ."[19] Nevertheless, the inefficiency of this method was considerable and planters knew it. An Alabama master expressed his discontent with the situation: "Three of my Cloverdale hands ran off a short time ago at the same time, but returned after spending a few days in the woods. Our police regulations are very defective."[20] Yet, on the other side, patrols ran the risk of giving offence to planters themselves by needlessly abusing and whipping slaves. Consequently, patrols were constantly near the heart of ill-feelings between blacks (bonded and free) and whites. Many slave conspiracies were, in fact, directed against patrollers, who often went out of their way to abuse slaves in the slaves' leisure moments, simply for the sport of it. They barged into slave social gatherings. They disrupted some religious meetings and even sexually assaulted some of the slave women. Slaves' derogatory remarks about the patrollers abound. Both free and bonded blacks sometimes killed particularly bothersome patrol members, but they might, more typically, hurl rocks from the shelter of the woods or "stretch clothes lines across the street, high enough to let the horses pass, but not the rider. . . ."[21] The patrollers, naturally, subsequently went about their work with added caution, fully conscious that they too were being patrolled.

The life of a patrol was usually short. Its members worked in rotations of two to three weeks in order to spread the responsibility for policing bondsmen evenly among slaveholders. The patrol's make-up and efficiency therefore could not be guaranteed. Some southern counties levied small fines upon individuals who failed to take a turn on duty, but many preferred to pay the penalty rather than serve. Numerous communities, in an effort to bypass these problems, hired men who served regularly, though their professionalism was generally not of a high grade. One slave was not at all friendly to the patrols he knew in bondage. They "are poor white men," he said, "who live by plundering and stealing, getting rewards from runaways, and setting up little shops on the public roads" to capture the illicit trade with slaves.[22] If a patrol caught a bondsman off his plantation without a written pass from his master, the consequence was thus not always dire. Many slaves persuaded patrol members not to whip them or turn them over to the jailers. They struck a deal, which could mean that the patrollers agreed to "take whatever the slaves steal paying in money, whiskey, or whatever the slaves want."[23] Policing of bondsmen therefore ran the gamut from strict control to collusion between established authorities and Africans. Slaves prompted much of the latter sort of activity.[24]

Because of the weaknesses easily detectable in these methods of slave control, it appears that the Old South utilized its police system as much for its ability to create the illusion of security as for its actual ability to restrain slaves physically at every juncture. This outlook betrayed the thinly veiled feeling that bondsmen were not quite as submissive and contented as pro-slavery spokesmen often insisted. There are also some indications that those bondsmen who were pushed into cautious submissiveness by stern slaveholders were the ones most easily bullied by their own fellow bondsmen. The care with which other bondsmen took notice of submissive behavior, critically disapproving it, has been largely overlooked. The slave's sense of kinship with his fellows was strengthened by common overlapping personal successes and failures.[25] A too-submissive slave could not easily share in these. Bondsmen who were courageous but not foolish commanded respect in slave circles, especially when their fellows saw their behavior as just.[26] Bondsmen broken by discipline were pitied by other slaves in a manner that seemed easily to broaden into antagonism. Experience taught many that these bondsmen were often the first to confess the details of the group's activities when pressured by masters.

The practice of hiring slaves out to work for neighbors on nearby plantations or in towns forced a further modification in the effectiveness of slave controls. Necessitated by the economics of bondage, this practice allowed and stimulated bondsmen to refine their work skills to make themselves more marketable; many times it gave them an opportunity to escape the tight personal confinement that could develop when a slave worked for only one master.[27]

Contracts of hire were not difficult to arrange. The Dismal Swamp Company of Virginia, a lumbering enterprise, employed the slave George for thirty dollars "for the year 1835." The company was to furnish him "with two Suits of good clothes, two

pairs of Shoes, Stockings, Hat, and blanket. . . ."²⁸ Transactions
of this kind frequently occurred with the active consent of the
slave. Moses Grandy's master gave him permission to hire his own
time, and Moses was able to pay "him out of my earnings . . ."
while "I maintained myself on the rest, and saved what I could.
In this way I was not liable to be flogged and ill-used."²⁹ The arrangements some slaves set up during these hirings considerably
modified their dependence on slaveholders.

A North Carolina bondsman, diplomatically pressuring his
master to see things his way, tried to negotiate the hiring of his
time in this fashion. He was a literate slave, and in a letter to
his mistress he confided, "I am not willing to live with Mr. White
and I hope that you will not make me live whare I dont want
to live for I do every thing to obay you that is in my power." He
bargained from the record of his past obedience to get what he
wanted: "I will pay you any way thay you want me to pay you
if it is by the month or by the Year . . . I wish you would answer it [my letter] as quick as you can make it convenient. . . ."³⁰
His was a kind of obedient resistance.

The occasional compliments good slave workers earned pleased
their masters much, though slaveholders sometimes neglected to
give the slave full credit for a job skillfully done. This was, there
is little doubt, very frustrating for bondsmen. One expressed his
annoyance succinctly: ". . . I hated the injustices and restraints
against my own initiative more than it is possible for words to express. To me that was the great curse of slavery."³¹ Subsequently,
this same slave worked for a while in a New Orleans foundry
where "I was put to work under a [white] foreman who did not
know his job. I knew then that my position was hopeless, because
I knew I was a good workman."³² His knowledge led to his extreme discontentment and eventually to open confrontation between himself and his superiors.

Other bondsmen were even more offended when their masters
pocketed most of the wages they earned. Many resented this intrusion on their earning power. A little-explored area of the hiring
out of slaves concerns salary arrangements. The usual practice,

it seems, was to pay the hired slave's wages directly to his master, who then gave the slave a share he deemed fit. Perhaps one notable reason for this was that bondsmen who received their money directly might not turn it over to their masters, and for this were placed in jails "for not giving their masters the wages they had earned."[33] Money these slaves gained from their own labors they believed to be theirs.

Clearly then, the slave possessed the potential for unsettling the Old South's tranquility.[34] John Mills, from his home in Bayou Sarah, Louisiana, reminded his cousin, "you must know, that unless there is order and subordination kept up, amongst negroes, they would soon be masters, instead of Slaves. . . ."[35] Most masters were only too aware of this possibility.[36] The situations that arose could be quite compromising. Linton Stephens, brother of Alexander Stephens, vice-president of the Confederacy, sought his brother's sympathetic ear about the serious problems he confronted in his slaves. "I have got a big row on hand with about 8 or 10 of my negroes for killing my hogs and sheep. . . . I have one of them in jail on bread and water. He tried to cut two of my negroes. . . ." This slave posed some special disciplinary challenges, for "he is the worst negro I have and has drawn his knife several times before on the overseer." Then why not get rid of him? Linton had the answer: "He was brought to me at the camp and the first thing I did . . . was to knock him down and choke him. . . . I would sell him if I could."[37] Alexander Stephens himself had a slave Pierce about whom his overseer raged after Pierce's brief imprisonment, "I am satisfied that his imprisonment has only tended to harden him. . . . I don't think he will ever reform. . . ."[38] Southern newspapers further reveal how concerned slaveholders were about blacks gaining the upper hand, not necessarily by insurrectionary means but by masters' failure to enforce firm rules of conduct.[39]

The short account of still another planter's difficulties with his slaves is illustrative. He had particular trouble with his bondsman John about whom he had "given up all hope of ever being able to make him an honest and obedient boy; whipping does no good

and advice is nearly thrown away—." John's recent activities as a
runaway had caused his master's current irritation. He determined
that when John was apprehended he should be "heavily ironed
and put to work."[40] Yet he did not really believe that even this
would correct John's disobedient ways.

The management problems on the above plantation assumed
many forms. During one weekend bondsmen belonging to the
Hamiltons, the owners, and their neighbors "gave a supper party"
without formal permission. According to one of the Hamiltons,
"just about the time they were ready to set down to tea I waked
them up with the Contents of my Gun—such scampering you
never did see, running over cordwood, tree tops, in ditches, & c."
The sight was, no doubt, comical to the rifleman. All but one of
the slaves managed to scramble to safety. He was the property of
a Dr. Smith and during the shooting was "very badly wounded
and may in all probilaty [be] disabled for life. . . ."[41]

It is surprising that such a gathering occurred at all in view of
the Hamilton's past record of harsh discipline. The bondsmen's
behavior was a direct affront to plantation guidelines. And gatherings of this sort required careful planning well in advance in order
that all guests might be present and the proper victuals prepared.
The need for such extensive pre-arrangements were what many
masters could not understand, but more revealing is the fact that
bondsmen believed they could engage in these forms of activities
at all. They were fully aware that such momentary enjoyments
would not go unpunished if found out, but nonetheless they went
ahead, throughout the Old South. Dr. Smith's slave—reminiscent
of the slave John—had been shot previously by a Hamilton who
explained, "this same boy has been shot twice this year. . . ."[42]

That slaves were discontented with their bondage is overwhelmingly documented by manuscript and narrative materials.
In some measure their uneasiness probably stemmed from being
the least of the Old South's sons. They were not always forgiving
of such inconsideration, and retaliated when they could. The
Reverend Charles Elliott, a northern minister, was among many
who wrote of "eye-servant[s]" who "do as little as they can."[43]

Illogic and bias mar his two-volume study, *Sinfulness of American Slavery*, published in 1857, but his conclusion that some slave laborers in retaliation for the "injustices exercised on them become the most expensive laborers" seems quite accurate.[44]

The bondsman Henry C. Bruce once commented haughtily that many of the companions he had known in slavery "took no interest in their master's work . . . and went no further than forced by the lash. . . ."[45] He referred to slaves who plowed furrows too shallow for proper planting of crops or deliberately overworked field animals. Overseers constantly encountered this kind of field hand. In the cotton country during harvest, many bondsmen might work through a cotton patch leaving some of the cotton boles purposefully untouched. It was easy for them to do so and blame their seeming inefficiency on an overseer or driver who pressed the work gang too hard. They did, of course, get whipped if they pushed such behavior too far, but not as often as one might suppose. "I have punished all the negroes very severely," was the remark of a Louisiana planter to his father. And it "would not surprize me, if they all left."[46]

An entire gang of slaves could agree privately to slow the work pace for a variety of reasons. Landon Carter of Virginia complained of this practice by his field hands. He noted that "the pretence is Nanny was sick one day. But even with overseers this is a constant excuse, if any one person the most trifling hand is ill but a day or a piece of a day, it generally excuses the loss of a whole days work of the gang."[47]

With lash in hand overseers threatened and disciplined slaves for working poorly or breaking badly made tools, but there were few acceptable alternatives to bent hoes, broken plows, and toothless rakes other than a slowed work pace, a fact which all too few slave managers appeared willing to allow. An overseer's salary and job security often fluctuated with the abundance of the year's harvest, and he occasionally worked bondsmen unduly hard to insure that his share of the take would be as large as possible. Some bondsmen died from overwork or abuse.[48] But in the range of contacts between overseers and slaves many overseers found themselves buffeted about in ways that compelled them to work harder themselves to insure their own salaries. On the large estates where overseers were usually employed, they could not make daily checks on the various slave gangs' work efforts in all of the widely separated fields. If one of their concerns was deliberately broken tools, an equal one was misplaced tools, for bondsmen would frequently disrupt the work schedule by leaving "plows and tools of all kinds, just where the[y] use them, no matter where, so that they have to be hunted all over the place when wanted."[49] Plantation managers tried vigorously to suppress such manifestations.

A relative of General John A. Quitman of Mississippi wrote him that the General's overseer was "getting to be, too sever[e] with the negroes—Too fond of his whip and the use of the 'Stocks. . . ." Fearing what the slaves might do he warned, "the negroes complain almost every day and many would have been run away, were I not at home."[50]

This apprehension had a much broader implication, however. The news of extraordinary disciplinary measures handed out to bondsmen spread quickly to slaves on neighboring plantations. Masters generally knew that such punishment made bondsmen uneasy, and many feared that disgruntled slaves might feel justified in seeking retribution, maybe by setting fire to crops, or, even worse, harming members of local planters' families. In Georgia one traveler observed, "Fires are continually occurring in this country."[51]

When they could, many slaves pooled their assaults upon the slave regime. In a cooperative venture dreaded by masters, some bondsmen gave food and furnished aid to runaways in their neighborhoods. Sometimes the runaways themselves raided plantation food storehouses. Two were hunted by the authorities in North Carolina after they "broke into Beaven's pantry . . . stole all his edibles, took a horse and departed. . . ."[52] Several more runaways committed a somewhat daring theft in the 1840's at the Magruder plantation in Louisiana. While the Magruders were away, slaves "rode in the yard and went into Fred's house made up and baked biscuit, made up a bundle to carry off when the bread was done, then went to bed to wait for. . . ."[53] They accomplished all this before the plantation's bondsmen seized and imprisoned at least one of them.

The action of the Magruder slaves in apprehending one of the runaways points up some of the intricacies of slave resistance behavior. By their thefts the runaways were, in part, jeopardizing the trust the Magruders placed in their own bondsmen. This trust is everywhere evident in Eliza Magruder's diary. Perhaps too, since these runaways were committing disturbances throughout the neighborhood, the slaves may have seen them as a possible threat to their own privileges. While at times slaves closely cooperated in thefts with those who "resisted" slavery, when the activities of a small contingency of resisting bondsmen threatened to give rise to general repression by whites, non-resisting bondsmen often chose to expose the offenders. Usually the ousted slaves had performed acts that endangered the security of the slave community itself before this happened.

Some slaves even occasionally captured runaways and turned them in to their masters or the authorities for rewards. A. C. W. Knott sent his slave Jim to a neighbor's "to get pay for ketching you Boy Oston. . . ." He recommended five dollars as a just reward and added, "I wil allways like to incurage negroes in betraying runaways."[54] Yet this appears to have been rare. The tendency was more to assist a resisting slave or leave him alone rather than betray him. Bondsmen were well aware that there was also the possibility that a runaway they turned in might escape his captors and return to punish them. This was another variable to consider.

For the planter, the runaway slave epitomized alienation from bondage.[55] The slave's theft was of his person, and whatever reason explained his departure the fact remained that his time away from work meant money lost and more: his absence spawned the master's fear that he "will spoil the rest of my people by his bad example. . . ."[56] The majority of runaways were temporary and were motivated, significantly, by slave efforts to force a change or compromise in their master's or overseer's treatment of them. In 1815 John Mc Donogh of New Orleans told a neighbor that he had at first believed that a slave of his who disappeared had been stolen by traders, but that later the slave got word to him by a friend that "he will give himself up on condition that his master will promise to forgive him for his past offence."[57] There is no record of a settlement being worked out. Such an arrangement would clearly have abridged Mc Donogh's authority while making the slave a minor hero among his fellows; other alternatives were often as unappealing. The slave Robin ran away from Landon Carter's Virginia plantation in 1773. "Robin has been out these three months," a notation in Carter's journal reads. "To be sure he is doing mischief about by destroying corn in the fields."[58] It is doubtful that Robin could have carried on his campaign without the knowledge of at least a few of the plantation's slaves, which raises the likelihood that ties between bondsmen on Carter's plantation were strong.

Several decades later a relative of Carter's commented on the collusion she suspected among her slaves: ". . . it is out of my power to discover which of the men introduced a runaway negro woman to my New Carriage as a sleeping apartment."[59] But South Carolina slaveholder John L. Bourquin dreaded a much more serious cooperative venture. Fearing an uprising by runaways, he solicited official help to prevent having to "quietly submit our Families to be sacficided by them and probably by our indoor Domestics—."[60]

Landon Carter had considerable trouble with his slaves, largely because of his inflexible managerial practices. A bondsman came to him in the autumn complaining of the treatment he had received at the hands of the overseer. Carter's response was swift: ". . . I drubbed him and sent him down again." Carter nevertheless seemed resigned to the manner in which the slave would react to this treatment: "I suppose he will go off."[61] Carter's troubles mushroomed in many directions. He accused the slave Sarah of feigning illness. When he forced her to work she ran away. When she was captured he locked her in a storage shed, but during the evening another slave freed her.

Throughout the antebellum period southern newspapers ran

advertisements on runaway slaves. Some of these ads dot front pages, and a single ad soliciting the whereabouts of a missing bondsman might appear in a local paper for many months. During the peak of the abolitionist movement anti-slavery agitators utilized these capsulized expressions of slave unrest as evidence of slaves' widespread dissatisfaction with their lot. But, in turn, many slaveholders saw running away as a natural, though troublesome, part of the slave's life in bondage. A few masters even turned the ocassion into a literary event, perhaps to mask real alarm. "Charity Is Gone!" was the title of an ad in a Charleston newspaper in 1793. This was the third time that Charity had absconded. "It is supposed she has left the busy city in disgust, and retired to rural quiet on the *banks of Stono*, to enjoy the company of Sable nymphs and swains who there cultivate the luxuriant pearly grain."[62]

A few successful slave runaways produced their own literary pieces. Some time after escaping from the Joseph Long plantation in Stephensbury, Virginia, Joseph Taper, a literate bondsman, wrote Long a lengthy letter, extolling the conditions of his new-found freedom in Canada. He emphasized, "I have been well contented, Yes well contented for Sure, man is as God intended he should be, That is, all are born free and equal. This is a wholesome law, not like the Southern laws which puts man made in the image of God, on level with brutes." He clearly wanted his former owner to know that he was succeeding as a free man, having been successful in resisting Long's efforts to return him to slavery. He mentioned that in one town "there was an advertisement put up there for me, 200, dolls reward while I was there." And later "I was in Pittsburg at the time that George Cremer was in pursuit of runaway servants." He summed up his feelings, appropriately, in a closing sentence: "My wife and self are sitting by a good comfortable fire happy, knowing that there are none to molest or make afraid."[63]

In the plantation South, however, specific means of controlling resisting slaves varied enormously. Many masters' basic intent, as pointed out earlier, was simply to instill some generalized fear.

Yet there were implicit dangers in this. Dr. Cartwright briefly and indirectly explored the problem in a letter to General Quitman. "Fear," he warned, "like a bad diet, want of comfortable clothing or over exertion, lowers the vital energies, and opens wide the door to diseases of all kinds."[64] The diseases of which he wrote might have included his *Drapetomania,* an ailment causing slaves to run away, "a species of mental alienation," he claimed, like any other disorder of the mind.[65]

It was not Cartwright's *drapetomania,* however, but slavery's severity that explains the resistance of some runaway slaves in Jefferson County, Georgia, in 1837. They first went on strike in order to protest harsh treatment at the hands of an overseer. Deeply distressed by their behavior, and, no doubt, fearful for his job, the overseer wrote immediately to his employer to let him "know that six of your hands has left the plantation—every man but Jack." He tried to justify his own position by noting that "they displeased me with their worke and I give some of them a few lashes. . . . On Wednesday morning they were missing. I think they are lying out until they can see you or your uncle Jack, as he is expected daily."[66] If his assessment of their motives is accepted, then here is a good picture of slaves trying to reshape the personal and physical relationships surrounding them. Was this at all a common tendency? The answer is most certainly yes, and is backed up by references in many slave sources.[67] In Virginia, for example, an overseer wrote the planter who employed him that the reason for two slaves running away was, ". . . they can not be allowed to do altogether as they please where the[re] is such a crowd [of slaves] requiring attention and they sometimes become offended." The two were Silas and Richard. The overseer claimed that Richard had no cause to run away "excepting being offended for a slight correction while you were here."[68] He did not reveal what the slight correction was.

Bolting the plantation, even if the slave had every intention of returning, might provide him a form of catharsis. Planters were knowledgeable about such things, sometimes punishing the slave only slightly or not at all. Bondsmen, however, rarely expected to go undisciplined for resisting the slavocracy's rules. Psychologist Gordon W. Allport reminds us nevertheless that catharsis by itself is not enough. "The best that can be said for it is that it prepares the way for a less tense view of the situation."[69] And running away might, in the end, have the opposite effect, bringing about closer regulation of slave activities. In addition, the planter often had an ace up his sleeve. Following the running away of one of his slaves a slaveholder observed, "he would not go any where remote from his wife, for whom he always indicated strong attachment."[70]

In the summer of 1854 an Alabama slaveholder sent a letter to his overseer requesting that his slaves be permitted to rest two to three hours at midday. The season was very hot, the kind of weather that makes the hair on one's head lie down with sweat, and some of his bondsmen had become runaways because of the failure of the overseer to adapt work loads to the season. He commented, "It is seemingly Strange that you can not whip or correct a negro belonging to me, without its running away. . . ." The overseer must have been startled at the tone of the message and have given some reflection to the line which read, ". . . hands always running away is no mark of a Good manager—and I am weary and tired of it, and want it Stopped."[71] Indeed, slaves did have a direct and not always silent voice in shaping plantation operations. Reprimands to overseers were recurrent, not always because they were bad managers, but because slaves' behavior persistently failed to correspond to rigid rules.

But what of the runaways who totally escaped bondage? The census returns do not set the number very high—only some eight to ten thousand out of a population of millions of slaves during the nineteenth century. And why is the figure so low? The answer to this question is not easy to come by.

Slaves who tried to remove themselves permanently from bondage faced a formidable undertaking. There was the initial planning, which might take weeks, months, or even years. But there was more to running away than just planning a method of escape. Perhaps the most important element was preparing oneself emotionally for a long, if not permanent, separation from relatives and friends. The thought discouraged many. Slaves also knew the eagerness with which the authorities and professional bounty hunters would pursue them. As one planter put it about a runaway of his, "I wish to have the Villain caught [so] that an example may be made of him to deter the other Negroes from Eloping."[72]

Another important consideration was the slave's conception of what American freedom was like. He glimpsed free blacks in his community and saw that many had a hard time surviving. Some slaves were, in fact, married to freedmen. Just after their release from bondage during the Civil War many ex-slaves expressed feelings of uselessness and fear. Isabella Soustan was one of these frightened ones. She wrote to her former master Manual:

> I want you if you pleas Sir to Send for me. I don't care if I am free. I had rather live with you I was as free while with you as I wanted to be . . . master pleas, oh, pleas come or Send for me. . . .[73]

Many ex-slaves chose to live with their masters after emancipation, some out of affection. However, others would not return under any circumstances, and the record reveals more than just an occasional reference to ex-slaves who wanted back pay for labors they believed had been extorted from them as bondsmen.[74] But considering the persistence of the plantation regime—into the 1930's—for many the choice of removing themselves from the plantation and purview of their former masters was not available. The arrangement, in some cases, was mutually consented to, a former master preferring to have his old hands and "friends" about him in preference to newly freed upstarts from elsewhere.

There were times, too, when slaves witnessed the hasty retreat of free blacks to the plantation's safety in order to escape repression by whites during periods of rumored slave uprisings. Elizabeth Jefferson of Mississippi remarked that her "grand father Let a negro free and gave him a trade. He was a competent brickmason.

Often he came to the plantation for protection Sometimes remaining there for weeks." And this was not all. "There was an old darkye freed by a relative of our family He was prosperous and finally bought his wife and children. He and his family on several occasions came to Greenwood for protection."[75] This was not an atypical situation. But despite these drawbacks the slave Francis Fedric could still observe, as he looked back on his own enslavement, that bondsmen "are almost always, when they have a chance, talking privately about escaping, and getting away. . . ."[76] During the American Revolution, an irate Virginia planter fumed, in anticipation of Fedric's claim, that "the manners of the Negroes down this way seems totally change[d] what with corruption from those who return[d] from following the army, the new fancy[d] religion, & the idea of being made free that there is no managing them to make them do their duty."[77]

Though the number of slaves who escaped to freedom was small, the number of those who actually tried to escape was sizable by any measurement. Not all planters advertised in local newspapers for runaways. An advertisement might set ruthless slave kidnappers on the trail. Instead, masters just passed the word to neighbors that a slave was out. Since a runaway's chances of making it to a free state were slim, the real worry was that he would remain in the neighborhood causing trouble among the slave populace.[78] Did elopement then constitute an attack upon slavery itself? It did in both a limited and a broad sense, for many slaves went out of their way to destroy crops and housing rather than merely lie low and blend into the countryside.

Swamps and caves were widely used hiding places. The Virginia–North Carolina Dismal Swamp, some thirty miles in length and fifteen miles wide, and the swamps in Louisiana, Georgia, and elsewhere were hideaways where communities of forty to fifty fugitives (maroons) at a time and perhaps more gathered.[79] They were sometimes aided by Indians in the lower South, and "they have even been known to clear portions of the wilderness and plant it with maize or Indian corn for their subsistence. . . ."[80] The whereabouts of these refugee slave communities were well-kept secrets. One group of slaves set up a retreat "at the head of a small Creek . . . and with a small Canoe found in their Possession, they had well stored their camp with Fish and Grain of several Sorts. . . ."[81] Others took food with them that lasted only a few days. When it ran out they turned to stealing from local plantations. But the opposition from whites they encountered in these exploits was likely to end in violence. To minimize such confrontations, runaways kept themselves well informed about the movements of slave patrols. In this they were assisted by the local slave populace. Gabriel Manigault, a planter, finding himself in the position of having to deal with such security problems in tracking down some runaways, wrote to his brother Louis that "it is *extremely* difficult to prevent runaways from being informed of a search after them being in preparation. . . ."[82]

It was hard to organize such searches in secrecy because of the trust that prevailed among slaves, stemming somewhat from fear but more often from genuine sympathy with one another's plight. Some were silently gratified—perhaps it boosted their self-esteem —by stories of runaways escaping their hunters. They both delighted in and felt uneasy about old-timers' tales of fugitives' acts of bravado. The stories did not exclude women, or even children, for both groups ran away and resisted slavery more than has been thought. On a Virginia plantation in 1787 the slave Sucky showed up carrying a knife. She had been cooperating with a male slave who appeared later that night but, unlike her, escaped capture. "I wish the neighbors wod fall upon some method to get in the outlying runaways," complained the plantation's owner. They "really are now troublesome to both whites and blacks."[83]

Women's motives for running away were as diverse as men's. Those who ran off, but only for a few days, often did so to escape the quarreling that so commonly underscored some slaves' relationships. They occasionally fled to be with husbands or lovers. Nor were they averse to staying away—despite the lash—for a few hours or days to attract the attention of a potential mate.

Parents also ran away with their children in attempts to shield them from an overseer's cruelty or maybe an unwanted sale. One fled with hers a few days after being burned on her face with a hot iron by her master. In an effort to identify and retrieve his slave he openly ran an ad to this effect in the *Raleigh Standard* in North Carolina.[84] The slave Moses Grandy remembered too that his "mother often hid us all in the woods, to prevent master selling us. . . . After a time the master would send word to her to come in, promising he would not sell us."[85] He later broke that promise and split up the family.

Slave resistance, endemic to southern bondage at all levels, challenged an uneven system of authoritatian controls. On the large estates where overseers were most often employed, bondsmen could usually appeal disciplinary methods to a master. And while this program of checks and balances might serve to safeguard bondsmen from extremely brutal treatment, in important ways it sometimes tied the hands of the overseer and resulted in slave challenges to his dominance. It took no great ingenuity to exploit the situation. In 1833 the overseer of William B. Randolph of Virginia wrote him that "as soon as you left the plantation I had much Trouble and vexation with the negroes they were unruly they were wondering about at night and in they day they ware sleeppy and it was almost impossible to make they do any like a days work."[86]

Slaves repeatedly forced planter-overseer confrontations.[87] A slaveholder learned much about the immense diversity of their behavior from these experiences. For example, two hired slaves complained about the management they received from an overseer. In turn their master quickly wrote a letter to the owner of the plantation where they worked, observing, "They say there is not barely time allowed them to eat their victuals which [are] very badly prepared for them. . . . They say more that he will sometimes not allow them time to get a little water to drink and upon the whole it will be impossible to continue to work under him."[88]

Often a planter tried to hide from other slaves knowledge so gained. A Baltimore master whose slave had come to him seeking asylum from the oppression of his overseer told the slave that he "could not listen to what he had to say, and ordered him to proceed immediately back to Bloomsburg. . . ." Charles, the bondsman, did not want to return, however, and would not therefore promise that he would "behave better in the future." Instead he "refused to return" and went willingly to jail.[89] His master then confided to the overseer, "I am conscious an example had become necessary to fix your authority."[90] But a concerned and economically motivated slaveholder would not forget the charge against his overseer, even if he momentarily disregarded it.

Nonetheless, simple disobedience does not easily explain Charles' behavior. His only alternative was jail, and by accepting it as a consequence of his behavior, he indicated that the conditions under which he worked were unbearable for himself if for no one else. His behavior throughout the incident was that of a mature and rational person caught in a bad situation. In a similar case, an overseer told the master, "I have bin with Negroes for Somtime, and I never have knowe nor heard tell of thar runing away to be put in Jail befor[e]."[91] But this they did.

Frequently, disobedience and resistance by slaves led to the dismissal of an overseer, although many planters elected to keep the basis for such dismissals to themselves when possible. A slave hired to work on the Mississippi plantation of General Quitman ran away and complained to his master of mishandling by Quitman's overseer. The general, from his military post in Texas, warned his wife that the slave should not be returned to the plantation. He reasoned, "It will be a bad example for the negroes, that the complaints of a strange hired negro, can effect the discharge of an overseer."[92]

There was always the danger to bondsmen that an overseer, fearing the loss of his job because of their misconduct, would discipline them severely in an effort to force compliance with his demands. But the result of such action was seldom to subdue the slave or, mold him into patterns of docility. On the contrary, harsh discipline spurred some slaves into what must be called open rebellion. As a consequence, many planters and overseers felt perhaps like John W. Brown whose slaves "have wearied out all the patience that I had with them now for nine years. . . ."[93]

In one rather revealing case, a Maryland planter, worn out by the disturbance caused by a neighbor's slaves, and knowing that the law held that a slave could be put to death for striking a white man, said that "he would swear that the negroes Struck him" when they had not if their master did not monitor their behavior more closely. The neighbor's "hands [were] tied because he was afraid of having his negroes killed—."[94]

Most planters, large and small, had difficulty with resisters at times. Slaves might first attempt to reason with managers to slow the work pace or provide them with additional rest time or privacy; their motives, of course, were not always above suspicion. But even so, the overseer or master who dismissed these complaints ran serious risks. A slaveholder in Louisiana promised his slaves "that the overseer would require nothing unreasonable from them . . ." after they "threatened not to live under his management." Another time slaves on this same plantation put forward a representative to express their grievances to the owner, Thomas Butler. They were at least perceptive enough to understand that they needed representation by their "best" member, according to Butler's standards, if their complaints were to stand a chance of serious consideration. But rather than listen, Butler punished Ned, the spokesman, for a previous offence—"running away when I discharged the late overseer."[95] The Butler family's records show that they continued to have difficulties with slave resisters down to the Civil War.

Considerable numbers of slaves clearly recognized their worth to plantation operations and pressed forward toward what they deemed new liberties, though they were not unused to setbacks. As agricultural laborers, slaves acquired knowledge that put them at a decided advantage when dealing with a newly hired overseer —regular hiring and firing of overseers was common[96]—or a master who took little interest in the actual running of his plantation beyond the level of profits made. They could, and did, hold back information valuable to the plantation's operations if it suited some personal motive.

The term "conspiracy" in its most common usage is too strong a label to attach to most of this activity.[97] Resistant slave behavior was generally intended to force masters and overseers to make some considerable adjustment in their relationships with slaves. A Virginia master, taking note of this, observed that his overseer "lacks authority among the Negroes to make up for which he is very industrious and works with them."[98] When whipping was used to control errant slave behavior, one ex-slave writes, slaves became "used to the lash as a remedy for every offence, and had no fears of it. . . ."[99] James Henry Hammond made a similar discovery one summer while managing one of his plantations himself. "I find Robert," he wrote to a friend, "a very hard hand to manage, and sometimes am resolved to return him to you. I have flogged him untill I am tired. . . ."[100]

On small and not-so-small farms dotting the southern countryside, entangled personal contacts usually evolved between masters and slaves. In these settings everyone was a field worker. The planter lived in a house that frequently had no more than three or four rooms, his slaves, making do the best they could, dwelt in rickety shacks constructed of little more than sticks held together by clay. The relationships that emerged often alarmed visitors to the back-country.

In the early 1860's Colonel Garnett Andrews, a South Carolina lawyer and slaveholder, traveled into the back-country of his native state. Stopping at a farm whose mistress owned just a few slaves, he met two other men who had paused on their way to court to partake of the hospitality offered by the farm's mistress. One morning, shortly before sitting down to breakfast, the mistress called out to Charles—who Andrews thought was her husband—to come and serve the gentlemen. Only after several minutes did Charles finally appear, and to the guests' surprise "instead of being the husband, or some male relative, as they had imagined, he turned out to be a big, very black negro." His manners were coarse, and when scolded by his mistress for his failure to respond immediately "as the gentlemen were in great haste to reach court, he answered, that he would take his time, let gentlemen wait, no more gentlemen than he, etc."[101]

Garnett Andrews realized that Charles' position "may seem a strange state of society for the great slave State of South Carolina, but was nothing uncommon. . . ." The symbiotic quality of master-slave relationships on farms altered the slave's role in vital ways. In his travels Andrews noticed that bondsmen and masters had reached compromises that not infrequently placed the slave on an approximate footing with his master, at least within the setting of the farm. It was not unusual, he explained, "especially in the poor districts where slaves were few—to occasionally find a nego with . . . the influence over a family or an individual, that Charles had over one, who, it seems was, or should have been his mistress—though Charles' was rather an extreme case I admit."[102]

At the core of such behavior was the slave's lack of accommodation to much that confronted him in bondage. Bondage continually worked against the bondsman, though he never left its functioning untampered with. The frustration was enormous.

Any group that is oppressed for an extended period of time rarely strikes out at its oppressor without also turning on itself, blaming itself, at times, for its predicament. Because so many of the slaves' attempts were frustrated, it is no surprise that their aggression spilled over onto themselves as well.[103] The most desperate of their acts involved self-mutilation, murder, and suicide. The record discloses some revealing deeds. One slave thrust her arm into a beehive and required treatment as an invalid. Another prime hand chopped some of his toes off to keep from being parted by sale from wife and children. Still another in Virginia "sharpened the hatchet with which he had been felling timber, and with his right hand severed his left from the wrist."[104] There were many opportunities for a slave to cut his hands badly enough to hamper his effectiveness as a laborer, forcing reassignment to lighter chores or postponement of a sale until they healed. A rock dropped on one's foot or broken bones (there were many such incidents) achieved similar delays and sometimes a master's careful reflection. The complex of motivations behind such deeds is difficult to analyze. Perhaps we view slaves most accurately simply by keeping this complexity uppermost in mind whenever we raise questions about them.

Some forms of slave self-mutilation were often just the first steps taken by distraught bondsmen who later took their lives. Slaveholders deemed suicide likely to occur among slaves recently arrived from Africa or during times when families were separated by the domestic trade. In several cases, slaves who had recently arrived from Africa sang songs in the evening and then some walked in a trance to the ocean and drowned while trying to swim home.[105] We have generally underestimated the frequency with which suicides occurred.[106] Slaves of all ages snuffed out their lives, and the evidence indicates that field and unskilled slaves were just as prone to do so as domestic and skilled workers. Reflections on suicide were perhaps not unusual with bondsmen. It was but a short time after being separated from his wife and children that Charles Ball entertained "serious thoughts of suicide so great was my anguish. If I could have got a rope I should have hanged myself in Lancaster."[107]

Emile Durkheim, in his study *Suicide*, writes of "fatalistic suicide" and its predetermined features and asks, "Do not the suicides of slaves . . . belong to this type, or all suicides, attributable to excessive physical or moral despotism?"[108] One may imagine that many slave suicides in the Old South were of this kind. They sometimes came on with startling suddenness. The entry in one master's diary partially illustrates this: "Freds Negro woman took it into her hed that She had lived long enough and between 12 and 1 o'clock hung herself . . . for no known cause."[109]

The suicide of another slave woman appears to have been a reaction to punishment. She was the aged domestic servant of a southern lady in Pecan Bayou, Louisiana. Her mistress "got mad . . . and gave the negro five or six licks with a whip." That same day the slave "cut a slit in her stomach. . . ." Her mistress summoned a doctor to treat her, and after the examination he advised that there was no reason why the mistress could not continue to punish the slave. The evidence does not reveal whether she chose to do so, but that evening the old slave "hung herself, and was found next morning at daylight."[110]

Slave suicides prompted a great deal of talk among bondsmen and neighbors as to slave treatment. Slaves viewed suicide sometimes as murder because they knew that so often harsh handling was its cause. To smooth over such acts planters occasionally tried to shower the suicide with shame or might report it to their other slaves, if they did so at all, as an accident while reporting it as suicide to the authorities.

The suicide web was an intricate one. Some had sexual overtones. A planter found that a female slave had hanged herself, and "from the evidence it appeared her master had whipped her for 2 nights before because she would not attend to the chickens & c." Further evidence in the case revealed a sexual relationship between master and slave. A diarist who recorded the tragedy wrote of the slave that "feeling herself slighted, & as she supposed set aside & imposed upon she preferred to die than live, thence the rash act."[111]

Runaways frequently threatened suicide to give their pursuers some cause for concern. The threat might be merely an attempt to make slave catchers carefully consider the consequences of their pursuit so as not to make themselves responsible for the loss of valuable slave property. A few bondsmen bluffed successfully with this threat. Many, as well, preferred death to returning to bondage.[112] One ex-slave recalled a dramatic confrontation of this sort: "He [a master] was so mean they [slaves] got up a plot to run off and they never come in till after twelve o'clock that night. They had plotted to go and jump in the Mississippi River and drown themselves. . . ." Their behavior apparently worked to their advantage, for ". . . after that he [the master] quit beating and knocking on 'em, and if he got an overseer that was too mean he would turn him off." But, as to whether the slaves would really have carried out their suicide threat: "They said they meant to drown, too, but they thought about their little children and come on home."[113] Others, fearful of punishment if caught or refusing

95

to return to bondage, did take their own lives. A Georgia doctor leaves us a record of one unsuccessful attempt. "I had a surgical case yesterday in a negro fellow who cut his own Throat," he wrote. "He had run away from Master, and when he heard the Dogs 'on trail' he made *Five* determined rakes at his Throat, exposing the Caratids and important nerves."[114]

A sociologist studying the impact of various kinds of behavior on individual identity in a modern black community offers a valuable insight applicable to the plantation scene. He observes that militant or antagonistic "attitudes" must certainly precede attempts to alter one's social surroundings and that changes in one's "self-conception" are in many instances most likely to come about as well.[115] His findings seem applicable to the world of slave resistance, where so often the conditions imposed by slavery tended to give slaves "consequence in their own eyes. . . ."[116] It seems too that some recognition of the slave's shifting rather than static identity is important to understanding why sometimes very little separated his minor acts of disobedience from his serious acts or threats of rebellion.

During periods of rumored or real slave disturbances, southern officials customarily arrested suspected bondsmen, free blacks, and perhaps a sprinkling of "po' buckra"—poor whites. Arrest was an alarming experience, especially for those slaves who had been faithful and reliable servants and who had earned reputations for good behavior. Upon securing their release from jail, masters might console them while deprecating the "rash" behavior of the authorities. Slaves therefore had several quite different reactions to themselves to evaluate. Even if they mistook their master's verbal castigation of local officials for faint approval of certain of their own acts, they were still able to see how and when he disapproved of fellow whites. In these instances, authorities were important "reference groups" against whom the slave might favorably measure himself.[117]

The general safety of local slaves was often endangered during disturbances. A white carpenter once apparently barely saved the lives of some bondsmen who had greatly angered neighbors by prior disobedient behavior. These neighbors had apparently planned to put an end to the slaves' ways.[118]

The statistics of the Vesey and Turner plots are informative.[119] Despite the fact that authorities uncovered Vesey's plans before the conspirators could act, Charleston officials executed thirty-seven implicated slaves. Although sixty white victims were claimed by Nat Turner's band of Virginia insurrectionists, reprisals against suspected slaves counted more than a hundred dead. The hanging of conspiring bondsmen followed by decapitation and setting of their heads on stakes for other slaves to see is evidence that masters saw violence as an effective way to influence behavior.[120]

Close brushes with the authorities at such times effectively checked many bondsmen's behavior. In one community a mistress commented that "all [her bondsmen] behave well but shockingly frightened at the Patrols being ordered out. poor little *Fan* is afraid to go after the geese without a pass."[121] Following the Nat Turner revolt, a writer in the *African Repository*, the primary literary organ of the American Colonization Society, reported that every freedman in Raleigh was arrested and some were "ordered to leave the city, because they could not give a good account of their mode of subsistence. . . ."[122] There was cause for blacks to be on their guard.

One Virginia slave later launched an attack on Turner, wishing, he said, that he "had better never been born than to have left such a curse upon his nation."[123] This slave had been a boy in the early 1830's and remembered that "we poor colored people could not sleep at nights for the guns and swords being stuck in at our windows and doors to know who was her[e] and what was the business. . . ." He also recollected that "at that time a Colored person was not to be seen with a book in his hand." Some burned theirs out of fear, but he kept several that his owners had given him.[124] Slave disturbances of an insurrectionary nature tended to divide the slave community in a way suggestive of some contemporary racial conflicts. There was a tendency among some slaves to sympathize with the aims of resisters without condoning their specific acts; to see an expression of violence as meaningful because it alarmed planters just as planters' acts of repression alarmed slaves.[125] And there were, naturally, a few bondsmen who hated the rebels, identifying more with slaveholders or at least desiring to avoid open conflict. Such slaves felt authentic concern for their master's family's safety while viewing resisting slaves with a contemptuous eye.[126]

News of slave conspiracies furnished exciting if alarming conversational material for the southern parlor set, especially during holiday seasons, when rumors were often rampant. Conversations frequently dwelt upon the large gatherings of slaves that milled about towns and clogged roadways, disturbing, some Southerners said, the holiday tranquility. Christmastime was a particularly tense period for slaveholders. In 1830, just after Christmas, Louisiana authorities hanged two slaves; the charge was conspiring to rebel. These slaves and two others were reported to officials by a bonded female acquaintance. One plantation source tells the not unfamiliar story that two of them escaped execution because "there masters were rich."[127] The slave system's response, therefore, was not simply to execute—mindlessly—known resisters or slaves suspected of conspiring to rebel.

An overseer on an Alabama plantation told his employer in 1853 that "six of the fellows had rebelled" against him "and there was some bloodshed tho no life lost. . . ." The slaves disarmed the overseer of his whip and "inflicted wounds upon him That he will probably carry to his grave. . . ." Such behavior was punishable by death under southern law, but these slaves met no such misfortune. Instead a friend, the Virginia planter Farish Carter, advised their owner merely to sell a number of his worst slaves. It is difficult to tell how many other individuals knew of these slaves' resistance. A third party, N. B. Powell, remarked to Carter, "If I were in his [the neighbor's] place I would take all those fellows that had rebelled and some half dozen women that always laid up a dead expense to him . . . and put them in the Market."[128] There was no mention of having the rebellious slaves put to death. The financial loss would have been staggering. Their rebellion was thus "absorbed" by the system.

Herman Melville, the nineteenth-century American novelist, perceptively sketched a picture of how such situations between slave and master might develop. In a passage of his novelette "Benito Cereno," he writes simply that "long-continued suffering seemed to have brought out the less good-natured qualities of the negroes [slaves on board a slaveship], besides, at the same time, impairing the . . . authority over them."[129] If, nonetheless, master's problems with their slaves still appear small as one looks back on the larger picture of slave life in the Old South, perhaps it is because the picture that researchers are used to looking at is in need of a few fresh brushstrokes.

We can help to supply these by looking at a Louisiana plantation in 1850. A "negro man," began a neighbor's diary notation, "broke open and robbed Mrs. Blacks house and was very insolent to her."[130] When masters were unable to keep the news of such disturbing acts from spreading to neighbors, ever curious about such things, the result was that plantation after plantation went on the alert, readying itself for similar occurrences. An alarmed planter of Parrysburg Parish, South Carolina, wrote to a state representative expressing just such a concern about the threat slave rebels in his neighborhood posed:

> I make no doubt but that you have heard of the many depredations which have already been committed by the runaway Negroes about here before our departure for Charleston, & which I can & do assure you that from their threats, unless their being extirpated I fear in a very short time the prospect of their obtaining provisions will not be their only object, as they have in my hearing threatened the li[f]e . . . help us as otherwise the matter may become of too serious a nature as hereafter to give ourselves further trouble about the matter. . . .[131]

It was less difficult then for planters than it has become now for scholars to disentangle the multitude of rumors that hinted at genuine slave unrest. Near Christmastime in 1852, John Johnston, a North Carolina slaveholder, observed to a relative "how very sensitive people are on the subject of negro insurrection. . . ."[132] They could hardly be otherwise; their sensitivity had an interesting past in the Old South. It stemmed from knowledge of such activities as those in Warren County, Mississippi, in 1857, where planters broke up a large unauthorized slave meeting. The slave gatherers, it was observed, "pretended to preach but it was found out they meet there for 12 and 15 miles round and were Laying plans for an inserrection. . . ." To add to their problems authorities discovered more than a dozen runaways said to be the leaders of the movement in a cave; and they put thirty to forty other slaves in jail. General slave response in this neighborhood was correspondingly intense, "and every negor in the hole County has go[t] above bein[g] whipe[d]. . . ." wrote John Johnston. One of Johnston's own slaves, Old John by name, stole some chickens "and went of[f] on Several ocasions to Sell his stole Chickens and Nealy [overseer] went to whip him and he whiped Nealy and Edmond both an[d]—Cut out. . . ."[133] Planters were in fact often jostled about by circumstances created by slaves more than they understood or were willing to admit—and much more than later observers have allowed for.

There can be little wonder that misconceptions about slave resisters abound. It did not always require the ingenuity and daring of the most intelligent slaves to plan and execute a serious slave disturbance, and for scholars to continue to hold to this notion is unrealistic.[134] The initiating spark might come from some ill treatment slaves regularly experienced, igniting a long fuse of past abuses. As the slave William Hayden put it, "I was determined to stand firmly upon the rights of my manhood . . . ," obeying the orders of his immediate owner but no one else.[135] Any slave motivated by such an attitude was bound to have difficulties. But as we have seen, the slave system was bound to have problems with him too.

Gabriel, Vesey, and Turner have been drummed into our collective consciousness to the exclusion of other slave "rebels"; the conclusion that there was generally little slave unrest in the Old South follows easily from this. Also, our research approaches to slave disturbances tend to demand quantification of both their frequency and the number of participants.[136] Yet the uncertain nature of slavery and its sources renders such precise estimations suspect; and before research goes too far in this direction there is a need to ask if our formulations and body counts coincide with slaveholders' perceptions of slave unrest. A tentative answer seems to be that in many cases they do not. Manuscript information especially indicates that slave disturbances were widespread; just how widespread requires further investigation. Many involved no more than one slave, but the response of slaveholders to even these limited disruptions was never gentle.

In a neighborhood in Texas in 1860 some slaves poisoned a family of slaveholders. This was a strategy many resisters used. It was apparently a large band of slaves, for they terrorized the neighborhood and attempted to "burn houses and destroy masters. . . ." One of the runaways, refusing to surrender, was shot, and it was discovered that he was a former local slave who "had been long sold from our vicinity. . . ." He had apparently returned to his old neighborhood to seek revenge. During the rebellion "his former masters building & barn & gin were set on fire & a horse was missing. . . ."[137] It is safe to say that bondsmen ignored as often as they followed the frequently given advice to submit to bondage. But if slaves plotted widely, why is it that these plots have not been publicized?

Often few individuals in the master class beyond the immediate circle in which disturbances occurred were even aware of their existence. Planters clearly did not want to give other slaves any ideas. Robert Carter of Virginia pondered in a letter to a local sheriff whether his runaway slave Charles would "Commit Violences in these parts, such as burning of houses and stealing from myself and others."[138] Indocility was a constant variable, not docility.

In many instances, at any rate, slave rebels achieved moderate success only because of their ties to and understanding of the workings of the slave community. Some probably saw themselves as leaders of a silent slave following, drawing upon that bounty of contempt that the oppressed invariably harbor—often behind smiling faces—for their oppressors. Near Windsor, North Carolina, authorities arrested more than twenty slaves in 1802 and charged them with plotting rebellion. In part of his courtroom testimony the slave Old Dair admitted that he was first approached with the plan by the slave Sam who "when he come up says I an very tired and weary . . . the Damn'd White people plagued him so bad they ought to be killed and shall . . . if he could get a great many to join him. . . ."[139] This feeling of kinship led, at times, to an exaggerated conception of the help one bondsman might receive from other slaves when fleeing for his life or trying to slow down or cripple neighborhood plantation operations.

Slaves mingled together intimately enough in the quarters to know that there were many among them who sympathized with the idea of attacking slavery as it had attacked them—directly. But they were also aware that a large show of force would lead to bloodshed in their ranks, with women and children being seriously hurt or killed. Slaves' decisions not to revolt in such instances are understandable in light of this reality.[140] It was difficult, too, to keep the details of a potential rebellion secret when more than a close ring of slaves joined in its planning.[141] There were slave informants, as mentioned earlier, bondsmen who for personal gain, revenge, or whatever, communicated or peddled information about slave affairs to planters.

An account of an uprising in Alexandria, Louisiana, in 1837 had it that bondsmen took advantage of prevailing sickness plus the absence of some masters from their plantations to revolt. Discovering the plot, irate slaveholders did not bother to hold a trial, but hanged nine or ten of the plotters forthwith; "not in a legal manner," wrote a concerned diarist, "but by a committee of citizens formed for that purpose without the form and contrary to law, setting a bad example. . . ."[142] A similar incident in Laurens, South Carolina, implicated twenty white men with five runaways. Authorities hanged the five slaves but jailed only one of the white men. They reasoned that "the poor white *trash*" only affiliated with the runaways because they "are jealous of higher classes and think inserection will place all on a footing and they get some plunder in the bargain."[143]

Slaveholders were able to keep watch over only the most visible forms of slave behavior. Did the slave work steadily and efficiently? Did he obey the plantation rules? These were the areas of behavior that mattered most. Many therefore expected that their contacts with bondsmen would be filled with a share of extremely frustrating encounters while master and slave were coming to know one another better. The demands of the southern work load did not, in most instances, however, permit a master or overseer to gain the close understanding of each slave that he needed to smooth his management. That there was some docility among slaves need not be denied. But it was not the norm. Masters and authorities repeatedly linked seemingly docile slaves to acts of resistance.[144]

A series of runaways from the Warfield farm in Maryland in the 1840's amazed unsuspecting neighbors who thought the Warfields' had "the happiest, and most social families of blacks." Yet Susanna Warfield's diary regularly recorded slave trouble, which the Warfields, true to the Old South's tradition, discreetly kept to themselves; and this was the reason that neighbors "did not think any of their boys would have done so."[145]

There was a threatening quality to the slave's resistance which the astute slaveholder recognized he would have to deal with. He cultivated a suspecting mind where bondsmen were concerned, not because of what he considered their childish antics, but because of their potentially menacing habits.

Historians might agree that an institutional framework that gave rise to so many conflicts—both interpersonal and with the system—was not a healthy one for slaves, or even for masters. Suppression of minor and serious slave disturbances by the slave regime did not erase slave disobedience for long. And planters' efforts to "advance the bondsman towards civilization" were too inconsistently applied and left too much to chance to lay claim to making slaves what they were. It was not that easy, and few masters ever clung to the belief that it was.

In noteworthy ways, the kinds of resistance that slaves chose to engage in indicate some clear behavioral patterns. In many of the incidents cited, slaves directed their actions at modifying the conditions of their bondage by prompting slaveholders to recognize some needs considered important by slaves. In cases where one to several bondsmen were involved in a disturbance, they were frequently endeavoring to reshape plantation management. When they succeeded, as they often did in small though ever accumulating ways, the circumstances of their bondage might subsequently be more favorably adapted to their work loads and private lives.

Again and again bondsmen attacked slavery. Even runaways, closely pursued by slave catchers, did not seem content just to elude the authorities and protect their momentary freedoms. They often struck back at their hated oppression by deliberately menacing local white populations. They stole from or burned a portion of plantation crops. And other slaves aided them by silent acquiescence in their activities or by active cooperation. To make plantation managers aware of some limits to their authority appears to have been a conscious slave goal, which, of course, brought white resistance and violence. Many times bondsmen made cruel overseers appear to be poor plantation operators by creating endless management difficulties. This, more than any other single factor, seems to explain why overseers were continually being fired throughout the antebellum years. An overseer's firing gave slaves another opportunity to strive for favorable modification of their circumstances with a new overseer.

Slaves did not take abuse passively. And to accuse them of docility because they did not constantly rebel against slavery is misleading. As the years passed, slaveholders' responses to bondsmen necessarily hardened in response to mounting concern for their own lives. Slaves attacked bondage at its core. And their deeds compelled tighter physical controls and more and more laws which, designed to restrict slave behavior, thus recognized its complexity. Slaveholders knew that there was more to fear than an occasional Gabriel Prosser, Denmark Vesey, or Nat Turner. A plantation's authority could quickly change form, if not hands. At any time during slavery's history after the American Revolution it would have taken an enormous effort (the Civil War?) to recast legally the role of blacks in the Old South. But the evidence is strong that slaves resisted by challenging the slavocracy at every level, and, perhaps, forcing it towards a breakdown.

5

The Household Slave

The class of slaves who occupied positions near the pinnacle of the slave labor system were the domestics. Theirs was the proud position, according to one Virginia planter, to which proper slaves might aspire. Domestics were the "aristocrats" of bondage, a title they wore with varying degrees of pride.[1] In their jobs they usually wore laundered dresses and pants, at least on larger plantations, in contrast to the tattered garments worn by many field hands. "Upon every Estate," wrote John Cocke of Virginia, "the young heir, or heirs finds a number of old domestic servants who have been raised about the persons & in the confidential service of the former owners . . . [and] by a long course of faithful service have established their claim to the character of humble Friends of the Family."[2]

Popular lore has sometimes labeled house servants "Uncle Toms," pawns of the slaveholders and betrayers of their slave brothers.[3] Such descriptions derive in part from two sources. First, it is claimed that domestics serving directly under a master's tutelage became nominal members of white families, generally received milder treatment, and thus were reluctant to relinquish the "good" life. John Cocke observed that domestics "naturally form a separate Caste from the common herd of slaves. . . ." And if their descendents prove "worthy [they] are the successors to the standing & privileges of their parents in the House or fill the most confidential stations in the outdoor work of the plantation or are instructed in the plainest mechanics arts."[4] Second, it is said that since many domestics were mulatto slaves—very often illegitimate children of a master or his relatives —they chose to identify more closely with their white than their black relatives. Linked with both of these claims is the image of domestic slaves obedient to their owners and lovingly bossy to young masters and mistresses.

Certainly, a high percentage of house slaves were mulattoes, but there were many more who were blacks of pure African ancestry. Among both groups there were those who were loyal and loving and those who were not. It was, indeed, not their parentage but the status domestics believed they held and the duties they performed that most influenced the development of their personalities.[5] As members of the slave aristocracy they were considered to possess, theoretically, the finest behavioral norms to be found among slaves. Correspondingly, those frequently commented upon character weaknesses that typified blacks—thievery, lying, some laziness—supposedly appeared more often and in a more pronounced degree among less cultivated field workers. Therefore, although field bondsmen, masters, and historians all have accused domestics of putting on airs while in the presence of less-priviledged blacks (and, in truth, domestics were guilty at times of very high-handed actions), they did not reserve their high-handedness just for other bondsmen; slaveholders, as well, came in for their share of jostling from domestics. Domestics supposedly lacked that troop-like quality so often described by observers of field hands. On the economically anemic but palatial estates of Virginia tobacco planters, and on the disease-ridden cotton and sugar plantations of Mississippi and Louisiana, the domestics rivaled the masters as topics of conversations among field slaves.

From the available records it appears that unrest in a master's household was at least as common as tranquility. It was apparently no easy task finding compatible slaves for the household. One important reason was that some slaves did not want to become domestics, despite the fact that "domestic slaves," as one planter noted, ". . . were better fed and clothed, and generally better treated than those employed out of doors. . . ."[6] Domestic slaves were often "liable to every call, early or late . . . ,"[7] and because of this, Hall discovered, ". . . everywhere the slaves preferred the fieldwork, chiefly, as I could learn, from its being definite in amount, which left them a certain portion of the day entirely to themselves. . . ."[8] The close scrutiny a domestic might receive from his master was another objection for some. A female slave noted: ". . . I liked the field work better than I did the house work. We could talk and do anything we wanted to, just so we picked the cotton. . . ."[9] Others felt torn between naturally developing affection for the planter's family and alienation, especially when the planter's treatment of them varied with each mood. Slavery shadowed and crippled the simplest and sincerest of relationships in the Big House.

A house slave's work routine was similar to a field hand's in its basic repetitiveness. Most learned their chores readily enough, though they usually found that their masters' behavior took a lifetime to adapt to. Often up before dawn, a few slept off to one corner in the same room with masters when the latter were sick or when ordered to do so, supplying nightly needs as they arose. More often, they occupied huts immediately adjacent to the Big House, or returned to the clustered security of the slave quarters.

There were few, if any, ways for a master to assure perfect casting of the domestic, for even the best house servants occasionally displeased their owners. In search of a cook for his household, G. Garrett confided to his wife, "it will be very hard to get a negro whose qualities are all good but my object is to come as close as possible. . . ." He was therefore not only seeking a good cook but someone with a "good disposition" who "will give you as little trouble as possible. . . ."[10] There was ample cause for such scrutiny. Bondage itself marred the domestic-slaveholder relationship. The day-to-day familiarity of master and slave was regularly offset by a lack of truly intimate knowledge of each other.[11]

A domestic might serve in a single household for years and never really confide in a master. "Almost every white woman feels," writes an anthropologist, "that she knows all about her cook's personality and life, but she seldom does."[12] It was not hard for the slave, with a little caution, to retain a certain amount of anonymity even while at work in the planter's house. A cook or a butler could perform his duties well and simply not volunteer information about personal matters. This was hard to do when he was kindly treated, however. Many won the genuine respect of a master and his children whom they might serve for decades. The Englishman Adam Hodgson complimented the house servants that he encountered, revealing his surprise at their intelligence and capabilities.[13] A large number of masters in every part of the Old South would have concurred with him. A mistress in North Carolina privately admitted to an aunt her good fortune "in getting ma's old cook, who knows a great deal more about her business than I do, but I try to prevent her from finding it out."[14]

Another slaveholder was a little more uncertain about his fortunes. He admitted in a letter to his mother that Ellen, his cook, "continues to try my patience." And then he attacked one of our nation's outstanding beliefs about blacks: "It is very difficult to get a negro who understands good cooking." Why? "If they do ten to one they have some bad habits or bad temper & are not fit to be about. . . ." But then his uncertainty raised its head. He explained, "Yet at times I think I can never be as well suited— Ellen is a *good milker*, a negro rarely is. She makes *good bread*, few can do it, or do do it. She makes Excellent *coffee*. . . . She cooks meats and vegetables well, but I might find others to do the same."[15] His complaints were thus mostly about her behavior or rather his inability to mold her behavior to what he desired. In this, he was, as he well knew, not alone.

In an effort to obtain a rounded view of domestics' behavior it is necessary to pursue numerous leads. The stories of house slaves who fell asleep while standing by their masters' sides at the dinner table, only to be suddenly awakened by a loud voice bellowing commands, have a quaint sound of hyperbole. And the tales of domestics who in the constant company of owners were totally oblivious to private conversations—which were none of their business anyway—take us back to a time which, except for literary imaginings, never was. Other leads are more fruitful.

It happened, on occasion, that the planter's household became a battleground for slaves and an irate master. During these times, if the master did not resort to extreme measures, the advantage frequently fell to the slave, for good domestics were hard to replace. Such a confrontation occurred on a Maryland plantation in the mid-1840's. Susanna Warfield, the young mistress who helped manage her parents' home, entered in her diary for October 28, 1846: "Elisa . . . in the Sulks made a mistake in the white hangings [drapes]—got mad—because I told her of it—abused me much—I left her abusing—She made a worse mistake. I made her take them down."[16] The struggle was not one-sided by any means. At times, when Elisa was criticized for the performance of her tasks, she retaliated by making life in the Warfield home unpleasant for weeks. When threatened with replacement she confronted the situation openly, flaunting her various skills in domestic affairs.

Elisa's difficulties in her role as a house slave continued through the years. She was constantly antagonistic to Susanna, and was adept at selecting the right words and tone of voice to deflate the girl's spirits. She made constant and effective assaults upon Susanna's character with but few recorded reprisals, and among these never a whipping. Her dominance, and this seems the proper expression, was nearly complete, yet disputed at every turn.

We often imagine that when domestic bondsmen were awakened by a master's request for anything from a glass of water to more wood for the fire in the early morning hours, they simply and uniformly responded to the summons promptly, and perhaps without question. It was after all an inconvenience they learned to cope with. Elisa, disturbed from her rest at eleven one evening, begrudgingly answered the call, performed the needed chores, and then returned to her hut. Yet this was not the end of the episode. The next morning she proceeded to make life miserable around the Warfield home, and continued for a succession of days. Susanna explained that Elisa was mad "all because the fire in Papa's Stove went down, and in passing a bucket to kindle it up—I upset it—and it went on the carpet—I wiped it up but Papa [who was sick] insisted on calling Elisa up from the quarters—."[17]

Susanna's diary also relates this incident: "Elisa has been in the tantrums this morning and has told me that I am no lady—that Miss Annal and Miss Lucretia Van Bibber are ladies, but I am no lady." Susanna was very upset by this. At another point, when she was about to reprimand Elisa for apparent negligence at her chores, Elisa successfully turned the encounter to her own advantage. She demanded that the Warfields sell her away "where she will never See any of us."[18] Despite their differences, Susanna was deeply hurt by this request and, it seems, gave in to some of Elisa's previous wishes.

Elisa attempted repeatedly to gain pre-eminence in the Warfield home, but her activities did not go unquestioned, even by other domestics. One challenger, in a limited sense, was the child Mag, whose habit it was to tell lies about Elisa, the slave Jane, and Susanna herself. "Little black Mag," complained Susanna, "has made mischief between mamma and myself this morning— She is a great story teller—and mischief maker— . . . She is always telling lies on the Servants and Papa and unfortunately Mamma credits her."[19] Sometimes Mag's behavior backfired and she received what appears to have been a well-deserved spanking. Once, however, when Susanna paddled her, Mag got a bloody nose and won the sympathy of Susanna's mother so completely that Susanna determined never again to lay a hand on her.

Nor was it unusual for domestics to be at odds with one another. They jockeyed for positions of favor with slaveholders and for positions of authority that might perhaps enhance them in the eyes of the quarters community. One master commented to his sister, "It was not very discreet to leave such incongrouous meterials together as Pet & Ebony [the cook and butler]. They are very sure to come into collision without a stronger power to hold them in check." He then added a not infrequent observation about domestics: "I take for granted that liquor was the chief motive power [in] the controversy between butler & cook."[20]

Naturally, most house slaves did not play as dominant a role as did Elisa; nor were they as pampered as Mag. But Elisa's stature in the Warfield household was fully acknowledged by the domestic Jane. One day Susanna overheard Jane tell Elisa, "you are a philosopher but I am an ignorant negro—."[21] Susanna was curious about the meaning of Jane's statement, if only during the moment that she wrote it down in her diary. But the observation does not appear so puzzling when taken within the context of how Elisa molded the conditions of her bondage. Elsewhere domestics held sway over planters' children, and had them jumping to orders more readily than did their own parents. A raised eyebrow, a hand signal, and youngsters scampered hurriedly out of sight.

There is no way to measure, on the average, exactly how busy masters kept their domestics. On large plantations where work tasks stretched before them in an endless procession, domestics were quite busy. The cook's chores on the McCorkle plantation in Alabama provide an illustration of the demands placed on some: "Rise at five breakfast prayers—milking kitchen breakfast —dishes—lamps . . . stove & kitchen cleaning. Arrange for The four o clock meal—Two meals a day are ampel for ordinary habits—children twelve o clock lunch." Lucilla McCorkle suggested further that the "mistress should herself know how to perform these & if she occasionally *chooses* to do *herself cheerfully*." Why should she? "It will have an excellent effect upon the house servants' behavior and probably show them that their duties are not so menial."[22]

A domestic slave belonging to Henry Watson, Jr., also of Alabama, completely managed the Watson home affairs, by no means an unusual practice. In a letter to his cousin Watson noted that an "intelligent faithful & house & man servant is our home keeper . . . I have put him at the head of affairs & he attends to Every thing, decides what we shall have to Eat at our different meals, provides, gives out & directs."[23] Still, to counterbalance those domestics who performed their duties efficiently in the household were those who had difficulty adjusting to the regimen. "Old Daniel," wrote a Louisiana slaveholder, "has disgraced himself and has become a field Negro again which has sunk his spirits very low."[24] The cycle by which house slaves were returned to the fields for misconduct and then later returned to house labors was a familiar one, though it seems seldom to have effected the desired change in behavior. Apparently, some domestics regularly doubled as field hands, so the punishment was no great hardship. "Nancy . . . an excellent house servant—a tolerable good seemstress . . . She is also an excellent hand in the fields."[25] This tandem work arrangement increased and nurtured contacts between domestics and field workers, closing the personal gaps that could otherwise have developed between them.

The distance between the harsh arena of the fields and the steps of the plantation house was often not very great in terms of the disgruntled interaction of slaves and masters. In the Big House domestic slaves displayed a corresponding degree of restlessness. Some masters complained that they continually had to scold and whip their domestics to get them to do their chores. But such methods often backfired because bondsmen worked sloppily under these pressures and had to redo tasks. One mistress, accordingly, wondered why "my cousin's wife, Mrs. Judge Sprage . . . gets twice as much work out of three female servants as I do out of six. . . ."[26] A successfully managed home appears to have required an owner who was sensitive, if not sympathetic, to the emotional needs and habits of his domestics. This did not mean that he had to recognize the slave as an equal, but it did require an attempt to understand the circumstances involved when a domestic failed to perform a deed to the slaveholder's satisfaction or behaved in a fashion not in accord with household harmony. If the master did not weigh these factors his home could become a battleground of unending pitched struggles. For the slave, like anyone else, responded to constant scolding by working poorly and showing defiance. In such times, slaves often conducted themselves so as to make very clear their contributions to the running of masters' domestic affairs. They were not easily put off by derogatory comments directed their way. "I suppose it must be my own fault," observed the sister of the planter J. B. Bailey of Florida, "that they seldom do as I want it unless I am looking at them not that I think them inferior to other *negroes*."[27]

A single unruly slave in the Big House could shatter its quietude. If the planter prided himself on being a good master—most did—then the news of a disorderly home spreading to neighbors might be somewhat embarrassing for him. It was perhaps a feeling akin to his attitudes relative to wealth. Advice in this regard often ran, as one father told his son, "don't *talk to* much about your poverty, it will bring You & the Plantation unto[ld] redicule."[28] Under this curtain of secrecy, bondsmen continually garnered privileges that ameliorated a variety of slave-master contacts and affected the nature of their bondage. The appearance of an orderly household was, by some standards, more the goal than was the actual realization of such order.

In New Orleans a planter who was renting a house from the philanthropist John Mc Donogh warned him that if "negress Sophia remains her[e] I cannot engage to continue—." Among her many faults, she "keeps in the yard and kitchen a constant disturbance quarrelling with this one & that one. . . ." Sophia's indiscretions continued to mount, but there is no report of disciplinary efforts to curtail her behavior. The warning continued, "and ther is at all times especially on Sundays & at evening a constant running to & from through the gate of men who[se] appearance to say the best of it affords no very favourable impression & keeps me in continual fear of theft et., etc." It is somewhat amazing that Sophia's conduct went uncorrected for so long, in fact, until finally the gravity of her deeds began to tear apart the fabric of domestic life. The final annoyance was a full day of disturbances near the house, peppered with "such conversation as in addition to its extreme vulgarity & obscenity was calculated to carry a very unfavourable impression to all who heard it from the street and neighboring houses."[29]

In trying to understand how its bastions withstood each instrument of erosion, there is little need to pay tribute to slavery's great flexibility. It remains, rather, that to explain these developments one must expand his appreciation of slavery's meaning for the slave—must, if he can, fairly weigh the slave's own impact on the institution. Nevertheless, this is not to exaggerate the freedom and initiative possessed by domestics in general. Examples abound where masters forced them to toe the line, to work without questioning though not without complaint, and to suffer the lash.

What we generally find, in any case, is an almost astonishing physical closeness between domestics and masters. The situation was hardly avoidable. Each saw the other at his worst. Insensitivity on either's part in this setting was not the norm, but frequently did occur. Sometimes contacts were close but impersonal, bordering on intimate burlesque. The slave Henry Bruce remembered being called as a boy to the side of his unclad mistress in her bedroom merely to pour additional water for a bath. She seemed, he recalled, aloof, almost unaware of his presence, though he clearly was not of hers.

Scholars have been quick to accuse domestics of upholding bondage, and even of being Sambos. No bondsman, one reads, in such close contact with planters could stay loyal to both his fellows and the master class. But the choice, when it came to that, was rarely so easily delimited.[30] The number of house slaves historians may label willing informants does not appear to have been large in proportion to the number of such slaves; Uncle Toms and Aunt Minnies were not in the majority. Putting on airs and feeling oneself better than field hands was a far cry from disclosing their secrets and deeds.[31] In the Big House planters discovered all too recurringly that talk about the sale of slaves, runaways, and resistance was communicated to the bondsmen in question by domestics. Charles Manigault believed that even small house boys and girls "communicate all that they hear to others, who convey it to the spies of the runaways. . . ."³² It is doubtful that house servants, child and adult, acted simply out of fear of field hands in conveying this information. It is more likely, in view of other sources of evidence, that they acted on the basis of personal identification with other bondsmen, knowing full well that their own positions would be jeopardized if their masters found out what they were doing.³³ One diary account reveals that a slaveholder had his personal servant Esther "whipped for not telling that she heard Flit (who has run away) talking in the yard" about his plans.³⁴

Many domestics, to be sure, were nominally members of the planter's family, a position by its nature confidential. This was the relationship that the slave Bush had with her Virginia master William Massie. He described her as "a valuable servant, & I at one time thought We would be able to confi[d]e in her to any extent. . . ." The association did not last in this form, however. Massie wrote with some regret in the same letter that "within the last year or two Foggyism has peeped through her skin in various directions."³⁵ By Foggyism he meant that Bush had begun to drift beyond his influence, disobeying his orders and neglecting her duties. She was, he suggested, falling increasingly under the baneful sway of her black companions. If this was true Foggyism had captured many slaves throughout the South. He added, "We do not want to sell Bush & never will, unless old Foggy should burst her open."³⁶

The affection that masters and domestics showed one another took many forms. At the death of Jinny, a "faithful servant," one of her owners, whom she had suckled in his infancy, experienced her loss deeply. He lamented that she "always felt more like a mother than a servant to me and was a kind mother to all my children."³⁷ Masters' feelings at these times seem to strip the slave's personality of any resemblance to stereotypes. Jinny's master continued his tribute as follows: she "was a kind mother to all my Children I frequently left them entirely in her care & always found her faithful in nursing & taking care of them & they all loved her as a mother & she loved them. . . ."[38] In other cases masters compared their domestics to relatives and friends: "True sister he was a servant, and you may be vexed or ashamed, that I should in any manner compare him with yourself . . . [but] altho his skin was black his heart was always in the right place."[39]

A favorite bondsman, domestic or otherwise, could cast a lengthy shadow of privilege and authority on occasion; and a few were well aware of the possibilities. Some body servants accompanied slaveholders to various vacation spots and later to the war. They were attentive; they had to be to maintain their jobs. Often there were as many body servants at vacation spots as there were planters. The time slaves spent at such places could be rather pleasant in some respects. In 1831 at the Red Sulphur Springs in Virginia, guests dined on venison, jelly, mutton, veal, beef, and ice cream: "every thing that can tempt the most fastidious appetite." We can make no one generalization about the treatment accorded body servants at these vacation spots. Some servants joined with white vacationers within limits, eating the same food. Others kept lower profiles, doing little more than was expected to please those slaveholders at hand. Slaveholders and nonslaveholders frequented such places to regain or maintain their health. An occasional favored slave might gain permission to accompany his master for the same reason. "It is no wonder," reflected a planter, "that persons in common circumstances so soon get well here, as the living is so much better than they have at home—I believe, they make it a practice to come here once a year to fatten. . . ."[40] Shortly after the presidential election of 1848, the slaveholder John Quarles, though not formally vacationing, wrote his wife Cornelia that the "only excitement we have . . . is occasionally a supper given by Some old favorite Negro who invites all the gentlemen old and young and leave it to the generosity of the guest to pay what they please."[41] A competition took place in this neighborhood, near Jackson, Tennessee, between favored slaves. It centered around who could give the best "fling" for the local gentlemen. Such rivalries could last for months or years, with weeks devoted to the preparation of a single outing. Each bondsman enjoyed the gatherings because they allowed him to display his organizational skills before a large number of masters, and make useful contacts with planters which might bring him some financial and personal rewards.

In Quarles' neighborhood in 1848, two slaves held a classic entertainment duel. "Night before last," wrote Quarles, "an old Negro Man Col Dire an old servant of old Genl. Dire . . . gave a supper in a large vacant Slave house. . . ." This was the opening move. He continued, "Next friday Night a servant of Col. Chisters Says that he entends to give a Supper in the Court house that will thow Col Dire^s in the Shade."[42] And on it went. These were good times for the domestic.

Still, in some ways, the most privileged domestic was the black mammy of the large estate. She "is in fact the foster Mother of he[r] Masters children and is treated with all the respect due to the faithful discharge of the duties of her Station—. . . ."[43] The mammy nursed them through their illnesses and watched them as they grew into adulthood. She also showered them with a loving affection, which they returned. Many whites mourned for her at her death. John Cocke gives one view of her in his excellent slave diary:

> She of course lives as well as the Mistress of the House & Mother of the children under her care. . . . She too like the foreman of the plantation, has her perquisites of office—and the privileges of bestowing small benefits upon her children & c the family and its visitors calling her Aunt—as Uncle is universally bestowed upon the Male House Servants.[44]

Cocke believed as well that many house servants were ready for freedom, a tribute no doubt to their close contacts with whites.

In the summer of 1845 M. E. Carmichael, a planter, noted with some distress, "my poor Harriet threaten very suddenly with dropsey she is a servant given to me by my dear father and of course a favorite one—We shall have her moved up tomorrow where we can attend to her ourselves."[45] This was the kind of affection that a mammy might command from her second family.

But some researchers have argued that the mammy possessed a dimension to her personality that other slave mothers rarely had. Her relationship to the master's children, wrote E. Franklin Frazier, "offered greater scope for the expression of emotions and impulses characteristic of maternal love than the contacts which she had with her own offspring."[46] At times, the mammy even provided the cohesion necessary to hold the planter's family together in trying moments. She mediated quarrels and gave helpful advice and an understanding heart. But, it is said, she seemed ill-prepared to apply these same talents to her own family's difficulties. How could this be? The mammy knew that a master's children required the special care that she was "employed" to give them. It is not too mundane to suggest that she was concerned with safeguarding her favored position as well. Stern discipline of the children was part of her duty. Yet many mammies were the victims of antagonisms born of parental conflict, and the master's children were not above pitting the authority of the mammy against parental taboos. For as many who were dearly loved, there were others who were spurned and ultimately removed from their posts.

It would seem, however, that the difference in the mammy's treatment of her master's children and her own were not nearly so striking as has been claimed. In the parks of Savannah, Georgia, the Reverend Nehemiah Adams of Massachusetts observed children "with respectable colored nurses" who were "superior in genteel appearance to any similar class, as a whole, in any of our cities" in the North. Besides noticing that these slaves did not have the manner of "hirelings," he commented, "the degree of seemingly maternal feeling which was infused into their whole deportment, could not fail to strike a casual observer."[47] Could a mammy turn such maternalism on and off at will—on with white children, off with black? Perhaps, but it is not likely that this was the case. The mammy instead transferred some of the expectations held for a master's children onto her own, not with the same goals in mind but with a hope of having them better their positions as slaves, maybe with an eye toward freedom. In many cases, she probably treated her master's children the same as she treated her own.

As in every area of slavery there were those wretchedly bad moments. Masters tortured and murdered some domestics, and house slaves killed slaveholders. Many acts against domestics went unpunished. For example, a slave cook and her husband were suspected of plotting to poison their owners. Rumors of the pair's intentions greatly alarmed local slaveholders; and one planter believed that though the slaves received no official attention, they "will probably be strung up in a quiet way"[48] by neighboring whites. A slave system like that found in the Old South could not avoid such tragedies.

It is not easy to generalize about house slaves. They were a diverse class of bondsmen who helped to shape and reshape the character of their servitude in the Big House. In some respects theirs was a special kind of enslavement marked by privileges that most field hands never experienced, at least not in the same way. They did not, however, give in to it. If they had, the slave John Parker's indictment that "if I had submitted I presume I would have been a good house servant"[49] might serve as an apt epitaph. The evidence shows that it does not.

6
The Black Slave Driver

Among those slaves most important to the functioning and harmony of plantation life, the slave driver (foreman) held a slight edge. His hut, perhaps a little larger and better furnished than those of his neighbors, sometimes stood in the center of the slave community. On farms with only a few bondsmen, although there might be no slave known officially as a slave driver, there was usually one who served from time to time as a field leader. His duties in the fields could have considerable impact on the behavior of fellow bondsmen and were crucial to the economic well-being of the slaveholder. One master wrote: "A man would do better to have a good Negro driver, than to have an overseer. . . ."[1] Another noted: "The head driver is the most important negro on the plantation."[2]

What manner of men were these foremen? One ex-driver said simply: "I allers use my sense for help me 'long; jes' like Brer. Rabbit. 'Fo' de wah ol' Marse Heywood mek me he driber on he place. . . ."[3] Slaveholders' comments provide some other insights. "Nearly every large plantation further South," wrote J. D. B. De Bow, "has a driver, who is a negro advanced to the post from his good character and intelligence." Good character meant any variety of things depending on the situation; most important, however, the driver maintained his position only if he also had the ability to extract work from fellow slaves. James Henry Hammond of South Carolina noted in his plantation book that the driver "is to be treated with more respect than any negro by both master and overseer."[4] Carefully conceived, the rule recognized the need to attach prestige to the driver's position. Hammond further commented on the unique relationship he thought a driver ought to have with master and overseer. "He is a confidential servant and may be a guard against any excesses or omissions of the overseer."[5] The driver was thus part of the checks and balances by which careful slaveholders looked out for all their interests.

Was the driver really so important to the slave scene? The death of Ismael, the slave foreman of Thomas Butler of Louisiana, elicited Butler's recognition that while Ismael was alive there was little fear that the plantation could have "suffered from the mismanagement of an injudicious overseer . . . for he was the best driver I ever knew."[6] The loss of a slave foreman prompted another master to fear that "his services . . . cannot be replaced."[7]

To be sure, slaves' responses to black drivers ran the full spectrum of contacts between men. The position was an important but ambiguous one, for the effective slave driver had to tread a path between master and slave, serving both whenever he could. Often this was not possible, leading frequently to driver versus slave or driver versus master-overseer confrontations. The driver might be the plantation "tough," but it was best if he stood up to bullies while forsaking that role himself. Besides, if he bullied the wrong slave there was no telling how the ensuing conflict might end. In one encounter recorded by the driver, a bondsman being disciplined "flong down his cradle and made a oath and said that he had as live die as to live and . . . he then tried to take the whip out of my hand. . . ."[8] In a more serious case, in October 1838 a planter wrote hastily—so his penmanship reflects—to a friend from his West Baton Rouge, Louisiana, plantation that "a few days ago a favorite Negro [a neighbor's driver], . . . was murdered by one of the other negroes he is said to have been horribly cut to pieces, the one that killed him has run away."[9]

Such incidents occurred now and then because in order to save his own back, remarked Francis Fedric, "the slave overseer very often behaves in the most brutal manner to the niggers under him."[10] The experience of another slave confirms this observation. He decried his treatment during one year when, as he emphasized, "he [the master] had a *colored slave foreman*, who had to do as he was commanded, and I hardly had so much consideration as from a white overseer."[11]

There were, quite naturally, many rules to regulate the driver's behavior. But often these rules were only as good as the man. His responsibilities were sometimes nerve-racking, and his temper flared, not unnaturally, when slaves failed to accomplish their tasks. He could be blamed for their shortcomings, and since all the hands knew this any one of them might deliberately antagonize him, compromising his position just as bondsmen regularly compromised the position of overseers.[12]

The Reverend Peter Randolph, an ex-slave writing in the 1890's, set forth an interpretation of drivers which, with minor variations, has passed from the pens and, it seems, through the minds of various scholars unchanged almost to the present. He observed that by placing blacks in the position of foreman, planters were able to point to them as co-initiators of cruelty on plantations. Yet for Randolph the driver was more like a soldier carrying out his orders.[13] The actions of James Williams, himself at one time a slave foreman, are partially illustrative of Randolph's position. Placed in charge of 160 slaves, Williams had "orders to supply the whip unsparingly to every one, whether man or woman." Failure to comply, he explained, left "myself subject at any moment to feel the accursed lash upon my own back. . . ." He admitted whipping a pregnant slave brutally: "I . . . gave her fifty lashes." Although at one point in his narrative he informs his readers, perhaps to ease a troubled conscience, that he "used to tell the poor creatures [females], when compelled by the overseer to urge them forward with the whip, that I would much rather take their places and endure the stripes than inflict them,"[14] he seldom seemed to hesitate in carrying out his instructions to the letter. In Fredrick County, Virginia, still another driver confided, "I was harder on the servants than he [his master] wanted I should be." His owner punished him for his cruelty, but his self-initiated disciplining of other bondsmen indicates how seriously he took his job.[15]

These statements support the charges of those who describe the driver's relationship with other slaves as despotic. Clearly, this side of the relationship did exist. It is worth mentioning, however, that it does not seem to have been the most prevalent side. The driver also served in another and far more important capacity—as confidant and mediator.

It is true that while some drivers nagged other slaves into making careless mistakes which they might then agree to cover up in exchange for small favors and even a portion of the slave's already meager weekly rations or hunting fortunes, others attempted to be helpful. The southern novelist William Gilmore Simms advanced an interesting, though limited, portrayal of the slave foreman in his 1845 story "The Loves of the Driver." The slave in question is Mingo, a many-sided figure. Simms describes him as of "not uncomely countenance" and as "brave as Julius Caesar in his angry mood."[16] Throughout the story Simms' characterization of Mingo is generally complimentary. He shows Mingo's ability to maintain tranquility in the quarters and to sustain the respect of bondsmen by his conduct before the master. Though Simms' characterization of Mingo is often historically flawed, it stands as an honest portrayal of the driver's functions as Simms saw them.

Mingo's multi-faceted personality angered many literary critics in both the Old South and the North who thought that Simms had overstepped the boundaries of artistic license by making a slave the hero of his tale.[17] Simms apparently was bothered by the criticisms, for in none of his later works do slaves play other than token, undeveloped roles. Nevertheless, his brief descriptions of plantation life and of black bondsmen demonstrate that at least for him slaves were more complex than the stereotypic bondsmen readers often encounter.

A driver's job was difficult, for despite the power granted him, the wise driver understood that he gained the trust or enmity of his companions from his associations with them in private just as much as in the fields. It was probably in these private moments that slaves made those agreements that help to explain bondsman Solomon Northup's and others' observations that the lashes of some drivers came close to but never touched the backs of certain slaves, even when the drivers had been ordered to work them vigorously and lay on the whip.[18]

The driver did, according to the testimony of one planter, have his "perquisites of office—and the privilege of bestowing small benefits . . ."[19] upon his fellows. The ex-slave Baskin, a slave driver, perhaps made other uses of the office. He bragged that when he went courting among the slave women, despite his small stature "I alers carry off de purties gal, 'cause you see, Missus, [along with being the driver] I know how to play de fiddle [for some drivers this was an important management asset] an allers had to go to obery dance to play de fiddle for dem."[20] Though this admission is innocent enough, a few drivers sexually assaulted slave women, though we can only speculate about how frequently this occurred. Drivers also worked out arrangements by which certain females were not required to work too hard at times and were given a few minutes' extra rest.[21] Within the shadow of the plantation a variety of agreements were grabbed at to help ease the conditions of bondage.

How was it possible for many of these agreements to come about? For one thing, many masters gave slave drivers great responsibilities and left important matters to their discretion. Walter S. Harris, who was born a slave in Virginia in 1847, reflected back in 1910 on the old days in a letter to his former master's son. He remembered that his "father (until we left in May 1864) was your Fathers head man on the home place." But most revealing are his remarks about his father's duties: "he sowed all the wheat, had charge of the hogs, in fact Master never at anytime know how many sheep or hogs he had."[22] Here is part of the answer. A driver might neglect to mention the precise number of livestock, allowing himself one or more head to trade on or off the plantation in exchange for favors or items of use to himself.

It is difficult, in fact, to explain extensive slave plantation maneuverings not in the interest of masters without positing driver complicity with bondsmen in a wide range of activities. For example, in the Parrysburgh district of South Carolina in 1787, according to planter John L. Bourquin, runaways were at his "Swamp plantation, & . . . they left us with the loss of our Driver fellow [who ran off with them], ten Barrels of clean Rice & myself slightly wounded in the hip. . . ."[23] Slave foreman George Skipwith recognized leaders in "resistance" among the field hands under his care in Alabama. He also knew that just because he was the leader chosen by his master he was not necessarily the one chosen by his fellows.

The possibilities for personal development within slavery stretched before slave foremen as for few other bondsmen. For purposes of slave community harmony he was usually a married man, and his household shared in the "perquisities" granted him as well as in the scorn he might receive from companions. Many drivers were married to domestic slaves—cooks or maids—thus setting up additional and important links between the field and the Big House. With each added privilege some drivers' grew less amenable to assault, less receptive to direct challenges "for daring to think."[24] When a slaveholder's support was withdrawn drivers often reacted in extreme ways—they ran off, sabotaged the estate, or turned on their masters physically. The ex-slave Walter S. Harris recalled that his driver "father disobeyed your father [a master] in a matter while he was in Charles City in May 1864, which caused an unpleasantness and one dark night, father taken us [his family] an slipped away."[25] This conversion to rebel was not a simple reflex. The driver's perception of himself had much time to develop as he carried out his duties. He could easily see that although society discriminated against him he was certainly as qualified as many whites to direct the course of his destiny. It is interesting too that often he did not see himself as unique in this regard among "field" slaves.

James Henry Hammond of South Carolina wrote a revealing sentence about drivers in the plantation book he kept. The driver, he stressed, "is on no occasions to be treated with any indignity, calculated to lose the respect of other negroes, without breaking [being especially cruel to] him. . . ."[26] Hammond conceived of the black foreman as a liaison between master and slave, plantation house and slave quarters. The driver could convey the complaints of bondsmen to the master; but he could do this accurately only if he had a sound understanding of specific individuals. He was not usually a spy, a dupe of the slaveholder, although he could become that. But if he breached too many confidences he found his management of slaves increasingly difficult and his private life somewhat censored. It was best to stay on the slave's side of the line.

The slaveholder John Cocke viewed the driver as a "humble friend of the master."[27] William Pettigrew of North Carolina, while consoling his driver Moses about the death of his uncle, reminded Moses that "our lot having been cast together her[e] [on earth] . . . I am a friend. . . ."[28] Yet neither Pettigrew nor Cocke appeared to convey by this that the driver was a dupe. They expected him to be an individual who had confidence in himself to perform his assigned duties. If he did this—often having great leeway in his interpretation of them—he was eligible to receive rewards for "himself & his family" in money, clothing, or other things he selected. Thus, the driver's potential for acquiring influence over his fellows and his master's interests was greatly expanded. Regarding remuneration for services well performed, Cocke recalled, "I have known the monied annuity to very from $5 to $100 a year." Where this practice was followed the driver might aid his friends in getting badly needed additional clothing or even food. But he could, as well, withhold his beneficence in a display of displeasure with their behavior. Appropriately used, his "freedoms" could be the critical element in cementing his authority.[29]

The slave Peter, identified in a letter from William Pettigrew to a relative as the one who "so well supplied the place of the worthless fellow [an overseer] you discharged," ran the North Carolina plantation of James C. Johnston in the mid-1840's.[30] The letter continued, "there are some instances in which negroes are not inferior to white men. . . ."[31] Years before, in 1803, an ancestor, Charles Pettigrew, had commented that "the negroes at the Lake plantation have commonly done better by themselves with a little direction than with such Overseers, as we have had."[32] James Johnston wrote in 1849: "I have three farms carried on entirely by colored men without the aid of a white and I think they are better managed than I ever had them when I employed white overseers. . . ."[33] In each instance, select slaves apparently served as both overseers and drivers. The practice was not unusual, since many times the duties of overseer and driver were virtually the same. The practice appeared to add to plantation harmony. An additional consideration on the Pettigrew estates was that the bondsmen were furnished more of life's material goods than slaves obtained on many other plantations. But of far greater importance is the part these slave managers played in shaping the outcome. William Pettigrew summed up his feelings this way:

> It is desirable, if the good conduct of my negroes will justify it not to employ a white overseer for preferring this I have several reasons . . . if one be so unfortunate as to emply a worthless man, then his negroes & his income both suffer; for the former with such a person soon settle into idleness, As far as I can, up to this time form an opinion. I think my people will, by the assistance of the two negro men who have heretofore been over them/Henry at Magnolia, & Moses at Belgrade/work faithfully, and conduct themselves well.[34]

Any number of planters around the Old South would have agreed with this assessment. A South Carolina slaveholder, a friend of James Henry Hammond, certainly did. He wrote to Hammond about a slave auction where a slave driver was sold. He mentioned that he was a man 35 to 40 years of age and was "so intelligent & trustworthy that he had charge of a separate plantation & 8 or 10 hands, some 10 or 12 miles from home. . . ." He concluded, "Such a man would be invaluable to me. . . ."[35]

Yet despite this evidence of his obvious importance to the slave scene, the driver has not received much attention from scholars, and in two recent studies about slave culture he garners only passing references.[36] On large plantations the driver's influence in slave affairs was often of such importance as to alter many perceptions we have about the total slave community. He has to be an integral part of our examination of slavery.

It will perhaps serve to illustrate this point further if we focus on the experience of the slave driver George Skipwith, who has left us, in his own words, a rather unique and detailed account of his experiences. From Greensboro, Alabama, George wrote his master John Cocke in 1847, "i hav[e] a good crop on hand for you both of Cotton and corn this you knoe could not be don without hard work."[37] For almost five years George managed the affairs of this particular plantation. He watched over the livestock, planting, and harvesting and handled the disciplining of his fellow slaves. This latter duty caused much animosity between him and his hands. He was also very protective of the authority he exercised and battled against whites and blacks who tried to compromise his position.

Admittedly, George Skipwith was an exceptional slave in many ways, not only by virtue of his status as a slave foreman. He and some of the other slaves on this Alabama plantation were among a group selected by John Cocke to be colonized from Virginia to Alabama and then, after a period of preparation, to be sent to Liberia in Africa. But many years were to pass before this began to happen, and in most cases these Alabama slaves did not escape bondage.

George's duties brought him into contact with whites in situations where his judgment weighed heavily. Often matters of supplies and care of the grounds were handled by him. The slave Moses on the Pettigrews' plantations had similar duties and at one point thought it "best to get Mr. Davis [a white man] to saw another [frame] on wich I have don so[me] thinking. . . ."[38] In many of these contacts, whites seemed to have responded to the driver as they might have to anyone in authority, though other whites in the neighborhood resented the prestige thereby accorded the driver. Some patrols harassed drivers when they left the security of the plantation to remind them that, despite their apparent freedoms, they were still slaves. In his comments to a relative, John Johnston complained that "some troublesome persons who have been appointed Patrol have given Peter [his slave foreman] some trouble. . . ."[39] His relative's reply was conciliatory: "I regret Peter has been annoyed by the improper conduct of the Patrol."[40]

George's services were invaluable, and few understood this better than he. He confessed to but one failing—an over-fondness for liquor. The slaves under his care, however, were quick to point out others. Trouble frequently arose in response to George's disciplinary measures. He wrote his master once in defense of some of these measures, stating that "among twenty or thirty hands there will be some times that a man will [have] to spur them up."[41] Most masters would have been in agreement with him on this point. During the previous month, when trouble had also flared, George observed, "i have whiped none without a caus."[42] The slaves disagreed. But George tells about his corrections this way:

Luky who i put to plant som corn and after She had been there long anuf to hav been done i went there and She had hardly began it i gave her Som four or five licks over her clothes i gave isam too licks over his clothes for covering up cotton with the plow. i put frank isham usually Dinah Jinny evenline [Evelyn] and Charlott to Sweeping cotten going twice in a roe and at a reasonable days worke they ought to have plowed seven obbers a piece and they had been at it a half a day and they had not done more than one abber and a half and i gave them ten licks a peace upon thir skins i gave Julyann eight or ten licks for misplacing her hoe that was all the whiping i hav done. . . .[43]

The slaves under George's care resisted him strongly when they believed his methods especially harsh. George told one group of slaves whom he had disciplined, "you do not intent to cut these oats until i whip every one of you." But the slave Robert responded by "saying that he knoed when he worked . . ." and that "he was not afraid of being whipped by no man."[44]

Robert did indeed get whipped, but it was only with the help of several of "the other boys" that George succeeded in doing this. Believing the matter at an end, he turned his attention to other duties. But in the meantime, Robert solicited the aid of a white minister whom the plantation's owner had permitted to preach among the slaves. George believed that Robert took his problems to the minister and his family "becaus he knoed that they would protect him in his rascality for he had hoered that they had said that they [slaves] were worked to death and that they were lowed no more chance for living than if they were dogs or hogs." George appears to have considered the accuracy of this statement and its implications for his own life as a slave. But he seems to have believed that his chance for freedom lay along the path he was following. Therefore, he focused his attention on the disruptive minister, noting in his letter to Cocke that Reverend Taylor had had a chat with all the slaves which, he believed, "was calculated to incurage the people to rebel against me."

George thus found himself in the unenviable position of appearing to uphold the institution of slavery while a white man championed the cause of freedom. How perplexing this could be! Yet he never really saw the conflict in these terms. Once freedom had been promised him by John Cocke, the issue was more a matter of preventing disruption of his authority. Reverend Taylor was a threat to his position, a white man trying to erode his authority and spoil his chance at freedom.

Reverend Taylor did possess abolitionist sympathies, which he

did not try to conceal, and several months after the above incidents was removed from the plantation. Trouble among the slaves
had continued to mount, and George had apparently convinced
his master that Reverend Taylor was responsible for most of it.
He confided in John Cocke, finally: "i knoe sir that mr Taylor has
don more harm amoung our people than he has don good for he
says that we are treated worse than any peopel in the world and
if there is any in the world treated any worse he has never herde
talk of them." These were the words that turned the heads of so
many of the bondsmen. George further observed that Mr. Taylor
said that "he will tell [this] to every boddy that ask him any thing
about us." George added, "i cant say that mr. Taylor was not a
christian but he aked very comical the time he was with us."[45]

With Mr. Taylor out of the way, George's attention turned to
more routine matters. It is clear from his correspondence and
from letters of members of the Cocke family that George recognized that other slaves possessed forceful personalities, and he
thought it best to meet these personalities head on when they
threatened his authority. He tackled the duties of the plantation
in the same manner.

In many ways, of course, George's letters to his master resemble
in tone and content those of a white overseer to his employer. The
main reason for this might be that they both operated within the
same slavery system and accepted many of its standards. But despite George's admitted disciplines, as well as his obvious self-
interest, he seems to have been genuinely concerned about his
people.[46]

George kept tabs too on the lives of slaves away from work. At
one point he noted that the "married people gets on very Smooth
togeathear and keeps themselves and thir rooms very clean." In a
later letter he wrote that "they have been disposed to act contrary with one another but was John has got them all to rights
again."[47] In this same letter he observed, with a touch of fatherly
pride, that the slave Lucy is "dutiful to her intfant school and she
says martha and my little george are the too smartist ons about
learning."[48] And lest he be criticized himself, he always men-

tioned how successful his crops were, and if they were not, what he planned to do to improve them: "my crops of cotton is as good a one at preasant as any man can shoe on Sandy land. . . ." He further commented that the worms were doing their best to harm thc crop "but I am no way Disincurageed yet."[49] There was a P.S. attached to this letter from George Cocke, John Cocke's brother, disagreeing with George's assessment of the crop.

When George was not in conflict with his fellows he seemed to "push" work nicely. There were several skilled slaves under his direction. Two carpenters put up a corn crib, and two slaves were engaged in putting chimneys "to the new houses."[50] Usually such skilled hands were nearly of driver status themselves, and George did have trouble with those under his supervision. They often possessed egos to match his own. On a Virginia estate a slave who had run away was called the "foreman of your carpenters." In this case, it was feared too that "he is urging her [his wife] to follow him & has given her the necessary instructions to accomplish this object. . . ."[51]

The complications accompanying life in bondage made the driver's job a troublesome one. Because some abused their stations or failed to comply with regular disciplinary regulations for slaves, they were reprimanded or deprived of their positions at intervals. This happened to George Skipwith; he found, like others, that it was impossible to abuse slave neighbors month after month and continue to receive friendship and cooperation from them. Under similar pressures many other drivers also fell from the master's favor and were demoted. The slave driver Mingo in William Gilmore Simm's story "was degraded from his trust, and a young negro put over him," though Mingo was not guilty of slave abuse.[52] The Charleston district bondsman Primus had the following written by his name in his master's listing of slaves, indicating that he too had once been demoted: "field han[d], & good Driver, but broke about two years ago by the overseer for talking too much, pushes business very well."[53]

George Skipwith attempted several defenses of his conduct but to little avail, for his management of the slaves was constantly jeopardized by his disciplinary methods. On December 1, 1848 he wrote his master, "i was in hopes that you would hear a good account of us all the hold year out but i cannot write any thing concerning our matters that will be pleasing to you for the state of things at preassant are such as i have never knone here beofore."[54] He worried that his master would take the word of the slaves against him and reminded Cocke that Cocke had assured him that "no fals reports could condem a man if he went right." But he continued to drink and abuse his fellows. He further observed that "they [the slaves] have raised report upon me once but missed thir ame. but here is the second one. . . ."[55] George weathered several new crises, but bondsmen's complaints continued to reshape his authority. John Cocke eventually removed some of George's disciplinary powers and placed them in the hands of Mr. Perkins, about whom George wrote, "Sir i think mr perkins is the very man that you take him to be he is kind to the people and whips none without a suffishent cause."[56]

In Louisiana in 1844 a driver balked at a particularly gruesome prospect. The incident involved the fate of the slave Tom, who was abruptly knocked down by his overseer when he complained of ill health. The overseer, Gillespie, then sent "for the Driver to whip him, when he was laying upon the gallery floor apparently dead & the blood running upon the floor. . . ." But "the driver expressed an unwillingness to whip him in this fix" and apparently declined to do so, whereupon Gillespie decided to "whip him [Tom] himself—Then had him taken to his bed, frm which he never rose—but died in a few days after."[57] Gillespie's employer tried to bring murder charges against him, though we cannot tell from the correspondence if he was successful. This account is also illustrative of the extreme situations that might confront the driver. Most of the circumstances he dealt with fell far short of murder, but he often had to decide on the spot whose thinking he would follow, his master's or overseer's or his own.

Thus, it was no surprise on some larger plantations to find several field hands who had formerly held the rank of driver or assistant driver over the past few years. Difficult as it is to measure how extensively this occurred throughout the Old South, the fact that it could and did occur suggests the pressures on drivers.[58] It was usually a driver's inability to "push work"—a matter heavily influenced by his relationships with other slaves—that brought about his removal.

Occasionally a driver's removal elicited a rather severe reaction from him. His ego and pride were, of course, deeply involved in his occupation. It is not difficult to suppose that his own sense of dignity could openly clash with his master's. Anthony, the "head man" (driver) on the plantation of R. K. Cralle in Lynchburg, Virginia, threatened suicide and fled when Cralle hired an overseer who then assumed many of Anthony's duties. He "cut some tremendous capers, and cleared out," wrote Cralle. And before leaving he "threatened quite bravely." Prior to departing, Anthony "said to the Overseers wife . . . that he should hang himself—and might be found by the *buzzards*."[59] By these threats, Anthony showed a self-confidence and scorn not uncommon to discontented bondsmen. His master vowed, seemingly forgetful of how much he had relied on Anthony before this incident, "If I get hold of him again, I will make him acquainted with the Climate of the West Indies."[60] We can only speculate about the impact behavior like Anthony's had on plantation slaves. It had to have some shock value at least, and they may have wondered why someone so trusted would simply abscond. But in any case, the slave driver's behavior was a further example that trust between a bondsman and a master in the slave setting was, indeed, delicately balanced.

7
The Shadow of the Slave Quarters

The social arena in which bondsmen of every station—field hands, domestics, drivers, artisans—came face to face was the slave quarters. Here slaves held center stage, and the larger the farm or plantation the greater the odds that the roles they played here would go largely unnoticed by many masters. The influence of the quarters was a strong one, difficult to measure in direct terms, but frequently an important factor shaping the quality of the slave's personality, his private life, and his bondage itself.

Although slaves generally lived in huts arranged tightly together around an open expanse of ground, the dwellings themselves varied greatly from plantation to plantation. A slave has left us with this vivid description of the slave quarters on one of the larger estates:

> The houses that the slaves lived in were all built in a row, away from the big house. Just at the head of the street and between the cabins and the big house, stood the overseer's house. There was some forty or fifty of these two room cabins facing each other across an open space for a street. In them we lived. There was not much furniture. Just beds and a table and some stools or boxes to sit on. Each house had a big fire-place for heat and cooking.[1]

This was the village-like setting he remembered, a physically tight community animated by the life within. In most settings the overseer's hut was not a part of this complex. When it was, of course, it was situated so that he might keep his eye on his charges. Perhaps an additional description is also worth noting. It comes to us from a slave, and in some ways describes the kind of living arrangement that was most widespread. Negro houses

> were constructed of logs, and from twelve to fifteen feet square; they had no glass, but there were holes to let in the light and air. The furniture consisted of a table, a few stools, and dishes made of wood, and an iron pot, and some other cooking utensils.[2]

But what of the fabric of slave life, its disappointments and its joys? One historian has written that in the quarters "there was much hospitality and sociability, much dancing, laughing, singing and banjo playing when the day's work was done."[3] A portion of his claim is correct, but his implications as to the bondsman's carefree existence are in need of revision.

For slaves, life in the quarters could be a welcome retreat from the prying eyes of overseer and master. To aid in securing this privacy many slave cabins had the conjurer's horseshoe brand or some other conjuring symbol on their doors to bar evil spirits and persons. And inside the door a "conjuring gourd" might be just within reach. A definite calm was often noticeable in bondsmen's deportment in this setting, as a result of their being here at leisure. The English traveler Captain Basil Hall once asked a master about happenings in the Quarters. "In answer to our question he told us that he interfered as little as possible with their domestic habits, except in matters of police."[4] At times this widely followed practice nearly gave the bondsman a free hand. Robert Carter, the Virginia planter, once chastised his overseer for whipping the slave Jerry for a disturbance in the quarters. The "offence you Charged him with," he angrily pointed out, "was a matter in his own house, last Wednesday night when two Negro men [belonging to neighbors] were very much disposed to fight on acct of

Negro Mary who lives at Jerry's house, but thro the means of Jerry these fellows were dispersed. . . ."[5]

In all slave quarters, of course, the presence of slaves of varying duties, strengths, talents, and temperaments living and socializing together caused some personal and managerial difficulties. Skilled laborers might not have to start their work with the first sign of dawn like other slaves; they were more likely to labor at their own pace, and usually had longer rest breaks. They were "slaves of significance" to the plantation's operations, fully aware of their special status. Animosities quickly developed between them and other slaves during non-working hours. Finding himself an unwilling onlooker to an emerging rivalry, an overseer wrote to his employer that "i have bin oblige to tell your mill handes that they had to leave the quarter at the same time those people did that is in my Charge."[6] The field hands did not believe that the mill laborers were working as hard as they. In a letter dated three days earlier the overseer warned that if some slaves "see negroes around them Ideling why they want to doe so two"[7] and would if given the chance, he believed.

Such disparities set the stage for the quarrels and fights that erupted in the quarters, sometimes becoming feuds that dragged on through the years, ending only when one or several of the feuding slaves died or were sold by the master. In a similar sense, a single slave could try to dominate the quarters scene, making life unpleasant for other bondsmen when he or she chose to. The Maryland slave Elisa was able to do this with some regularity. "Jane says," reads the diary of Susanna Warfield, that "she rules in the quarter—When she gets angry it is no use to Say any thing to Elisa—She will whip every child in the quarter until she satisfies her vengeance."[8] With a slave like Elisa around, some difficult situations might develop between her and other bondsmen during their important leisure hours. Her impact, directly within the quarters, was probably more important at times than the Warfields'. Elisa worked steadily to consolidate her position, acting like a combatant to whom the engagement is new but the footpaths well worn.

Her position was different from, for example, that of the "old people" of the quarters, who with approaching age traditionally assumed places of respect among slaves. That this did not always hold true in a favorable sense, however, is clear from a runaway slave's unsympathetic words about "old Milla." He wrote to his former master in his own hand, "I expect [she] is dead & gone to the devil long ago, if she is not, I think the imps are close at her heels, & will soon put her where there are nothing else but *nasty, stinking black dogs* a plenty."[9] The emphasis is his own, and he perhaps alluded to supernatural forces because some of the old ones were known to be powerful practitioners of the occult. Throughout southern neighborhoods many were known as "oracles" of considerable influence.[10]

For children and adults the old peoples' memories were the cultural storehouses of those tall tales that they loved to hear so much. As some huddled around a crackling fire in the evening (the fire was often used to ward off evil spirits), the old ones would frighten them with stories about snakes, their tails tucked neatly into their mouths, rolling in pursuit of human victims and upon catching them, stinging them to death with the end of the tail, or nearly so.[11] Listeners followed the stories closely, for who knew when it might be *his* turn to retell them, winning the admiration of companions? In these settings, the slave's West African past frequently raised its head. "Most of these stories," remembered Charles Ball of his own experiences, "referred to affairs that had been transacted in Africa, and were sufficiently fraught with demons, miracles and murders to fix the attention of many hearers."[12]

Sometimes slaves acted out various parts of the story, and often dancing, story, and music were blended into interesting folk operas. One visitor to Virginia was so enchanted with the folktales he heard that he not only argued, amidst some sarcasm, that slaves were "our ONLY TRULY NATIONAL POETS" but enthused, "A tour through the south, and a year or two of plantation life, would not fail to reward the diligent collector; and his future fame would be as certain as Homer's."[13]

After these sessions slaves retired to their own huts where, depending on the season, "Sometimes we sit around the fire all night. We could have a big hot fire, as much as we wanted, and we would sit up sometimes to keep good and warm."[14] Storytellers were usually elderly men as opposed to elderly women—the reason why is not clear—and they were important contributors to quarters harmony, especially during times when abuse accompanied by long hours of work and widespread disease escalated bondsmen's emotions and suffering to new peaks. This was the wonder of their folktales. The themes spanned a vast variety of circumstances and slave and master character. Frequently they combined a wide range of emotion in the same tale; good and bad, the happy and the sad were overlapping themes.

Keeping in mind sociologist Howard Odum's valuable perception that "treasures of folk-lore and song, the psychic religious, and social expression of the race, have been permitted to remain in complete obscurity,"[15] let us pursue some of the slaves' storytelling. Freedom and its necessary accompaniment within bondage, resistance, received extensive embellishment in the slave's folklore talk and give us insights into what slaves really thought concerning life's experience. And contrary to what some interpreters have written, the slave was not always the super-cunning winner in his tales. He was more real than that.

Bondsmen throughout the South told variations of the now-famous Br'er Rabbit stories, most of which have some particularly significant parallels in slave life.[16] Important in this regard is the story "De Reason Br'er Rabbit Wears a Short Tail," found in South Carolina and elsewhere. In this account, Br'er Rabbit (the slave) learns that cunningness is not always rewarded. Br'er Rabbit plans to trick some fish away from brother wolf (the master) for use by his own family. So often in these stories the slave's attention turns to food, perhaps as an indication of a want of sufficient and varied edibles in his daily life. Br'er Rabbit gets the fish from the wolf by lying on the road pretending to be dead while the wolf, the dominant force in the neighborhood, puzzles over his sudden death and momentarily leaves his fish unattended. We cannot deny what some might call the lazy aspects of Br'er Rabbit's character, for he preys off others' efforts, though he does not victimize the weak or helpless. On the contrary, he is usually generous with his "rewards," sharing them with his friends. But in this instance the wolf takes revenge on Br'er Rabbit and his family. Discovering the loss of his fish, he goes to Br'er Rabbit's house and sets it on fire, driving Br'er Rabbit, his wife, and children to the rooftop. When the fire finally reaches them they are forced to leap off the roof one by one into the arms of the wolf, who viciously cuts them to pieces with an axe—an allegorical rendering of the splitting up of the family by the slave trade. Br'er Rabbit, of course, stays on the roof till the last moment when he leaps off into what seems certain death. But his wits save him. Just as the wolf is about to ax him, he spits some chewing tobacco—a familiar commodity of slave life and conjuration practices—into the wolf's eyes, with the result that the wolf's aim is deflected and only Br'er Rabbit's tail is chopped off.[17]

The story is less amusing than most of the Br'er Rabbit variety, but perhaps this is because it bears a more realistic resemblance to slave life and experiences. The personal price that Br'er Rabbit has to pay merely to survive is a high one. The story recommends caution as a slave virtue, yet it also continues the theme of quick thinking and constant alertness, for it is only through these attributes that Br'er Rabbit manages to survive at all.

Indeed the Br'er Rabbit stories and other tales in the slave's folklore repertory are deeply concerned with power relationships. Beyond this concern with power and intertwined with it is the amazing amount of energy that Br'er Rabbit has to expend to accomplish his aims. He must often risk all to implement his cunning. He is, in effect, a rather daring personality, attuned to his own weaknesses and vulnerabilities as well as to those of others. Yet, Br'er Rabbit's triumphs are transitory. He outsmarts, but the powerful, momentarily outsmarted, still maintain their power. In contrast, Br'er Rabbit's power is momentary and totally dependent on the recognition and manipulation of transient opportunities. His view of his life is, in fact, an accurate one, and he sees behind life's surface realities to what may be possible for him even in his present condition. He possesses more human qualities than those who possess mere raw power; or, as an ex-slave story-teller noted in "Cooter an' Deer," "Cooter got de gal an' de whole county see him beat Deer in de ten-mile race for all Deer hab shich [such] long foot."[18]

The slave turned his storytelling abilities to many topics, and mixed them with those endless comments (aphorisms) that many bondsmen liked to make up on the spur of the moment. Especially in the quarters, they might sit back and momentarily reflect on their lives: "Tain't no use o' sp'ilin de Sat'day night by countin' de time to Monday mornin'."

By its nature the aphorism is a telling observation about one's existence. And the slaves made some interesting observations about their situation. Of their labors they said simply, "Sharp ax better'n big muscle." The hard labor of plowing on a hill received the comment, "Nigger don't sing much plowin' de hillside." And most slaves would have agreed, even when masters failed to understand, that "You can't medjer a nigger's wuk by de 'mount I' singin' he does at de shuckin'."[19]

These examples make up, along with the slaves' other folklore (music, dance), a continual dialogue that slaves kept up with one another in the quarters and elsewhere. These were more than ingredients for "pep-talk"; they served to ease the bondsman's lot by promoting those images of themselves the slaves wished to assume in their own ranks. Children especially received this continual diet of images from the slave community, being in some measure reared on them. We can only speculate about the impact such accounts had on the slave's self-concept but, like many other things in his life, they clearly helped to shape the responses he made to his bondage.

Slaveholders' manuscript sources confirm that many of these accounts were told to white children by domestic slaves. What impact they had on young minds then and after slavery is hard to assess but should provide a fascinating field of exploration.

Many of them are extremely revealing: "Tomorrow may be de carridge-driver's day for ploughin'." The slave turned his attention also to his very important spiritual life. In fact few things escaped his humorous jibes and telling comments: "De people dat stirs up de mos' rackit in de meetin' house ain't always de bes' kis'chuns." And they observed as well, "Folks dat go to sleep in de meetin' house do heap o' late settin' up at home."[20]

The close living space in the quarters itself elicited some perceptive slave remarks. Probably because of the social events they sometimes held there, at which liquid spirits were served, they could see that "licker talks might loud w'en it git loose fum de jug." They also had this sage advice about the well-known practice of dirt-eating: "Ef you bleedzd ter eat dirt, eat clean dirt."[21]

The settings that served as backdrops to the slave's folktales approximate his varied life situations. We know that these tales were told in the slave quarters and at work in the fields. They often turned into folksongs, helpful in cushioning slave labors. The slave John Parker remembered that bondsmen in a slave gang on the road just after an auction consoled themselves with stories and songs.[22]

Folklorists of the slave past have uncovered a number of recurring themes; with further research into this rich reserve we will be able to advance considerably our understanding of slave culture, the African background, and the plantation system. One important theme concerns the cunning or intelligent slave who was frequently called John. The slaves of the John tales bear a resemblance to slave drivers (favored slaves) in that they often serve as mediators between Old Marster and the other slaves and escape the heaviest chores. In support of this interpretation it might be helpful to turn to an ex-slave driver who was something of a folklorist. He claimed that because he was the driver ". . . I aint hab for work so hard as de res'; some time I git mo' ration ebery mont' an' mo' shoe when dey share out de cloes at Chris'mus time. Well, dat com from usin' my sense."[23] The parallel is not a precise one, and there is much of other slaves in John. But there is enough of the driver to suggest his hold on the slave imagination: "Old Marster had this main fellow on his farm he put his confidence in, John."[24]

In the John and other folktales, unlike the Br'er Rabbit stories, the slave is not quite as successful in outsmarting his master. His triumphs take on a more deliberate note, for the tales granted masters their share of victories and kept the slave wisely aware of the realities of his situation.

Among the most interesting in the slave's stock of tales were many that had to do with relationships between slaves themselves. One of the most noteworthy in this regard is called "De Tiger An' De Nyung Lady." Recorded among South Carolina slaves along the seacoast, the story line, as backed up by other evidence, was certainly not unique to these bondsmen. The focus is on a brazen young woman who vows that she will marry no man "what gets a scratch on him back" from whipping. She is warned about her inflexible stand but steadfastly sticks to it. One day a tiger overhears her boast and with the help of a little conjuration determines to teach her a lesson. He turns into the perfect man, marries her and then carries her off to his lair in the swamps and leaves her for three days. She is eventually rescued by an Uncle Sambo, who, unlike the stereotype of that name, shows amazing courage before the tiger. But the tiger does not want to fight, and gives the moral of the story: "I aint gwine hu't her. I only married um for le' um know dat a woman isn't more dan a man, for de word dat she say, dat she 'Wouldn't married a man what gots a scratch on him back.' " Uncle Sambo returns the girl home to her mother, who gives her this advice: "God had nebber made a woman for the head of a man."[25]

Such slave traditions, elements of which now seem picturesque, were only slightly altered on the modest farms of lesser slaveholding whites. The scale of things was smaller, and one looks in vain for the Big House. There were, too, some physical differences in the layout of the slave quarters, if there was a place with that distinct identity. To be sure, that was the main difference. Seldom were there huts set apart on their own ground. Instead, a few unimposing shanties fanned out from the master's house—little more than a shanty itself sometimes—like fingers on a hand. The activities of the quarters were not entirely separate from farm life.

It was in the quarters, wherever they might be, that slaves learned the advantages of pooling their efforts and resources. During all seasons of the year bondsmen collected firewood, "and they often have to go to' the swamp for it."[26] It was safer to travel with friends. Some slaves shared their fortune at hunting or fishing with others in exchange for reciprocal favors. The making of clothing is a case in point. During some evenings women sewed additional clothing for themselves, their men, and their children. They cooked together occasionally also, utilizing the skills and energies of the quarters in many joint efforts. In much of this, naturally, a few bondsmen sponged off the efforts of others and made a mockery of others' attempts at self-improvement, but this was exceptional.

When they were in the mood, members of the master's household shared in the life of the slave quarters, particularly during holiday seasons. "We visited the 'Quarters'—went into' uncle Bob's Cabin: ' had lots of fun."[27] Whites sometimes went down to the quarters to seek advice on quite serious matters. They wanted consultation on affairs of the heart, plantation operations, business, and in a few instances, even murder. Yet visits of a social nature to slaves' cabins occasionally prompted neighborly criticism. Many slaveholders feared that management difficulties would arise from too close a familiarity and comradery in certain things. Perhaps it was for this reason that the owner of a Louisiana plantation directed his overseer to keep the overseer's relatives away from his slaves. With the receipt of this communication the overseer advised an uncle to tell one "Uncle red" of the "impropriety" of going down to the quarters. He ended his advice by noting that "the doctor stoped his own Brother from cuming to the plantation for the sam[e] cause . . ." and added, "I mean yong men that wood bee in the quarters where the negroes are dancing."[28] Some members of the master class had sexual rendez-vous on these visits, and most appeared relieved and uplifted to find bondsmen gingerly enjoying themselves.

We get a wide range of descriptions about quarters happenings from whites who observed life there. In an instance which evokes the flavor common throughout the South on festive occasions for the slaves, a visitor witnessed a persimmon beer celebration in a hut.

> Here the banjor-man, was seated on the beer barrel, in an old chair. A long white cowtail, queued with red ribbon, ornamented his head, and hung gracefully down his back; over which he wore a three-cocked hat, decorated with peacock feathers, a rose cock-ade, a bunch of ripe persimmons, and to cap the climax, three pods of red pepper as a top-knot. Tumming his banjor, grinning with ludicrous gesticulations and playing off his wild notes to the company.

The banjo player's costume is worth further comment. Red rib-bon was often worn by bondsmen to keep evil spirits away. The three-cocked hat is a familiar symbol of the world of conjuration, as are feather and red peppers, which were familiar items in the pouches (mojos) many slaves carried. The description continues:

> Before him [the banjo player] stood two athletic blacks, with open mouth and pearl white teeth, clapping "Juber" to the notes of the banjor; the fourth black man held in his right hand a jugy gourd of persimmon beer, and in his left, a dipper or water gourd, to serve the company; while two black women were em-ployed in filling the fire-place, six feet square, with landed persimmon dough. The rest of the company, male and female, were dancers, except a little squat wench, who held the torch light.[29]

What passed for slave quarters in southern cities were simply rooms in the backs of stores or small out' uildings a few steps away from an alley or the rear of a master's residence, which itself fronted the main street. "The slaves in the cities do not fare so hard as on the plantations," said an ex-slave. "All can dress well, have comfortable homes, and many can read and write."[30] It was true that some city slaves—not many—had private homes that rivaled those of small country slaveholders in space and rustic luxury; however, the confined nature of most urban bondsmen's dwellings—in Charleston high walls frequently encircled them—moved the life of the quarters into the streets.[31] Slaves gathered in groups on corners, blocked walkways, and held night meetings despite black codes which prohibited everything from walking on the wooden sidewalks of the city to being on the streets after eight or nine o'clock in the evening. On weekends and holidays white Southerners lodged a constant flood of complaints with local officials about the behavior of slaves who pushed and shoved on the meager walks, lacking the common sense to step into the street, if need be, to make room for gentlemen and ladies.[32]

Richard Wade has given examples of social mingling of blacks and whites in cities. A good example occurred in Charleston in 1795. On November 7 bondsmen, free blacks, and whites held a dance in a private house in the downtown section of the city, with festivities carrying on well past the curfew hour. A sworn affadavit indicates "that between the Hours of Eleven & twelve the Patrole discovered a dance of Colored people in the House lately occupied by Julius Smith deceased." The patrol "demanded admitance & was refused by two negroes from within . . ." but after a brief scuffle "made a forcible Entry—" when, to their surprise, Captain Cunnington, a white man, "descended the Stairs & demanded in an angry tone 'who dared to enter the House.'" He explained that he had gained previous permission to use the home from its owner and "that there were none in the house but friends with the Circle of the Neighborhood, who were amusing themselves."[33] The patrol's members, however found his explanation unconvincing and arrested all in attendance.

But what real influence did the quarters have in its most important location, the plantation? And who were some of the slaves who helped to mold the course and quality of its life style? Shaping the quarters environment were two very powerful presences that were fixtures of the slave's life, religion and music.

About slave devotional periods bondswoman Harriet Jacobs said: "Precious are such moments. . . . If you were to hear them at such time, you might think they were happy."[34] The experiences of Frederick Douglass and other slave narrators support her observation. Indeed, the happy slave conclusion was the one that many planters came to. They had taken the measure of the slave and decided that religious occasions of all kinds held a wonderful fascination for him. And there was an abundance of supportive evidence. "Quite the largest crowd of Servants assembled below My House at Fowlers brick yard Cystern to see a Baptising," wrote P. H. Pitts of North Carolina.[35] To be sure, the slave's religious practices and observances took up a great part of his hours away from and, on occasion, at work.

Some slaves reported being moved by the spirit while working in the fields. They would be spiritually reborn, they said, after being struck dead by God to sin in this world. If, as historians are fond of observing, "a noted spectacle" of the harvest was singing, we might say also that certainly a not infrequent spectacle of work in the fields was the "shout" when moved by the spirit. Some bondsmen testified to seeing visions at such times, many dealing with their own sinful ways. For other slaves there were conditional aspects even to these spiritual influences. Apparently they believed that if God saw fit to give them a new life, then perhaps He should be expected to make that life better than the old one even if this required attempts, as one bondsman expressed it, "to make him bow to my own will and notions. . . ."[36]

White settlers met the first slave arrivals to Jamestown and New England determined to cleanse them of their African cultisms. Organized religion saw the task in part as one of the fresh challenges of the New World. Missionaries and slaveholders rushed ahead, rationalizing the moral dilemmas posed by the coexistence of Christianity and slavery.[37]

The arguments many employed often tried to justify most aspects of slavery. For instance, when the value of slaves rose, it was seen as the will of God working to bring about His Providential Government. Christianity was, as well, frequently linked to the economic success of southern crops. Cotton, the chief southern staple, was king of the commercial world in the nineteenth century, but for many slaveholders its dominance was attributable to more than just business acumen and the need for clothing. One master had a ready explanation for cotton's successes: "is not this as much a part & parcel of Gods providential government as the Institution of Slavery with which it is connected?"[38] The "History of the World will prove that the Institution of Slavery has done more in Christionizing in the heathen than all the missionary Society in the World besides."[39]

Slavery thus had its good side for some. In 1859 Joseph Jones, the son of Charles C. Jones, wrote his parents, "Some of the happiest, most profitable hours of my life were spent" in an Augusta, Georgia, sabbath school instructing slaves in the ways of the Lord.[40] The presence of pious slaves could be uplifting to one's spirit, and some masters credited the slave population with a considerable religious inclination. For every pious master there were ten pious slaves, ran one estimate, for "as a class the African Race, are more religiously inclined than their owners. . . ."[41]

Religious experiences were admittedly quite important to both masters and slaves. In a letter to Lewis Tappan, the New York abolitionist, James Henry Hammond assured him that he had both Methodist and Baptist churches for use by slaves on his South Carolina lands. A few other slaveholders—but not many— could make similar claims. Hammond neglected to mention to Tappan that one of the rules in his plantation book sought to exclude all forms of slave religious practice beyond singing and prayer. It stipulated further that religious observances should not "conflict" with the work schedule and that religious gatherings of any kind must be approved by the master or overseer.

In North Carolina the gleaming white chapel on the Orton estate stands about a hundred feet to the left of the plantation house and has a commanding view of the Cape Fear River. Here masters and slaves communed on Sundays at the same hour, the front pew being reserved for the Ortons. On another plantation, belonging to the genteel Colonel Morris of "Old Charlestown," a South Carolina minister remarked with pride, "I had the pleasure of preaching to this venerable Man, and his Servants in the same house."[42]

The wonders of religion were many, John Cocke believed, and properly used by bondsmen, could influence the way a slaveholder treated them. Thus he observed, in a controversial sentence, "A wicked Master has often been converted to christianity by his gang of pious negroes." We cannot know how many masters were so converted, but an example he cites concerns a "cruel master" called Bishop R. It is one of those events that slave sources occasionally hint at but rarely describe. A religious revival took place among Bishop R's slaves, apparently initiated from within their own ranks. Like many other masters, he opposed such developments but was unable to prevent his bondsmen from holding "prayer meeting during the late hours" in the quarters. One night "he heard them praying for the salvation of his Soul" and was so moved that he changed his ways. It would help if we had Bishop R's version of this happening, but even though some readers will find it hard to believe, we nonetheless have Cocke's assurances that slaves did much to shape the behavior of individuals they came in contact with.[43]

But formal religion per se was not entirely successful in commanding the slave's attention. The published letters exchanged by Reverends Richard Fuller and Francis Wayland in 1845 help reveal why. Southerner Fuller, in reply to a charge leveled by Wayland, wrote that ". . . a man may be held in bondage, and yet be treated in every respect as . . . a Christian brother, and his conjugal and parental relation be sacredly respected. . . ."[44] Apparently he had not carefully observed life among slaves, for his was an old argument, easily refuted by the realities of the master-slave relationship.[45] Showing no sympathy for the slave's lot, one slaveholder told the slave Francis Fedric, "you niggers have no souls, you are just like those cattle. . . . White persons only have souls."[46]

Though many ministers and slaveholders praised slaves' devotional habits, they were quick to tell visitors that if bondsmen were the easiest to bring to Christ, they were paradoxically the first to fall by the wayside. The members of the Flat River Primitive Baptist Church in Person County, North Carolina, accused "Negro Dinah" of lying. They then "agreed not to admit her to baptism but to exclude her as an uncommunicated woman."[47] Dinah's fate was common for the slave in the Old South. Elsewhere, the congregation of the Globe Baptist Church excluded sister Betty Hayes "from fellowship of the Church . . ." for stealing from her master.[48] Slave church-goers, too, made complaints about one another.

Most of the examples of formal slave church membership come to us from the records of Baptist, Methodist, and Presbyterian congregations, in that order. Bondsmen were first sought out by these denominations—particularly Baptists and Methodists—as lost souls in need of rescue, though southern churches actively helped fashion the pro-slavery argument. There were some anti-slavery wings among such groups throughout the antebellum years, but being anti-slavery seldom meant being anti-racial discrimination or anti–physical separation in church seating arrangements. Since slaves and freedmen never escaped these discriminatory manifestations, they could not easily identify with church systems that helped trample them under foot.

One thing was clear: there was an inescapable second-class side to bondsmen's church membership, a fact that turned many of them away from white religious groups and practices. One slave, annoyed by the treatment received each Sunday, sharply questioned a minister as to "the reson you always preach to the white folks and keep your back to us." He wondered, did God "direct you to keep your face to the white peoples constantly or is it because they give you money[?] . . ."[49] His queries are indicative of thoughts that must have flashed through other slaves' minds all too often.

But blacks, slave and free, often did more than just ask questions. In South Carolina in 1861 some free blacks got it into their heads to run off an "anti colored preacher" and did so even though he was apparently liked by some of the whites. When his similarly inclined replacement appeared, "they even went so far as to get up a war . . ." to drive him away.[50] Such acts give credence to another slave's statement concerning the ability of bondsmen to ". . . discern the difference between the truths of the 'word' and the professed practice of those truths by their masters."[51]

Christianity never worked as many changes on slaves' behavior as masters hoped for; it held out many promises of a pacification it could not achieve. Its ideal was probably the one expressed by W. M. Kenney, a member of the Maryland State Colonization Society. He wrote that

> a certain planter hired an overseer, who was a professor of religions. Upon entering on the duties of his office, the new overseer called all the slaves together, and read to them a portion of the word of God, and then kneeled down and prayed for them. This was a novel spectacle to the poor slaves. The same solemn service was repeated again in the evening—and so on in the morning and evening, during the whole year.—The effect on the slaves was like that produced on the 'Savage breast.' They loved their overseer—they felt that they were men, and though in bondage had souls to save, and might be free in heaven.—Their change in their conduct, habits, appearance and industry was noticed by all in their neighborhood.[52]

Whether the event described by Kenney did or did not take place is not of prime importance; for if it did it is certain that the overseer had to do much more than kneel in prayer each day. He had to be willing to make considerable concessions to slaves to accomplish the described end.

In this same connection we perhaps need to revise some of our assessments of the role Catholicism played in softening the slave's bondage in Latin America and North American areas like Louisiana and sections of Maryland and South Carolina.[53] Though slaves knelt frequently at the same altar with their Catholic masters while receiving communion, there is very little evidence that Catholicism cushioned the treatment bondsmen obtained from that point on in the Louisiana sugar cane fields. Catholicism did have more ritual and, with its emphasis on saints, widened the slave's choice of divine intermediaries. Indeed bondsmen could probably better relate this variety of spiritual agents to the large number of spiritual figures found in the West African traditions that came down to them. But the plantation evidence is not persuasive that U.S. Catholics treated their slaves more humanely than did slaveholding Protestants. Many complained about the slave communicants in their churches, and for such reasons blacks generally preferred separate congregations. Planters saw that though the "stamp of degradation is obliterated from the forehead of the slave, when he beholds himself admitted to community of worship with the highest and noblest in the land,"[54] this practice could raise disturbing questions in the bondsman's mind and lead to serious management problems.

In the course of their efforts to bring slaves to God, planters sometimes instructed them in reading, thus providing the only formal teaching many bondsmen received in a lifetime of bondage. Legal restrictions placed on the education of slaves not only frustrated them but some masters as well. Virginia's John Cocke, for example, believed that laws prohibiting bondsmen from reading involved slaveholders in the unenviable "position of virtually refusing the word of God to a portion of his creatures." He added, "Thus 'conscience did make cowards of us all' & we have recorded on our Statute Book what will ever stand as a monument of our shame. . . ." For him at least it was wiser to educate slaves than to keep them in total ignorance. The slave system, he believed, could at least encourage Bible reading for the "more religiously & intellectualy the Slave is made the better for himself his master & the public."[55]

The common practice of religious instruction for slaves was to have them memorize the answers to a catechism, which they would recite on cue at some future date. "The Black people answered there questions," observed a diarist.[56] The minutes of a

Zionist church in Tennessee in 1850 disclose that a few congregations set up Sabbath schools for teaching free blacks and even slaves who had their master's permission to read. "Some have great ambition in this respect and may truly be said to be greedy to learn."[57] Yet this manner of religious help was usually opposed in the Old South.

At any rate, second-class status in religious matters was not good enough for slaves. They had their own preachers, official and otherwise, who had risen from their ranks, and who "generally have an air of superiority to other negroes," according to Frederick Law Olmsted.[58] Black preachers, self-styled and planter-approved, had great influence among slaves. Thus many a slave who learned a few scriptures or mastered some of the mysteries of conjuration immediately launched himself on a career as a self-styled preacher, knowing that "if he be a person of reputation and intelligence, he is accorded a distinction unknown elsewhere."[59] Many charlatans were in this way attracted to the profession. A surprising number of bondsmen received a "calling." Sometimes several men and women on a single plantation would claim to be the spokesmen for God or other spiritual agents. Religious practices thus furnished much more than just passive spiritual and emotional solace. They were one of the primary outlets leading to personal attainment and satisfaction. Even children learned this from an early age, as many of them were destined by some sign or mark on their person (such as quick intellect, a caul, being born at a certain time of the year) to be spiritual leaders.

If a slave was so inclined, to obtain official sanction for his preaching he went before the membership of a local congregation or simply preached on a plantation with his master's consent. The former method was employed by the slave Harry, a member of the Flat River Primitive Baptist Church. The "church after talking with him gave him liberty if he felt to do to pray with and Exort his fellow creatures (and as he can read) to Read the scriptures and Explain them but to take care that his Explanation there on agree with other parts of the Scripture. . . ."[60]

Black preachers like Harry sometimes conducted religious services for both whites and blacks. While traveling in Mississippi, Samuel Agnew, a slaveholder, stopped briefly at one of these services:

> Went in and hear the negroes conduct a prayer meeting and' remained untill and old negro commenced preaching. This was the first time I ever saw "Afric⁵ ebon sons" conduct the public services of the sanctuary. I tried to keep my mind in the proper frame for such services but the "Kings English" was so mercilessly cout up that often I could scarce restrain a smile "Dis" "dat" "warship" "scource" "retentions" are given as specimens.[61]

Another black preacher's sermon—the evidence does not indicate whether he was bond or free—brought a biting remark from an Englishman visiting a Methodist church in Baltimore. He suspected, he wrote, that the minister could not read, "and that suspicion was confirmed by the amount of nonsense which he soon uttered."[62]

However, the self-styled preacher man was the most common spiritual counselor. The Old South's churches could not physically hold an outpouring of its slave population. Bondsmen's weekly or monthly treks to church or those infrequently held religious field gatherings were not enough religious involvement for most of them. Some knelt each evening in prayer in the seclusion of their cabins and in the morning just before going to work. Others held daily religious meetings in the quarters or came together two, three, or more times a week to share religious experiences. "Sometimes we would, unbeknown to our masters, assemble in a cabin and sing songs and spirituals."[63]

One of the most interesting links with the African past in the slave's search for religious solace was the hushharbor, bondsmen's secret church in the woods, the sounds from which were muffled by walls made of trees, brush, and wet blankets hung from branches. Here bondsmen communed with the spirit world in

ways echoing African traditions made all the more appealing by
lives whose futures slavery encircled. In hushharbors throughout
the South bondsmen summoned and dwelt with restless spirits.
They talked, shouted, and sang, testifying to the glories of the
spirits and frequently bemoaning the cruelties of masters and
overseers.

Such events were not as completely "unbeknown" to slaveholders as some slave witnesses believed. Masters were fascinated
—and not just for security purposes—by slave life styles and
sought many opportunities to observe them even within the privacy of the slave quarters: "As soon as the white folks heard the
singing and shouting they came running. They would sit and
listen until everything got quiet. Sometimes they would ask Uncle
Link or the others to sing a favorite song they liked to hear. Then
everybody went to bed."[64]

On a Virginia plantation a young mistress recorded in her diary
that "after supper we all went down to & stood near one of the
servants quarters to listen to one of their [religious] meetings—
They were singing most of the time we were present—some of
which was good." She added, "uninviable as is their lot they
seemed to enjoy themselves a good deal." But while the slave
quarters setting was definitely strengthened by such gatherings,
masters often wished that the community of slaves would only
manifest itself in such limited forms. "How much better is it for
them thus to meet together & spind their evenings in singing &
prayer, than by runing over the neighborhoods as is generally the
case with most of them."[65]

The slave James L. Smith has left us with a vivid account of
these moments of religious fervor:

> The way in which we worshiped is almost indescribable. The
> singing was accompanied by a certain exstasy of motion, clap-
> ping of hands, tossing of heads, which could continue without
> cessation about half an hour; one would lead off in a kind of
> recitative style, others joining in the chorus. The old house par-
> took of the ecstasy; it rang with their jubilant shouts, and shook
> in all its joints.[66]

The quarters accommodated these practices nicely and usually "walled" in the participants from the watchful eyes of whites who continually attended formal religious sessions to make sure that nothing inflammatory was said.[67]

Slaves had extensive religious gatherings in spite of masters' watchfulness. One slave tells us:

> At night, especially in the summer time, after everybody had eaten supper, it was a common thing for us to sit outside. . . . Sometimes someone would start humming an old hymn and then the next door neighbor would pick it up. In this way it would finally get around to every house and then the music started. Soon everybody would be gathered together, and such singing! It wouldn't be long before some of them got happy and started to shouting. Many of them got converted at just such meetings. There was so much fire among them why they started to praying and shouting, clapping and shaking hands and shedding tears, something had to move.[68]

There were many slaves, however, who were not attracted to this form of gathering. On one plantation a correspondent reported that there was a division among the slaves into a dancing party and a praying party: "The dancing having it to night & the other party will hold forth tomorrow [Sunday]—They are very selfish and never attend each others meeting."[69]

"Tricking," "conjuring," "obeah," and "voodoo" (usually pronounced "hoodoo" by bondsmen) were all part of the quarters' spiritual repertory. Gathered in a hut, a traditional metal pot turned down in the center of the floor to help muffle sounds so they would not reach masters' ears (often this did not work) and to serve as a dwelling for spirits, slaves performed secret ceremonies, talked in tongues, and sang. A bondsman did not have to be a participant in any of these rituals to know the intense emotions and feelings of kinship they aroused. The sight was strangely animated and also useful to the slave community. Sometimes a "Hoodoo" preacher, a conjurer, was in attendance, occasionally visiting each hut in the quarters to recite some chant. He had a well-known reputation in the slave South stemming mostly from his interference with slave discipline. While there were some slaves who professed not to believe in ghost stories or hoo-doo, even these bondsmen knew slaves who "have been known to be so perfectly and fearfully under the influence of some leader or conjuror or minister, that they have not dared to disobey him in the least particular. . . ."[70] Sensitive to the influence of the spirit world, the rebel Denmark Vesey relied heavily upon the conjure man Gullah Jack to win the support of followers. Perhaps with Jack's aid he was able to convince many slaves that they "were not inferior to Whites. . . ."[71] The environment itself had a hand in stimulating the world of conjuration as well as con-temporary theological thinking. The seasonal visits of tornadoes and hurricanes that swept through portions of the Old South were thought by some slaves and masters to be displays of dis-pleasure by an avenging spirit or God. An unknown number of bondsmen saw these storms as avengers on the slave system. Tor-nadoes made their initial appearances in the spring. Many con-jurers claimed credit for the paths taken by destructive funnels as they did their frightening dances around the countryside, ter-rorizing slaves and masters or side-stepping populated areas, per-haps conveying a warning by destroying only crops.

Watching such developments taking place about them, some slaveholders noted how "exceedingly superstitious" slaves were. In certain regions of the South they observed that some bondsmen thought it bad luck to start planting a crop on a Friday and that other bondsmen did not address anyone by the pronoun *you* be-cause they thought it insulting and linked the addressee with the devil in some way. But masters showed added concern when con-jurers sought to manipulate the situation.

On an estate belonging to Z. Kingsley in Florida in the early nineteenth century, the slaves—direct from Africa—were, at first, very manageable. But following the arrival of a slave preacher in their midst they formed a compact infused with the supernatural, in which women were not to bring children up under slavery. Women tried to avoid giving birth, but when they did they put the children to death immediately, before Kingsley could intervene. The preacher's voice was most influential, and he taught his followers that slavery was evil and it was wrong to contribute to its ends in any way.[72]

For many slaves who believed, there was both a practical and a spiritual side to the workings of hoodoo and Christianity. But perhaps most important, spiritual practices gave them a sense of worth. A stanza from one slave song entitled "Hoo-Dooism" captures that feeling:

> Ef dey wants you to get 'em well, Hoo-doo
> Dat is de han' at moves de spell, Hoo-doo
> Take it out before der eyes,
> An' you mus' be awful s'prised
> *And dey will think dat you is wise, Hoo-doo.*[73]

Even for the slave slightly more inclined towards Christianity, seeming to have some partial control over his existence was very important, and he often turned to hoodoo to help secure it.

A Virginia slave of Christian leaning wrote in this vein: ". . . in relation to my Conduct I can only say that I done every thing that was bad I sometimes felt really agravated with god him [self] and thought that I had done all that I had a Right to do for him and that he had [not] done his part toward me and therefore I tried to insult him by a very wicked action. . . ."[74]

There were many available means to help such slaves vent their anger. For these occasions many bondsmen, poor whites and an unknown number of masters carried mojos on their persons. And when the mojo did not contain the proper elements for success, there was always the collective knowledge of the quarters to tap for purposes of good and bad. One might take a piece of a person's hair, a piece of his clothes, or even dirt from his tracks and mix these with tobacco, clover, snakeroot, or Jimson weed, or pieces of animal flesh, fur, feathers, or bones. In North Carolina even the puzzling Venus fly trap was used. When these items were wrapped in fur, red flannel, silk, or wool they caused bad things, but when "made into such things as luck balls or jacks, they are good tricks."[75] This kind of behavior appears in the entire span of bondage, as the slave tried at every turn to control and shape the contours of his and others' lives.

The relatively small number of Muslims (we have no good count) who were brought to North America as slaves usually clung steadfastly to their distinctive and highly formalized religious practices. These often called for public displays of fidelity, such as praying to Allah five times a day and not eating any pork, one of the slave's chief sources of energy. Muslims were ridiculed and abused by masters for these practices, yet their strong traditions have carried down to our day in certain sectors of the black community. Some slaveholders believed Muslims had a disruptive impact on slave management akin to that of any self-appointed slave spiritual leader. Others felt that Muslim or not, a slave was a slave.[76] A few educated captive Muslims were displayed by the slave regime in attempts to expose and exploit their cultural differences from most other bondsmen. But this kind of ridicule often simply masked underlying fears which recognized that these differences could lead to resistant behavior that was strengthened by a Muslim tradition that to give in to infidel Christian masters would be the ultimate betrayal of Allah and self.

Many planters tried to curb orthodox and unorthodox religious practices among their slaves, believing that they were a stimulus to disorderly conduct.[77] From the Biloxi, Mississippi plantation of William S. Hamilton, his daughter Penelope informed him of the effects of religion on their slaves: "I expect Mr. Parkenham did the Negroes more harm than good. . . . It was very strang[e] all the scamps on the place joined the church. I think they had religion for a cloak to hide their villainy."[78] They were not all "scamps," and the religious experience she described was not exceptional. But similarly, having some difficulty with General John A. Quitman's slaves in the fall of 1843, a relative claimed that an overseer had "spoiled" them "during the summer with a religious excitement." He supposed now that "The negroes [are] determined if possible to have the upper hand and so far They have absconded for the most trifling causes. . . ."[79]

When death paid its visits to the quarters, religion and the slave preacher or conjurer could play a most influential role. He soothed slaves' emotions, assuring critically ill persons of the security of the future to come or reminding relatives of the dead that all was not lost. Some led prayer groups or hoodoo sessions to distract bondsmen surrounded by the dead during an epidemic. Slave religious leaders also extended their many services beyond the plantation. Some tried to console the black prisoners who populated city and local jails, leading them in prayer. For many bondsmen death was a welcome retreat from an existence they paralleled to hell: "dis is hell, dis is, I calls it. . . ."[80] Others, throughout their time in bondage, had little notion of hell or heaven, an approach to life consistent with some elements in their African past.

When accident or disease caused a slave's death, funerals, accompanied by their share of pomp, were the object of extensive preparations. Caroline Gilman, "a southern matron," remembered that "the ceremony of interment is commonly [per]formed by a class leader, a pious coloured man, who is the spirited teacher of the neighborhood. . . ."[81] He was admired among slaves, and looked to as perhaps the only person who could see the corpse safely to rest. He usually did not disappoint anyone. As a symbol of particular authority he had few rivals. When he died himself, his followers might compare his death "to the crucifixion of Jesus,"[82] or at least someone very important, and hold prayer meetings and say encantations for days. Nat Turner was so honored and was known as the Black Christ in certain slave circles.

"Plantation negroes prefer to bury their dead at night or before the sunrise," noted a contemporary.[83] What were some of the reasons for this? Bondsmen felt that it was easier to communicate with the needed spirits in the evening; and also at night they were free from work and could come from throughout the neighborhood to take part in the ceremony. It was a time of mourning, but, as with many slave functions, of socializing too. Slaves brought parcels of food, corn liquor, and other items.

The most important factor influencing the tone of the burial ceremony and the kind of accompanying events was the nature of the death. If it was from natural causes the affair would likely be marked only by solemnity and accompanied with assurances that the dead had heaven as a reward, though often the preacher made no mention of such a place. But if the dead had led a wicked life and ignored the advice of his fellows to reform his character, or if mysterious circumstances cloaked his going, bondsmen showed much concern, perhaps more for their own sakes than that of the deceased. Some feared that his restless spirit would return to affect their lives adversely. On occasion the rumor spread that someone had conjured the corpse to assure that his spirit would find no resting place and would spend a time in mischievous wanderings and wrong-doings in the quarters. Accordingly, if "any one died they will say that someone has bewitched and very often will go to the gran devil man . . . and get him to tell who . . . [and] if he choose to tell them a lie on any person, they catch the person and give him what the[y] call Sassawood."[84] This observation was made by a Louisiana planter visiting West Africa; but both he and his famous father, John Mc Donogh, were struck by its similarity to the American slave setting.

Rumors sometimes resulted in the leveling of the deceased's cabin or a general cleaning of the entire quarters to disperse the conjuration.[85] Preceding this, a sign that there was something wrong might appear at the funeral—a pallbearer slipping, an unexplained rock formation in the path of the procession.[86] A large turnout of slaves would come to see for themselves that the burial went off without a hitch.

Slaveholders usually made allowances for their bondsmen to attend a few neighborhood funerals during the year. It was advisable to do so, for refusal to permit attendance in certain cases confirmed slaves' fears that someone had tampered with the dead party. The resultant anxiety often led to deliberately inefficient work habits or all-night quarters disturbances that ended only when a master allayed suspicions; severity was rarely the answer. The slave driver might aid him in this, but sometimes a master had first to convince the driver that the death was natural. The driver then went among the slaves to persuade them that all was well. One slaveholder's solution, conveyed to his son, was to "Make George[, the] Driver[,] have the House cleaned out & put him in it *at once*. After any thing of the kind occuring in a house if it remains shut up any time the Negroes will get up a story of its being haunted. . . ."[87]

In significant fashion, then, slaves' religious and spiritual beliefs and the behavior these inspired point to personalities lacking in docile and childlike features.[88] They reveal situations in which bondsmen had chances to reshape their lives, giving them definition and purpose. The pressures of life in bondage could not be escaped, but religion and the security of the quarters could prevent these forces from always bearing down with crushing force.

8
The Rhythm of Culture

While the seclusion of the slave quarters provided some sanctuary from life's harshest realities, it is readily apparent that the bondsmen's creative energies took them beyond folktales, religion, and childhood games into other forms of expression. As we look at the various cultural avenues along which the slave trod, what stands out are the rhythmically musical elements that helped express so many of the bondsman's hopes of triumph and fears of despair. We need not be concerned that this observation will stereotype the slave or the black experience once we observe how much music and other cultural expressions helped bondsmen survive and even transcend the cruelest aspects of their bondage. These expressions may be seen as that marriage of great necessity and native talent which become the parents of creativity.

Without doubt interpretations of slave music are important approaches to understanding the bondsman's sense of life's worth, for music was nearly inseparable from his identity. His existence was built around repetitive work and rest rhythms which, through music, he translated into poignant expressions of life's direction and meaning. Through music he expressed the depths of his frustrations and the heights of his joys: "Outwardly we sung, inwardly we prayed."[1] Nightly, music emanated from the quarters; and daily, it accompanied many slaves at work in the fields where, one slave claimed, "We used to sing and have lots of fun."[2] Forty-one years after the close of the Civil War, the historian Albert Bushnell Hart, reflecting upon the condition of the slaves of old, wrote, "The only art in which the negroes excelled was music. . . ." Music in general, he believed, and "their songs" in particular "were their chief intellectual efforts. . . ."[3] Dr. Samuel Cartwright, probably after hearing some of the same melodies, argued to the contrary. "There is nothing in his [the slave's] music addressing the understanding; it has melody but no harmony; his songs are mere sounds without sense or meaning," he said.[4] But he had not been listening very attentively.

Planters themselves made many uses of the slave's musical talents. Fiddlers and songsters whose skills had been sharpened by practice in the quarters were in demand at social gatherings; playing at these events gained them privileges they might otherwise not have had. Some visitors to Virginia from the Carolinas were alarmed by one such spectacle: "they were so shocked by this exhibition—a Black man in a slave county singing love songs in the presence of their wives & daughters, that they, and with them, all the other Carolinians, marched out of the room."[5]

The talented bondsman often used his position to stretch his bonds. The slave Ben, who belonged to a Louisiana family, "got himself into trouble" in this way. He "was allowed to go to Mr. Archer's last night to play the fiddle, and did not get back till to night."[6] It is unfortunate that slave sources leave out many of the details about the extent and form of this kind of slave activity.

Disobedience resulting from his special status as an excellent fiddler precipitated an interesting encounter between the slave Lewie and his master, Colonel Garnett Andrews of Georgia, in the early 1860's. Colonel Andrews hired Lewie out to play in saloons and at neighbors' social outings. So great was Lewie's popularity that in "consequence . . . his pockets were full of quarters and his head of the fumes of drink. . . ." According to Colonel Andrews, Lewie lived the high life as a slave, and "he was a man of talents, and soon understood his importance and the high respect in which he was held on account of his broadcloth and accomplishments."[7] Admitting his great affection for Lewie, Colonel Andrews allowed these activities to go on for a while, but eventually, angered by his conduct, sold Lewie in haste to a slave-trader who in turn sold him to a planter in Mississippi.[8] Colonel Andrews later regretted this decision, for he never overcame his fondness for Lewie. Growing lonely with advancing age, he tried to retrieve him after the Civil War, pleading in newspaper advertisements for Lewie to return to him of his own choice, "if you will forgive me my anger. . . ." The evidence does not reveal the outcome.[9]

It was the slave's gift for entertainment that helped provide solidarity to the ranks of bondsmen when long hours of work and discipline made life agonizingly uncomfortable. Instrumental music and songs of all kinds were vitally important in these periods. To relieve their tensions bondsmen might join together in song and dance and conversation.

Harold Courlander, a leading scholar of Haitian affairs and black folklore, has written about "songs and dances in the Americas which parallel or have almost the same form as songs and dances in Africa."[10] Many southern slave songs and dances are ample proof of this. They were slaves' surviving link with a past their masters did not deny. Taking us still further in this direction is the interesting observation of one white Southerner:

> During my childhood my observations upon a few very old negroes, whose grandparents were African born, and early came to the conclusion, based upon negro authority, that the greater part of their music, their methods, their scales, their type of thought, their dancing, their patting of their feet, their clapping of hands, their grimacies and pantomine, and their gross superstitions came straight from Africa.[11]

To entertain one another and to pass on the latest news or gossip were the motives for holding numerous musical gatherings.

Bondsmen from neighboring plantations showed up at both sanctioned and unsanctioned events within the quarters or at some predetermined rendezvous in the woods. A few women came abundantly draped in several layers of garments intended for bartering. An exchange might be made for a conjurer's secret about how to keep from being whipped. Bragging was the habit of many, who took special delight in telling how they had outsmarted "ole massa."

The ranks of slave musicians and songsters were never thin. Bondsmen saw that vocal and instrumental ability captured the fancy of both whites and blacks. At some slave and planter parties, musicians played competitively, catering to the whims of those in attendance. Members of the audience called out tunes for them to perform. The slave who played the best at white parties received additional money for his few hours' work plus his share of appreciative glances. Slave musicians regularly entertained in the quarters spontaneously, and some of the better ones practiced diligently for weeks, preparing themselves for an anticipated slave outing. In the evening, whatever the season, the night air floated varying qualities of sound from the quarters up to the Big House.[12] It did not, however, always fall upon appreciative ears. We know from slaves, travelers and masters that a few planters tried to ban musical instruments. On one plantation alone the master had confiscated twenty fiddles within the past year. He could not, fortunately, do the same to slaves' voices.

If one searches for patterns in the bondsman's cultural-musical life, perhaps what appears most revealing is the high degree of both group and individual expression. In an area of achievement where bondsmen are conceded by researchers to have excelled, one encounters a sharp divergence from the slumbering docility slaves have been accused of. Strikingly, their musical performances were distinguished by efforts to attain peak levels of proficiency as individual entertainers. There was also a great amount of improvisation. This was due in part to the fact that since most slaves could not write, many of their tunes were never noted down. Thus the same tune might have a few lines added, dropped, or changed from plantation to plantation. It is a tribute to the survival potential of human personality that when left to their own devices slaves developed so personally revealing an art form.[13]

With reference to one talented quartet of bondsmen, a master reasoned that their skills were "a Confirmation of the views of intelligent slaveholders, that Slavery itself is the most effective mode, as far as it Concerns the African race of creating among them the most effective civilization."[14] But he reasoned too well. His slaves' merits spoke persuasively in their own behalf.

Expressing his reluctance to extoll the quartet's achievements for fear of appearing "egotistical," planter Manning did so anyway while trying to hire out the "services of my musicians for your annual exhibition of the 'Institute Fair.' . . ." He praised the slave Robin "who is the leader of this Lilliputian band of Musicians . . ." and who had begun his musical career playing with bows made out of twigs on horses' hairs strung across pieces of wood. Other slaves made their own instruments as well. Some made drums, banned in many parts of the South because of their message transmitting qualities, beat on gourds and metal pots, with sticks or clicked bones together. Some slaves even created "trumpets" out of bulls' horns simply by cutting off the tip of the horn and blowing into it.[15] Robin made such rapid progress on his own that after a time his master engaged the services of a friend, Dr. Frampton, "authorizing him to procure for him [Robin] the best masters upon the violin." Meanwhile Robin continued to improve: "At home without a teacher, & without any knowledge of music on my part his progress astonished myself & those of my friends who watched his improvement."[16]

Seeking to refine further Robin's talents, his master later employed a Mr. Dauer who, during the course of two summers, helped to advance Robin's musical education. Mr. Dauer also instructed Robin's brothers—Sanders, Edward, and Henry—who later joined the quartet. But before this happened "the three lat[t]er were taught chiefly by Robin without assistance from a superior teacher untill Mr. Dauer tooke charge of them under whose care they have arrived at the excellence which they now exhibit."[17] No doubt sounds from the practicing quartet provided many enjoyable hours for the plantation's slaves.

As performers at local functions the quartet brought themselves and their master widespread acclaim as well as money. To reward Robin his owner decided finally to leave the quartet in his sole management, "and to give him such remunerative returns as they may make by their skill, untill he shall be more than compensated in addition to the regular Salary which I have paid him."[18] There was no mention of freedom. Robin's bondage seemed light. His abilities and circumstance lifted him to a plane that not only accorded him special treatment but also compelled others to acknowledge and respect his humanity. In a passage of his letter which he tried to cross out, Robin's master concluded: "I will venture to say without a design to boast my, good Sir, that Robin who has been taught three years, Sanders by Mr. Dauer & Robin two, and Henry & Edward about eight months, can play together in a quartette with more precision upon the flute violin"[19]—perhaps than most white orchestral groups who had received similar or better training. The end of the sentence is conjectural; that portion of the letter has been torn away.

Although Robin's players were not a minstrel group per se,[20] slave minstrels were used by the slave regime. Slave musicians and singers performed regularly together, mixing their performances with dancing. Other slave entertainers performed throughout the slave period in cities and on the plantation as the chief entertainment on many occasions. On plantations, to be sure, though some masters played the fiddle or other instruments at some of the slave functions, it was the bondsmen who provided much of the social and cultural life for everybody. Some of the minstrel groups spontaneously toured plantations during the holiday seasons. Especially at Christmastime they expected gifts as tokens of thanks for the entertainments they provided. They were not always rewarded, and when they were not they frequently sang very biting tunes as an expression of their displeasure. Some were run off plantations they visited for this behavior, but it daunted their spirits little.

The slave's self-expression spread beyond the limits of musical instruments into song. But even on "light" occasions, when a span of holidays stretched out before slaves, their songs might have a somber quality. "They depressed my spirits and filled my heart with ineffable sadness,"[21] wrote Frederick Douglass. For him, the lyrics were reminders of the dehumanizing features of slavery. Some plantation owners may have also recognized this. Fanny Kemble, an anti-slavery sympathizer, commented in 1839 "that many of the masters and overseers on these plantations prohibit melancholy tunes or words. . . ."[22] But this would have been most hard to do. Still others believed that certain songs might lead to unwanted slave behavior, for these songs constantly called to mind the suffering bondsmen endured.[23]

A historian of songs has written that before 1832 "slaves sang that their warnings against militancy came from the devil . . ." but after that date modified their views.[24] Another writer has remarked that slave songs "speak with convincing finality against the legend of the contented slave."[25] It appears ironic that many of these songs were composed more or less under the planter's nose—in the fields and in the quarters.

In 1895 the famous European composer Antonín Dvořák paid high praise to slave musical efforts in an article in *Harper's Magazine*. He suggested that black melodies could serve as the foundation for a serious American school of music, explaining:

> I was led to take this view partly by the fact that the so-called plantation songs are indeed the most striking and appealing melodies that have been found on this side of the water. There is nothing in the whole range of composition that cannot be supplied with themes from this source. Among my pupils I have discovered a young colored man of talent upon whom I am building strong expectations.[26]

Dvořák's "New World Symphony" takes its lead from the black melodies.

> In the Negro melodies of America I discover all that is needed for a great and noble school of music. They are pathetic, tender,

passionate, melancholy, solemn, religious, bold, merry, gay, gracious, or what you will. It is music that suits itself to any mood or purpose.[27]

Indeed, songs accompanied bondsmen at worship, work, and play, tapping all their moods. Joseph Jones of Georgia used a "Colored quire" in his sabbath school teaching. "The African are very fond of music & I think that the cooperation of the Colored quire will be valuable to the school."[28]

The slave's spiritual efforts were more of a help to themselves, however. They often took the traditional "call and response chant form" whose roots go back to West Africa and whose reach extends into our times. Its pattern was simple. A class leader—often but not necessarily a preacher—chanted an evocative expression, spoken or sung, to which the congregation or audience chanted an answer. The preacher then moved to another expression. In many of these folk spiritual songs the words are of little importance. The rhythmic intensity of the music shaped and reshaped by emotion provides us with a better approach to understanding the message conveyed. Such moments tapped a well of emotion that blossomed into a beautifully cathartic experience. Slaves in various parts of the Old South fashioned different words to fit familiar music, and, as victims of the slave trade, carried these versions from place to place. Some have testified about the sense of brotherhood and community they experienced upon arrival in a strange area when the slaves there broke forth with familiar music. The scene was frequently an agitated one accompanied by handclapping and shouting.

Several capable researchers have accurately pointed out that the predominant body of allusion in the spirituals is to slaves themselves as the chosen people, the children of God, a captive people. Other peoples have, of course, similarly described themselves, with notable fervor. But this should not detract from the slave's claim. Many of the spirituals also directly protested against bondage: "I'm a-Rolling Through an Unfriendly World," "Go Down, Moses," "Steal Away to Jesus," "Nobody Knows the

Trouble I See, Glory Hallelujah!," "Before I'd Be a Slave I'd Be
Buried in My Grave," "Nobody Knows Who I Am," "Who
Will Deliver Po' Me," "Walk Together Children," "Do You Get
Weary," "Children We Shall Be Free," "Didn't My Lord De-
liver Daniel?," "Many Thousand Gone," "Keep Me from Sink-
ing Down," "My Way's Cloudy," "Don't You Grieve after Me."

Many slaves' songs are thus virtual blueprints of slaves' values
and guides to their most safely guarded fears and desires. Perhaps
they sought to explore the question of their identities in "Nobody Knows Who I Am."

> O, no-bod-y knows a who I am, a who I am, till the judg-ment
> morn-ing! Hear'n bells a-ring-ing, the saints all a-singing, Hear'n
> bells a-ring-ing in my soul, O, the soul.[29]

Edward Pollard, the southern journalist, observed that most of
the songs "relate to the moment of death and in some of them
are simple and poetic images which are often touching."[30] Thomas
Wentworth Higginson would have agreed with Pollard and tells
us that the favorite tune among the blacks he commanded for the
Union at the outbreak of the Civil War was "Hold Your Light":

> Hold your light, Brudder Robert,—
>   Hold your light,
> Hold your light on Canaan's shore.
>
> What make ole Satan for follow me so?
> Satan ain't got nothin' for do wid me
>   Hold your light
>   Hold your light
> Hold your light on Canaan's shore.[31]

No single explanation serves adequately to illuminate the whys
surrounding the sadness of slave melodies of all kinds, so many
sung with heavy hearts and troubled spirits. Evaluation of the accumulated evidence needs the skills of thoughtful interpreters.
But there are many clues embodied in their lyrics, reminders of
suffering that slaves lived with: "I'm a Rollin' Through an Un-

friendly Worl'." All these suggest a distinctive view of life's meaning for the bondsman.[32]

Slave spirituals are replete with references to Canaan, the ship of Zion, redemption, and the last Judgment:

> Oh Canaan, sweet Canaan
> I am bound for the land of Canaan.

Masters criticized bondsmen for dwelling too often on things beyond, for finding little satisfaction in the present. But indeed these songs assisted the slave in coping with the present. Still others revealed a lasting discontentment. A favorite, according to one ex-slave was "Oh the keys, oh the keys, Lord." It referred to loosing the chains of bondage: "somebody would holler 'Steady yourselves children. My God! The keys! Let's find them tonight.' "[33]

Outside religious settings, singing was sure to accompany bondsmen at their labors. "Wherever negroes may be, if in tolerable spirits, they always sing as the[y] work."[34] Slaves composed some of their tunes on the spot, the presence of onlookers suggesting the theme. While watching some bondsmen at work in the fields, the traveler Abigail Mott was witness herself to one of these improvisations. The field hands caroled:

> Go, white man, go
> but with thee bear
> The negro's wish, the negro's prayer
> Remembrance of the negro's care.[35]

The end of the harvest season brought a flood of new songs in celebration. It "really does me good to hear them" singing, remarked a North Carolina mistress.[36] A noted spectacle during the harvest was "the husking and the gathering into barns of the yellow maize or corn."[37] Here was a signal for general celebration. Slaves came from nearby plantations to husk and socialize, to sing into the early morning hours. "The tunes they sing are always slow," wrote the planter Henry Watson. He also observed that they refer to themselves as "the down-trodden; slaves" and added:

> They make a great deal of noise. . . . They then keep time with their song & do not feel their fatigue, & in fact are not fatigued as they otherwise would be. The[y] work more cheerfully. As all keep time, the lazy ones keep it without being sensible of their exertion, besides they might otherwise, and often do, fall asleep at their work.[38]

Martin R. Delany, the black separatist leader of the 1850's, made a worthwhile observation about working slaves and singing in Louisiana:

> In the distance on the levee and in the harbor among the steamers, the songs of the boatmen were incessant. Every few hours landing, loading and unloading, the glee of these men of sorrow was touchingly appropriate and impressive. . . . If there is any class of men anywhere to be found whose sentiments of songs and words of lament are made to reach the sympathies of others, the black slave-boatmen on the Mississippi River are that class. . . . they are seemingly contented by soothing their sorrows with songs apparently cheerful, but in reality wailing lamentations. . . . In the capacity of leader, as is their custom, one poor fellow is pitiful tones led off the song of the evening. . . .[39]

Many of the slaves' songs obviously had much meaning hidden even to some slaves, though they continually stressed the basic discord in the bondsman's life. They were his "articulate" expressions of what it was to be a slave.[40]

Although some planters happily believed that melodies coming from the quarters meant subdued and peaceful slaves, the tunes of songsters occasionally concealed night visits to other local plantations. To say in this connection that the slaves' songs and music often communicated their activities to slaves on other plantations is barely to scratch the surface. "We boys," the slave Silas Jackson claimed, "used to take the horne of dead cow or bull, cut the end off of it, we could blow it, some haveing different notes. We could tell who was blowing and from what plantation."[41] Music was used to communicate such things as warnings to runaways and the movements of the slave patrols. From the earliest years of slavery in the New World this pattern—if it can be called that—is readily observable.

In their speech and songs slaves spoke several languages within the English they had learned in America. Their split syllables and fuzzy intonations are well known. Bondsmen shifted syntax with ease, created a vast variety of additional words (neologisms) blended with Africanisms, and gave new meaning to old words.[42] Their assimilation into the American scene was fragile and imperfect.

Most important, the language of the slave's speech and song was the embodiment of his community. His broken English protected his communal feelings exceedingly well, even in the presence of whites. He could understand them, their use of large words aside, but the same could not always be claimed by them. Slaveholders repeatedly complained that their slaves might speak better if only they put their minds to it, but slaves often had other interests. They sometimes even called each other different names than those used by their masters. An employee of two South Carolina planters tried to make an inventory of their slave holdings according to age and skills. But finding his task a hard one, he wrote to them, ". . . I find it somewhat difficult to get a satisfactory list of them [the bondsmen] oweing to their being called by so many different names among themselves. . . ."[43]

Slaves' songs mirror their perception of the expansion and restriction of their bondage at various times. Quite naturally, an individual seeks first to manage successfully his immediate surroundings. To accomplish this, an accurate assessment of the realities of one's life is essential.[44] Slave songs clearly reveal a mature and accurate assessment of their woes and needs. Their songs were highly selective in this respect, attempting to place in perspective those features of bondage that troubled them most.

Bondsmen sold to the Deep South or out of their immediate neighborhood did not expect to see friends and relatives again. They might chant:

You may beat upon my body
But you cannot harm my soul;
I shall join the forty thousand by and by.

You may sell my children to Georgy,
But you cannot harm their soul;
They will join the forty thousand by and by.

Come, slave-trader, come in too;
The Lord's got a pardon here for you;
You shall join the forty thousand by and by.[45]

A slave claimed, too, that he heard the following lyrics:

See wives and children sold apart
Their children screams will break
    my heart
There's a better day a coming,
. . . .

Go sound the jubilee.[46]

If the songs themselves did not immediately infuse the slave's existence with the "satisfying meaning" he wanted, they did represent his attempt to move in that direction.[47] In great measure they tell us how slaves inveighed against efforts to stigmatize them as inferior, and they also demonstrate that most bondsmen were extraordinarily sensitive to slavery's meaning. "What is of pivotal import [too] . . . is that the esthetic realm was the one area in which slaves knew they were not inferior to whites."[48] To be sure, there is no longer any need to limit this generalization to esthetics.

Historians have written of the happy-go-lucky slave, but he was rarely the slave who appeared in song. "Perception," a psychologist observes, "is profoundly influenced by two additional factors: social and cultural custom, and the personality of the perceiver."[49] Just what part each factor plays is difficult to determine, for their effects would seem to join hands. The personality can be judged by the evidence it leaves of its perceptions, and the songs reveal the slave's personality to have been mature. The songs were at least palliative, and large numbers were somber attacks on slavery and slaveholders. They add to persuasive evidence calling for rejection of the infantilism-of-slaves thesis. Though most slave tunes were simple and melodic, the words lay bare much of the slave's vindictiveness.

What these songs best disclose, considering the setting that inspired them, is that bondsmen did not see one another as passive agents in a prestaged drama. Many were astute participants in and critics of southern civilization. The slave fittted his musical tendencies to immediate needs in the quarters and in the fields in a remarkable display of resiliency. This resiliency is remindful of what Frederick Law Olmsted wrote about slaves' music: their "power of . . . improvising . . . is most marked and constant."[50]

The slaves' cultural expressions spread forcefully beyond the slaves' ranks into southern culture at large. The important influence of their spiritual and work music is undeniable. In fact much of the cultural flavor attributed to the Old South owes a debt to the black presence. The sources occasionally disclose a slave artist or sculptor. The cultural art forms slaves created for themselves added dimension and substance to their work-weary lives. But as in other things, life in bondage never allowed the slave totally to divorce his cultural forms from the mechanical arts the slave system nurtured and needed to help it function properly. Some bondsmen even designed their own huts and made clever innovations in both slaves' and masters' homes.

In the broadest cultural terms the slaves' ranks were filled with persons to whose talents and skills the slave regime reacted ambiguously. Certainly in the eighteenth century, and perhaps down to 1830, the slave's dominance in the mechanical arts in the Old South was not challenged.[51] But after this date, some have argued, skilled slaves came under attack from competing white workers and thus declined in number. This interpretation is certainly supported by much evidence, but it cannot be convincingly substantiated. A careful observer of the southern scene, the industrialist

C. G. Memminger, made this interesting comment to James Henry Hammond in 1849:

> I find an opinion gaining ground that slaves ought to be ex-cluded from mechanical pursuits, and everything but agriculture, so as to have these places filled with whites. . . . The planters do not perceive how it effects their interest, and very frequently chime in with this cry . . . which is in truth, the only party [cry] from which danger to our Institutions is to be apprehended among us. Drive our negro mechanics and all sorts of operatives from our cities, and who must take their place[?]"[52]

Hammond ignored his warning and began to support legislation in his home state outlawing the employment of most skilled slaves.

Skilled slaves' contribution to the southern culture and econ-omy throughout the antebellum period is easy to document, though many find it difficult to accept. In 1777 R. Carter ob-served to a friend, "John Holt, Stocking Loom maker, is my Servant & has long to serve, who will always have my favor and protection, so long as he continues faithful and diligent." While slaveowners' journals have references to whites hired to do skilled labor on plantations, this seems not to have been the norm, and the manuscripts themselves do not give this impression. Frederick Law Olmsted's observation in the 1850's, while it cannot be taken generally, provides a valuable lead. A Mississippi overseer told him that

> he once employed a white man from the North, who professed to be a first class workman, but he soon found he could not do nearly as good work as the negro mechanics on the estate, and the[y] despised him so much, and got such high opinions of themselves in consequence of his inferiority, that he had been obliged to discharge him. . . .[53]

This was the risk any planter might run, for the slaves were proud of their talents. A number of planters expressed the belief that it was best to let slaves do all of the plantation's work if possible. Captain Eggleston of Holmes County, Mississippi, according to agriculturist Solon Robinson, had "all of his mechanical work . . . done by his negroes upon his plantation."[54] He even owned two slave carpenters who were so accomplished at their trade that he could hire them out at $40 each per month. This was in 1845. Nor do I cite these examples because they were exceptional; they are not. William Pettigrew of North Carolina was engaged in quite a bit of building on his plantations, Belgrade and Magnolia, in 1849. He noted that slaves did the work and that "Jim is the foreman of the carpenters, being quite efficient in that capacity."[55] A Maryland slave, born in 1844, remembered that her father was a carpenter whose "services were much in demand. This gave him an opportunity to save money." She spoke with pride, indicating that he did repair and building work for both whites and free blacks and was able to save more than half his income.[56] All this he did in a state where work competition from whites was keen. Among the exceptional slaves to be sold to a planter in 1845 were "a superior Blacksmith, a wheel wright, a shoemaker who understanding tanning, a weaver, a plain cook, and a pastry cook."[57] These slaves could not but know the contributions they made.

Proportionally, southern towns and cities were dotted even more than the countryside with slave men and women of skill. Southern civilization, with its emphasis on service, demanded it, and these bondsmen contributed much to the Old South's genteel tradition. A writer in the *Southern Literary Messenger* in 1837, reviewing Harriet Martineau's *Society in America*, was quick to point out that "some of the best tailors and mantuamakers in the southern states are slaves. In the cities, all of the hair-dressers and barbers, many of the butchers, and sundry of the tavern-keepers, are slaves or free negroes."[58] Conditions did not change that much down to the war years.

Many of the skills possessed by slaves related to more routine tasks. These slaves cannot all be classed as artisans, but the slave did not find it easy to separate art from work, and thus in many cases, sometimes with planter prompting, blended the two. Although the W.P.A. survey taken in the 1930's cannot be stead-fastly relied on in many matters concerning slaves, it has some excellent comments about slave artisans. On ornamental iron-work in Alabama it noted that

> . . . occasionally some of the best examples were wrought by local craftsmen, usually Negro slaves. The delicate patterns beaten out over a forge were among the most artistic creations of the Negro during early slavery days. . . . One of the best ex-amples of this wrought iron is in the French Double House, at 58 Conception Street, Mobile, built in 1824, which has delicate iron balconies on each wing.[59]

The same is true in New Orleans. Many of the wrought iron bal-conies in the historic French Quarter are the handiwork of slave artisans. The W.P.A. notes further about Louisiana:

> The metal work used in the construction of the first Ursuline Convent, now known as the old Archbishopric, was forged by slave labor, and through later years both slave and free forge workers made grills, guards, rails, gates, and other wrought iron pieces that survive in Louisiana's time-worn buildings. . . .[60]

James Porter, an outstanding student of black art, goes even fur-ther, arguing for a strong African influence in wrought iron struc-tures throughout the South.[61] We know that slaves did much of the building in the Old South, and evidence also suggests that they designed some of the smaller structures, of whose originators we now know nothing officially.

Skilled slaves carried their heads high with pride throughout the slave states. The bondsman J. W. C. Pennington tells us about his job as blacksmith that "I sought to distinguish myself in the finer branches of the business by invention and finish; I frequently tried my hand at making guns and pistols, putting blades in pen knives, making fancy hammers, hatchets, sword-cases, & c., & c. . . ."[62] For nearly all of slavery's work tasks the slaveholder turned to his slaves for assistance.

The slaves who possessed these various skills often responded to the conditions of bondage similarly to those who did not possess the skills. J. W. C. Pennington, later a runaway, said that his skills and privileges made him somewhat content with his lot. But others, as noted in a previous chapter, found it frustrating to be as capable as many who possessed their freedom yet still be slaves. And too, their futures were sometimes no more certain than those of slaves without recognized skills. One especially talented bondsman ran away in 1856, for which his owners wanted to sell him to John R. Liddell of Louisiana.

We have a very likely Mulatto Boy 22 to 25 Years old . . . has run Our sawmill by himself nearly a year except a little help in filing the saw occasionally, he understands running an Engine very will and is a tolerable Blacksmith and is very handy at any kind of work & very fast for a negro We have owned him about 3 Years has never been whiped by us or by any one else since we owned him[63]

But the skilled slave John Parker took another approach. While working in a foundry he decided to dabble in inventions. In his own unique manuscript he wrote:

I had been quietly working for some time on a new idea of a circular borrow or clod smasher, which was a very important farm implement of that period with so much new land to break up. Being handy with tools on my own time I secretly made a model. It looked so good I showed it to the superintendent. . . . [but later] in my presence the superintendent claimed both the idea a[n]d the model was his. . . . The words were hardly out of his mouth when I had him by the throat. . . .[64]

Parker was forced to quit the foundry and seek employment elsewhere.

The slave's creative life thus not only nurtured some of his most rewarding feelings but gives us some of the most direct evidence about his personality, which was most certainly vibrant.

9
A Family Folk

Few aspects of the slave's bondage have come in for as much speculative writing as the impact of slavery upon the slave family. Researchers in many disciplines have argued that bondage rent asunder this most basic of American institutions, injured black identity, and left scars to haunt black Americans down to our day.[1] But all this needs further examination.

Planters usually evidenced concern and not a little ambivalence, as several historians have preferred to put it, when reaching the decision to split up a black household. The practice was in sharp contrast to what many felt to be right, though planters consistently overcame nagging doubts. An agent representing John Mc Donogh of Louisiana complained to him that a slave trader "refused to give me a little negro boy and girl from belonging to the Mulattresses, claiming that he could not separate the families. . . ." He added bluntly, "It was a poor reason. . . ."[2] It cannot be denied that the slave family took a tremendous beating; its members were sold to satisfy creditors and purchased to increase personal wealth. Yet the historian U. B. Phillips has written that the "domestic slave trade was merely a readjustment of population within the United States. . . ."[3] From the slave's point of view his observation more than missed the mark.

"I seen better times in slavery than I've seen since," confided an ex-slave, "but I don't believe in slave traffic—that being sold."[4] For bondsmen the slave trade was a too-frequent reminder of near helplessness in bondage. The overseas trade had bothered the conscience of the nation—both South and North—forcing its shutdown nationally by 1807 and long before that in most southern states.[5] But despite the termination of the overseas trade its domestic counterpart continued to flourish legally. Slaves constantly experienced—directly and indirectly—its pernicious influence, and would no doubt have abolished it as a first step in ameliorating their bondage.

Activities associated with the slave trade gave many planters a bad name, both among disapproving friends close at hand and among many more than just abolitionists in western society at large. Still many acted as they personally saw fit. "My plan in selling a negro that I want to get rid of is to take a price under his real valuation," wrote a Louisianian.[6] Most masters were not so open in their admission; and a substantial minority sincerely tried to sell slaves, as one wrote to his mother, to a "man said to be a most excellent master" since "it will be most gratifying to my feelings. . . ."[7] One slaveholder expressed a "desire to make their [slaves'] situation as Comfortable, & happy as in my power, and am sure they could not be more so than with you. . . ."[8]

To avoid the public disapproval that increasingly attached to putting slaves on the auction block, some masters sold their bondsmen privately. For the slave, however, the impact remained the same, and scenes of mothers crying because they would never see their children again are more than products of historical imagination. George Tucker, a nineteenth-century Virginia novelist, offended many of his southern readers by writing, "One not accustomed to this spectacle [an auction] is extremely shocked to see beings, of the same species with himself, set up for sale to the highest bidder, like horses or cattle; and even to those who have become accustomed to it, it is disagreeable."[9]

Historically, the auction block has both real and symbolic importance. The lyrics from a slave melody, "No more auction block! No more, no more," capture both meanings. For slaves it meant a parting—often final—from relatives and friends. Unable to face such doubtful futures some ran off or mutilated or killed themselves. To curb such occurrences planters sometimes gave only a day's or even just a few hours' notice to bondsmen selected for selling and then guarded them closely or locked them up. One master, no doubt guilty of understatement, conceded that his ". . . Negroes will probably be somewhat distressed at being sold." He therefore advised his son, "you must say what you can to reconcile them."[10]

Slave traders held auctions, advertised well in advance, several times during each year in local towns and cities.[11] A great throng of slaveholders or potential slaveholders attended each session, accompanied sometimes by their wives, who might be clad in stylish dresses. It was, at the larger slave auctions, a time of gala social functions running through the day into late evening. The traders sponsored most of these events and invited planters up to their hotel rooms for pre-auction drinks and casual conversation. There was much imbibing and not a little carousing. Gangs of youths roamed the streets shouting names at free blacks, perhaps indicating a desire to see them returned to bondage. All had a good time except members of the black community—slave and free.

Of course the bondsman's participation in the auction began much earlier than these social functions. His psychological preparation started at the moment his master told him that he was to be put on the market. Parents gathered children too young to understand their fate around them and told stories of going on a long trip and not seeing one another for a great while. It could easily be the infants and adolescents who were being put up for sale, for nearly "all traders dealt in those from 10 or 12 years of age and many advertised for those from 6, 7, 8, and 9. . . ."[12] A Virginia agent wrote to a prospective buyer in 1850, "Boys and Girls are selling *best*."[13] For this reason Harriet Tubman, the underground railroad heroine, recalled that while she was in bondage, "every time I saw a white man I was afraid of being carried away."[14] The domestic trade, few would deny, was a basic reason for some bondsmen having only faint memories of their parents and of children growing up under the adoptive care of childless slaves and other foster parents. Frederick Douglass's well-known confession is emblematic: "I never saw my mother to know her as such, more than four or five times in my life. . . . I received the tidings of her death with much the same emotions I should have probably felt at the death of a stranger."[15]

Some bondsmen, waiting to be sold, abandoned their work duties, trusting that masters probably would not whip them, for the lash marks might not heal before the auction arrived and would raise potential buyers' suspicions about the slave's rascality. Slave owners did, of course, cut the rations of some disobedient bondsmen and physically restrain others, but there was always the possibility that discipline so close to the time of sale would leave a tell-tale sign and affect a slave's value adversely.

A few bondsmen became angered that after faithful years of service to a master he was about to sell them away for no apparent reason other than negro speculation.[16] Some bondsmen were indeed bred primarily for the auction. Southern newspapers ran ads expounding the "prolific . . . generating qualities" of slave females. Most informative is a letter from a North Carolina slaveholder to his grandfather in 1835:

> There is one fact generally admitted in support of the view I have taken which is that negroes are unprofitable in this country except for their increase and I believe there are few persons having as many or half as many negroes as Father has, that would be willing to take your negroes or an equal number from any one else and keep them on a farm and use them well, for *all* the profits arrising from them.[17]

To soothe those slaves intended for auction planters sometimes explained their reasons for selling them, hoping to win their confidence. Dr. James Marion Sims of Alabama wrote to his wife about an impending sale: "Let them understand that it is impossible for us to keep them . . . already are there mortgages on some of them and there is no telling when they may be foreclosed. . . . Let them know too that it lacerates our hearts as much as it does theirs to be compelled to the course we suggest."[18] Masters also promised not to allow reputedly cruel planters to purchase aggrieved bondsmen. Was this merely deception? In many cases it undoubtedly was. Yet there was not always cause to view a master's promises suspiciously, for some tried to keep their word. On a Georgia plantation the mistress, Lysie, noted that her slaves were very disturbed at the prospect of being sold. She further observed, "Most are family negroes that never knew what it was to be sold. I have cried with some that come to me with their troubles about going."[19] Occasionally a favorite slave got caught in the web of contradictions slavery created. John W. Abraham of Virginia claimed that his slave "Harriet is the best Servant we own & when gone I never expect to get her place filled." But he faced, he told his wife, an agonizing dilemma: "she [Harriet] is worth too much for us to keep and the balance of our negroes are in families which I hate to part."[20]

The time finally came for slaves to travel to the auction. In preparation, masters plucked out some of the older slaves' gray hairs or painted them over with a blacking brush. This was an illegal practice, but nonetheless widely engaged in, and traders delighted in outsmarting one another and uncovering the hucksters' deceptions.[21] Masters also had some slaves grease their bodies to make their muscles or a smiling face shine, but also to cover up recent or old marks of abuse. At the larger slave markets such as Richmond, Natchez, New Orleans, and Wilmington, North Carolina, bondsmen were placed in slave pens to await the arrival of auction day. The abolitionist James Redpath visited the one in Wilmington in the 1850's and reported it filled with slaves of both sexes.[22]

In accord with their interests, shortly before the auction was to begin, some planters visited local clothing shops and purchased new garments for slaves being put on the block that day. "I dressed up your Negroes," wrote a trader to the slaveowner he represented, "and made them look their best but could not screw them up [in price] any higher."[23] A few slaves on the block often rivaled their purchasers in neatness of appearance. Masters literally dressed some females in silks and satins and fitted men in neatly pressed, though inexpensive, suits. In New Orleans a traveler characterized some mulatto girls put up for auction as elegantly adorned and not at all like slaves. John Parker confided in his autobiographical account, "If I do say it myself I was very much better dressed and more intelligent looking than the white men, which pleased my vanity and modified my anger against my inveterate and hated enemies."[24] Less prized slaves, out of self-pride, tidied their own appearances. At one auction,

> the women, true to the feminine instinct, had made, in almost every case, some attempt at finery. All wore gorgeous turbans, generally manufactured in an instant out of a gay-colored handkerchief. . . . The little children were always better and more carefully dressed than the older ones, the parental pride coming out in the shape of a yellow cap pointed like a mitre, or a jacket with a strip of red broadcloth round the bottom.[25]

The auction block could be a peculiar spectacle indeed.

The sale began as the auctioneer's voice boomed out over the crowd's noise: "Now gentlemen, who bids for Tom? . . . His only fault is that he has a great idea of his own reserved rights, to the neglect of those of his master."[26] Several slaves were on the platform. The auctioneer commented on each one's relative value and merits, "and when the hammer at length falls, protests, in the usual phrase, that poor Sambo has been absolutely thrown away."[27]

An historian has written that many slaves were apparently unaffected by the auction experience "and were proud of the high prices that they brought."[28] This would seem to be an oversimplification of how slaves actually felt. Many, though colorfully dressed, wore somber expressions on their faces. At the Charleston market Captain Basil Hall noted a puzzling air of indifference in the slaves' manner.[29] And another observer, on a different occasion, remarked that "the poor victims did not seem to think hard of this matter, but regarded it as a matter of course . . ."[30] In reality, some slaves had simply resigned themselves to being sold, and saw little need for a display of emotion that might later bring them punishment.

But it seems that many slaves determined ahead of time to take an active part in the direction of the bargaining. They looked over the buyers, as the buyers did them, and selected several preferable ones. Often their decision hinged upon a knowledge of the planter's wealth and the living conditions and work load he would subject them to. They learned the needed information by keeping alert, quizzing other slaves, and sometimes confronting purchasers directly with rather blunt questions. Some were deliberately offensive to small planters, believing that slaves owned by them lacked social status and also life's necessities.[31] The slave John Parker explained: ". . . I made up my mind I was going to select my owner so when any one came to inspect me I did not like, I answered all questions with a 'yes' and made myself disagreeable So far as I was concerned the game was on, and I began to play it. . . ."[32] William Hayden claimed that because of his "utter indifference and apparent independence" to the events around him when he was on sale at an auction in Natchez, Mississippi, many prospective "purchasers were at a loss to know if, in reality, I were a slave, and subject to the hammer."[33] Slaves not as well attuned as Parker or Hayden to fine points of bargaining were less subtle. They might even kick or spit on buyers they did not like, and, according to the traveler E. S. Abdy, even shouted, "You may buy me . . . but I will never work for you."[34] Such threats turned many buyers away, but others were willing to accept the risk, confident in their ability to handle any bondsman.

Another method employed by slaves was simply to complain of imaginary ailments to every buyer except the desired one. Prospective purchasers often believed these stories because of those real instances of doctored-up slaves whose masters sought to dupe the unsuspecting buyer. Female slaves acted the coquette, offending planters and the sensibilities of accompanying wives.[35] They bickered and nagged at masters, convincing many that they would be a disruptive force in any work gang. They also made threats not to bear any children while owned by an undesirable master, and even to put infants that might be born to death. Only planters somewhat unfamiliar with slave management took these warnings lightly. For most, there was always a faint memory of a time on one's plantation or on a neighbor's when a slave had carried out an unheeded threat.

Occasionally, entire families stood on the auction block together. Attempts to separate them did succeed, of course, but the assault might meet with a volley of the foulest language from the slave, or with crying, hysterics, and threats of searching for the separated members and stealing them away. Some women, frantic, held tightly to their children, insisting they would not part with them. Other slaves consented to the sale when assured that husband, wife or child would only be a few plantations away. In a private sale one planter left instructions to tell the slave Davy that "the judge will make him a good master and that he not be far from his wife."[36] Basil Hall wrote about a slave awaiting his sale, "What struck me most was an occasional touch of anxiety about his eye as it glanced from bidder to bidder. . . . It seemed to imply a perfect acquaintance with the character of the different parties competing for him. . . ."[37] It is easy to see why purchase by a chosen master could bring a sigh of relief, and, at moments, joy.

But before a buyer sealed his purchase of a slave, he usually wanted to examine him physically. He looked at his teeth, limbs, and back, felt and poked muscles. Often buyers touched female slaves in most familiar ways, and the auctioneer and members of the crowd told obscene jokes. An English observer at Richmond noted, "I beheld with my own eyes a man . . . go and examine a poor African girl . . . grasping her arms and placing his course hand on her bosom!"[38] Many domestic slaves were unprepared emotionally for such examinations, and when they occurred many broke into tears, almost as if for the first time the full weight of their bondage pressed down upon them.

For more intimate examinations, a small yard was set aside. Slaves carried back there, according to the ex-slave Solomon

Northup, were "stripped and inspected more minutely."[39] Buyers looked for scars or signs of syphilitic ailments, for example, and examined the pelvic areas of females for purposes of speculation on their future as childbearers. The ordeal was especially difficult for husbands who were powerless to assist weeping wives. Yet bondsmen submitted reluctantly to such examinations if they provided the chance of being purchased by a preferred owner. Prospective buyers also compelled slaves to jump and dance as further proof that their limbs were operative.

With the auction over, buyers sometimes marched bewildered slaves on foot for several days or weeks to another auction and placed them on sale again, hoping to make a profit on a first investment. William Waller of Virginia wrote his son David that his slaves had "greatly improved in appearance although they have been walking for twenty five days. . . ."[40]

It was these marches, especially into the lower South, that often increased slaves' fears of never seeing loved ones again. They knew that some of them would die on the trip, and this knowledge fired those rumors of exceedingly harsh treatment down below. The rumors take on credibility, however, from the slave traders' correspondence about such events. In business-like fashion they simply estimated the percentage of slaves that would be lost in transit.[41]

Slaveholders boarded other bondsmen in local prisons or jails while they made additional purchases and then marched them off towards home. A member of the abolitionist-oriented National Liberal Club of London, arriving at the close of an auction in St. Louis, Missouri, observed "slaves that had just before been sold, who were then being bullied and threatened with punishment if they did not cease fretting and crying at being parted from their relations and friends."[42] Planters were quite aware of their feelings and often chained several or all of them together to prevent their running away, which happened often.[43] In one of these groups John Parker, "as a child of eight, [was] chained to an old man" and marched in a gang from Norfolk to Richmond, Virginia. "This old man was kind to me," he wrote, and "made my weight of the chain as light as he could. He talked to me kindly, because I was broken hearted at leaving my mother."[44] The favors slaves bestowed on one another at such times served to strengthen the bonds between them. Some perhaps reminded themselves that all was not lost; they would weather these hardships.

However, despair was not the only mood expressed on these occasions. Slaves purchased by a chosen master were sometimes cheerful, as were husbands, wives, and children who remained together. Some boasted that they had chosen their master, not he them. Masters watched all members of the gang closely, nonetheless, and cautioned them not to speak with blacks they met along the roadside, for if given a chance, "the negroes living along the route would gladly harbor refugees."[45]

News of the amounts that slaves sold for spread rapidly among planters and bondsmen. Slaves prided themselves on being sold at a high price, but not for the reasons that some researchers have almost casually advanced. A high price merely recognized the slave's special skills or potential as a good hand. For many it served to confirm the considerable opinion they already held of themselves and their abilities, and often secured better treatment from the planter interested in protecting his investment. Shortly after the purchase of the slave Polly in Baltimore, slaves stopped her and her new master on the road and asked if they knew of the slave lady in Baltimore who had been sold for a thousand dollars. Polly responded that it was she and that the purchase price was much larger than a thousand, whereupon "they gased upon her with *amasement* and collected all the per[sons] about the house to come and *look at her!*"[46]

Because of the frequency of auction block scenes, the composition and stability of the slave family has been the subject of much confusion. Was the family in a state of constant disruption? And if this was commonly so, what impact did such disruption have upon the development of its members' identities and general mode of being?

The primacy of one's family relationships in shaping one's

character is axiomatic among today's social theorists.[47] Family members gain personal strength from being loved and trusted by one another, and the family unit serves as a shield against outside attacks and the feeling of emptiness that often comes from being alone. The principles are easy to understand, but the elusive nature of the slave family makes them difficult to apply. Even the concept "family" as it applies to slaves needs reconsideration. With regard to them we might view it as several overlapping concepts. Slavery made it essential that the slave family be a great deal more inclusive than its white counterpart. Its ranks included not only blood relatives but also "adopted" relatives. Few slaves seemed lacking in aunts or uncles, real or otherwise.[48]

The odds against survival of the slave family intact were formidable. To begin with, marriage was not legally binding between slaves in any of the southern states. As late as 1855 there was a petition before the North Carolina Legislature requesting "that the parental relation . . . be acknowledged and protected by law; and that the separation of parents from their young children, say of twelve years and under, be strictly forbidden, under heavy pains and penalties."[49] Though such memorials were frequent, legislators never heeded them, for their implementation would merely have served to increase the moral questions that bothered many slaveholders, as well as greatly restrict the domestic slave trade. In the main, masters dictated the rules governing slave unions. What they were not able to dictate, however, was the seriousness with which bondsmen took their vows.[50] These a sizeable majority stood by steadfastly.

Slave marriage ceremonies varied from the symbolic jumping over the broomstick to the official-looking gatherings conducted by a white minister. Interestingly, a twist in the broomstick ceremony in some regions of the South was that if the couple did not jump over the broomstick at the same moment, they had to begin courting all over. We hardly need doubt that deliberate sabotage of the ceremony was at times tempting. Other bondsmen told of rather sordid marriage ceremonies in which they became husbands and wives after being forced to have sexual intercourse in a master's or overseer's presence.[51] Slaves, however, usually requested marriage by the planter, the ceremony followed by some festivities. One ex-slave remarked about still another possibility: "The field hands are seldom married by a clergyman. They simply invite their friends together, and have a wedding party."[52] Masters often encouraged or even insisted that slaves marry. Many offered a bounty of several dollars to the newlyweds, while others compelled slaves to marry individuals whom they were not interested in. But in most cases bondsmen selected their partners and went to great lengths to have the marriage solemnized "officially." One mistress wrote of a group of slaves coming through "mud, rain, and darkness to be married. . . . The bride and bride's maid were dressed in white swiss with wreaths of snow drops and evergreen on their heads."[53]

Once married, separations were usually not a matter of impulse on the slave's part. The domestic trade annulled an inestimable number of unions, but in the instance of voluntary separations some planters wanted to know the causes for the disunion and, in the case of James Henry Hammond of South Carolina, believed in disciplining the offenders. Slaves, nevertheless, have gained a reputation for licentiousness and immorality that is out of proportion, considering the circumstances under which they lived. There were, of course, slaves who had several wives or husbands. But ulterior motives of both slave and master often spawned these arrangements.[54] One planter thus discouraged his slave Peter from marrying a woman on another plantation because of "temptations to get into the rascality or meanness."[55] He perhaps suspected that such a marriage would lead to eventual disobedience by Peter should their judgments differ on when Peter might visit his proposed wife. And he probably feared Peter's performing some unauthorized errands. Yet other slaveholders sometimes reasoned that preventing a slave from taking a wife of his choice could lead to serious managerial problems with him. At any rate, slaves whose spouses died often remarried as soon as they could. The practice was not uncommon among planters and overseers as well. It was "very common among slaves themselves to talk of" marriage, wrote ex-slave William Wells Brown. What bothered him was that after marriage, "some masters, when they have sold the husband from the wife, compel her to take another" almost immediately, ignoring her personal feelings.[56]

At the center of the controversy over the slave family is the bondswoman. Her image usually stands in direct contrast to that of the plantation mistress. While her mistress was pure and dignified, she was tainted and uncouth. The mistress was ethereal and supposedly "begins from the earliest years to think herself a lady"[57] whereas the slave woman was all too earthy.[58] One mistress listed desired behavior for southern women in "A marriage Platform." Rule two called for virtue and discreetness, and rule seven emphasized "setting a right example of the cardinal virtues—meekness, temperance, faith, and love with an eye to Heavens reward her *chief end.*"[59] All this and more—except heaven's reward—seemed lacking in work-weary female slaves. Capping the entire contrast was the sensuality supposedly characteristic of slaves. Mysterious in its workings, it was thought to make them excellent breeders.

I have tried to capture an argument presented all too frequently, trusting it is clear that the portrayal misrepresents both mistress and slave. The image of slave women as somewhat less than what a woman should be immediately puts in doubt their role as effective members of a family. In fact, the entire slave marriage relationship calls into question the interaction of wife and husband and parent and child in slave culture.[60]

Many past and present researchers have assumed that the slave family was a very loosely organized group whose primary cohesion was provided by women. The black sociologist E. Franklin Frazier capsulized this interpretation in his 1939 study when he characterized the slave mother "as the mistress of the cabin and as the head of the family." Frazier also mentioned that the mother had a "more fundamental interest in her children" and was able to develop "a spirit of independence and a keen sense of her personal rights."[61] His canonization of slave women catapulted them to the forefront of modern discussions about the slave family.

Was he correct in his conclusion about the matriarchal structure of the family? His picture seems somehow too inflexible, for the slave family developed in ways which Frazier seems not to have imagined.

Under some conditions—when slave children were infants—southern laws provided that masters could not divide slave families. What these laws sought primarily to prevent was the separation of child from mother; the father might still be sold.[62] Indeed, when planters spoke of slave families they often referred to husbandless women and their children. The logic rings familiar even today, in that when a husband and wife legally separate the wife normally obtains custody of the children. We seldom assume, however, that the husband has been a passive agent in the family. Why then should we assume this to be so in the case of the slave, when there is no significant precedent for such an assumption in the slave's African past or in many of his American associations? Of course, this is not to deny that a slave father was a great deal more helpless than a free father today.

A variety of circumstances determined the position of the slave mother as well as the father. If women were the heads of the households, they rarely gained that dominant status among slaves at large. Women worked side by side with men at nearly every task on the plantation, but there were certain duties considered women's work that men declined to do. Some male slaves refused to do washing for this reason. Cooking was usually the task of women, as was sewing and some forms of child care. Sometimes masters punished males by forcing them to work with women labor gangs in the fields or compelling them to wash the family's clothes and attend to house-cleaning. So great was their shame before their fellows that many ran off and suffered the lash on their backs rather than submit to the discipline.[63] Men clearly viewed certain chores as women's tasks, and female slaves largely respected the distinction.

In the evening, back at the slave quarters, women gathered in sewing groups to make quilts and small items of clothing. Single females flirted, but the slave community generally deemed it improper for them to be too aggressive.[64] Yet the whims of lovers were fully displayed:

> We would just sit and talk with each other. I told him one time I didn't love him; I hated him, and then I told him again that I loved him so much I just loved to see him walk. You had to court right there on the place 'cause they had paddlerollers and if you went out without a pass they would whip you.[65]

The interplay often disturbed the quietude of the plantation and quarters settings.

Love potions were a major sales item of local conjurers, whose clientele included married as well as unmarried slaves.[66] Planters and their wives experimented with potions as well in order to enrich the content of their love lives, too often rent asunder by adversity. Emotional relationships took place at a frantic pace at times; the relationships of slaves particularly must appear unduly hurried to observers who do not reflect upon the uncertain features of their existence. Often females went to great lengths to beautify themselves. When courting ran its full course without intervention by the master, male slaves went all out as well to impress females with their strength and daring. Males showed their bravery by leaving the plantation without passes to hunt or run errands for the current "flame." The women enjoyed the attention paid them. Some of their more robust sisters, nevertheless, had difficulty attracting men, whom they daily embarrassed with outstanding work records.

A family's welfare sometimes compelled fatherless young women to assume male duties at an early age, in order to raise the family's standard of living. Many hunted with great success, for example. Their behavior may have contributed to some general uneasiness male slaves experienced when having their own accomplishments belittled by a comparison with a female's. The contrast might stimulate the male slave to work harder but also gave rise to a good deal of bitterness. At such times, the behavior of the female was vital. If she worked hard because it was her nature, and not to gain any special favors from a master or overseer, bondsmen might not seriously question her conduct.[67] Some females worked hard to attract the attention of men, perhaps to persuade them that they would continue to be industrious in marriage. This was particularly true of duties they performed for their families. The word passed quickly that they did their share.

The often peculiar marriage and dating relations of bondsmen have caused many scholars to doubt their morality. Females have borne the brunt of unfavorable conjectures. Scores of mulatto children fathered by masters have been used to support arguments that bondswomen were indiscriminate in their selection of male sex partners. Added to this was the fact that in the "southern states the prostitutes of the communities are usually slaves, unless they are imported from the free states. . . ."[68]

Motherhood in bondage provided extremely difficult tests of a slave's energies and identity. The slave had to play the role of wife and mother under circumstances that marred her effectiveness at each. Her plantation duties eroded the time she had to spend with husband and children. Distractions were infinite. This was akin to the condition that some planters' wives found themselves in, trapped in a continuous cycle of chores.

Slavery struck most directly at bonds of affection joining husband and wife. The slave trade occasionally separated slaves married only a few weeks. We may suppose that some slaves were reluctant to love anyone deeply under these circumstances. Yet most spent several years with one owner and one husband or wife, and came to know their fellow bondsmen well. Thus when slaves married it was often the consequence of courtship extending over some time. The resultant marriage was steeped in emotional attachment. "Our affection for each other was strong," wrote a slave of his marriage, "and this made us always apprehensive of a cruel parting."[69] The slave Sam, like so many others, ran away from his Virginia master because he thought "it a hard case to be separated from his wife. . . ."[70]

Planters understood such affections. "You have a woman hired in the neighborhood whose husband we own," began a letter to

Colonel Barksdale of Virginia. His "name is Israel, he is our Blacksmith, and he seems to be so much attached to her we [would] like very much for her to be hired near him . . . would you sell the woman?"[71] A sound marriage meant a better worker for the planter and often a sense of purpose for the slave.

But slavery compelled an uneven husband-wife relationship. A master could physically discipline either while the other stood by helpless, at least for the moment. Slaveowners worked both hard, and they often had little time left to enjoy each other's company in the evening. The relationship nonetheless had many interesting potentials. "A slave possessing nothing . . . except a wife and children, has all his affections concentrated upon them," wrote Francis Fedric.[72] Occasionally, the marriage partners focused so much attention on each other that the slightest change in the routine of one tended to disrupt the other's habits. Sickness is a good example. Wives and husbands often insisted that they nurse each other back to health, fighting bitterly against efforts to force them into the fields when the possibility of a loved one dying existed. Slaveholders severely punished many and accused them of merely trying to escape duties—but discpiline was seldom an effective deterrent. A planter could, of course, make arrangements for such times; expecting that wives and husbands might be off work briefly or difficult to manage during days when important personal matters came up. Sometimes a sick husband would prolong his sickness by refusing to take medicine from any but the hands of his wife, whom he could also trust to find out if someone had "hexed" him.

The marriage and family bond endured an additional hardship when masters hired out either partner, though often slaves saw being hired out as a means of bettering the quality of their lives. The slave Noah Davis was a preacher in Virginia. His master allowed him to travel and deliver sermons to raise money for his freedom. Davis' initial reaction was, "how can I leave my wife and seven children, to go to Baltimore . . . I thought my children would need my watchful care. . . ."[73] Other slaves hired their time to earn money for purchasing additional clothing and articles for the home.

The arrival of children served in large measure to solidify the slave marriage. Yet some parents feared that slaveholders would mistreat offspring or sell them away. A few adults also refused to assume parental responsibilities. They married and had children, but declined or allowed others to take care of them, and were occasionally abusive parents. Still, most assumed parental ties eagerly and were, according to a Mississippi mistress, "all so proud of showing their children."[74] While discussing the possible sale of a slave to an Annapolis slaveholder, Charles Ridgely wrote that she "is married in the neighborhood and has a family of young children, and would I think now be extremely unwilling to be separated from them. . . ."[75]

In Africa "tribal customs and taboos tended to fix the mother's attitude toward her child before it was born," making children greatly appreciated, and such tendencies were not absent in American slaves.[76] Few women probably did not want children, though they were aware they might not be able to devote the attention to them that would be required. The emotional outbursts of mothers following the deaths of infants, and their resistance to being parted from offspring, indicate that female slave attitudes in this regard were not markedly distinct from those of mothers world-wide.

In fact, many disruptions of the workday stemmed from slave parents' requests to tend their children. Masters set aside a period during the day for the nursing of babies, but there was also frequent disciplining of bondswomen when they failed to return to their duties on schedule. Yet mothers repeatedly risked the lash in order to allow their body temperatures to cool down enough for effective milk nourishment. Still Moses Grandy observed that overseers forced many to work in the field carrying full breasts of milk. "They therefore could not keep up with the other hands," and when this happened overseers whipped them "so that blood and milk flew mingled from their breasts."[77] It does not appear that he was merely trying to achieve literary effect with this dramatic statement. But often mothers got their way, for it was difficult for a master to justify, either to his conscience or his hands, children found dead from want of care. The slave's human increase was also an owner's most valuable form of property. On many plantations masters periodically assigned one or two slaves to furnish the nursing needs of all infants. They also hired slaves to nurse their own offspring.

Most planters were probably never able to solve the problems of mothers working during the day while their children languished back at the quarters or under nearby trees, or crawled and kicked "in the filthy cabins or on the broiling sand which surrounds them." A similar dilemma, though lesser in degree, confronted their own wives, especially on small farms where everyone had chores to perform. Many small slaveholding farmers were perhaps better able to understand the immediate problems confronting motherhood in bondage. They needed only to look at their own wives' workload for several months during the suckling period. Some permitted mothers to finish their duties in the early afternoon so they might spend the remainder of the day with their children. They also permitted, sometimes insisted, that husbands work overtime to make up the slack caused by their wives' partial absence from the work force. Usually men did the extra work rather than see their women suffer, though not without complaint. Adolescents also served in this capacity, taking up their mother's tasks in the afternoon, while learning one further example of family cooperation. Thus in the midst of this swirl of life's events, slaves improvised the conditions of the family as best they could.

In bondage, the varieties of adult family behavior served as the most significant models after which slave children patterned their own actions. We know that "where a variety of behavior or models is available, selection can be influenced either by affection and rewards, by punishment, or by awareness of what is appropriate."[78] All these factors operated with peculiar force within and upon the slave family. J. W. C. Pennington, the fugtive blacksmith, experienced what he called a "want of parental care and attention." By way of explanation he added, "my parents were not able to give any attention to their children during the day."[79] While this was not unusual, many parents did devote their evenings and weekends to family affairs—a first duty of which was to teach children the limits placed on their conduct. This was no simple task.

Pressures from within and outside the slave family further encouraged its members to identify with one another. Planters sometimes tried to compel the association. Beginning in January, 1847, William Ervin of North Carolina ruled for his bondsmen that "each family [was] to live in their own house."[80] This was the same suggestion advanced by several writers in *De Bow's Review*. But Ervin enumerated some minimal duties: "The husband to provide firewood. . . . The wife to cook and wash for the husband and her children. . . ."[81] Slaves who failed to carry out these chores were subject to immediate correction. But actually bondsmen needed little prompting in this regard. They realized that a division of labors was essential to a family's survival.

Contributing to family unity on plantations was the absence of the condescending glances that shadowed the daily lives of urban bondsmen. In contact chiefly with other slaves, there was no need for them continually to compare their family life to that of whites. Charles Ball observed of his bondage that despite the equality of slaves as slaves, "there was in fact a very great difference in the manner of living, in the several families."[82] The ways parents viewed their roles could affect this difference. Many husbands hunted in the evening to furnish additional meat for the family's diet. Ball "understood various methods of entrapping rackoons, and other wild animals . . . and besides the skins, which were worth something for their furs, I generally procured as many rackoons, opossums, and rabbits, as afforded us two or three meals in a week."[83] This type of activity identified the male as the "bread-winner" in the household. His wife and children tended to trust his abilities to provide for them, and to appreciate the risks—such as leaving the plantation without a pass—he took in their behalf. But Charles Ball notes too that not all slave families were as fortunate as his; many lacked motivation for the kinds of activities the Balls engaged in. "Many of the families in the quarter caught no game. . . ."[84]

Sometimes children accompanied their fathers on a hunting expedition. J. W. C. Pennington tells us as well that he assisted his "father at night in making strawhats and willow-baskets, by which means we supplied our family with little articles of food, clothing and luxury. . . ."[85] The impact of these minor activities was telling. Some families began to think of themselves as better than their neighbors, though their members worked daily at the same jobs. They might think of families less "affluent" as lazy. Children picked up these prejudices and, at the behest of their parents, were sometimes very selective in their playmates. Feuds between families of a mild nature could result and ironically serve to link husband, wife, and children in a family closer together, though disrupting the quarters.[86]

For the young slave, family life was vastly important. His early years somehow slipped past with the idea probably seldom if ever occurring to him that he was but a piece of property. His main worries related to minor chores assigned to him at about age five or six by parents and master; and adult slaves at times bore much of the burden of these. Children also escaped much of the stigma of racial inferiority that whites attached to the personalities of their mothers and fathers. Concerning his childhood one slave reminisced, "let me say to you that my case were different from a great many of my colore so I never knew what the yoke of oppression was in the early part of my life. . . ." He was relatively carefree and innocent, he explained, until "the white boy . . . began to Raise his feathers and boast of the superiority which he had over me."[87]

There were several kinds of observations relating to black children that both slaves and masters were quick to make. After much consideration Dr. Samuel Cartwright of Louisiana noted, "Negro children and white children are alike at birth in one remarkable particular—they are both born white. . . ."[88] The similarity struck him as odd, if little else, but might receive another interpretation among slaves. A few bondsmen may have jokingly drawn a comparison between the light child in their midst and his darker counterpart in the master's house. They knew, however, that in a few weeks the child's changing skin color would begin to reveal the true status of the new arrival.

Slave parents paraded their young ones before visitors to the plantation, some of whom observed that these infants were all their parents were not—likeable and bright. Yet this supposed difference appeared strange to few. "The young negro acquires readily the first rudiments of education," noted a Georgian who attributed such achievements to memory and mimicry. But at a later age "for any higher effort of reason and judgment he is, as a general rule, utterly incapable . . . except in the case of mulattoes, where the traits of the white parents are sometimes developed."[89]

Parents channeled most of the child's efforts into harmless activities (games) and labor at first.[90] What he did not lack in these early years was the "firm sense of belonging" so essential to survival as a slave.[91] Following the bitter neglect that might accompany a weaning interrupted by long parental work hours, an old slave took the child into a group of children under her care for pampering and disciplining.

The Reverend C. C. Jones observed in his travels that "negroes on plantations sometimes appoint one of their number, commonly the old woman who minds the children during the day, to teach them to say their prayers, repeat a little catechism and a few hymns. . . ." But regrettably the "instances are however not frequent. . . ."[92] On a Virginia plantation the child Molley, age two, was in need of a nurse. Her master wrote to his overseer, "I understand that Negro Payne 71 years old of the Forest Plantation is the grand father . . . I now direct that Payne be ordered go to Cancer Plantation & live at Suckey's house he to have the Care of both his grand Children. . . ."[93]

It was not true that when black children learned to walk and then play with the master's children their "first lesson is to obey everything that has a white skin," as one bondsman claimed.[94] Some masters' children learned this lesson the hard way when they tried to boss the little "niggers" about: ." . . every time they crossed me I jumped them," recalled one ex-slave about his white playmates.[95]

Frequently the tendency among black and white children was towards a general equality. They played marbles together, and the slave children themselves spent many hours at this game: ". . . my favorite game was marbles."[96] They also played sheep-meat, a game of tag played with a ball of yarn that was thrown by one child at others running about the grounds. They enjoyed a great variety of childhood sports. Sir Charles Lyell, the English geologist, witnessed slave and white children playing, "evidently all associating on terms of equality. . . ."[97] One slave narrator remembered too that he was very close to a son of his Virginia master: ". . . I was his playmate and constant associate in childhood." He learned the alphabet and some of the elements of reading from him. "We were very fond of each other, and frequently slept together."[98]

On large plantations communities of children were largely autonomous. Slave narratives relate that often one of the bondsman's earliest recollections of slavery was the sight of his mother or father being whipped or his brothers and sisters standing on the auction block. But this side of childhood can be overplayed. Fear did not perpetually pervade the environment. There are accounts of seeming childhood contentment which, though occasionally overdrawn by some interpreters, are to some measure accurate. The slaveholder did not constantly try to shape the character of slave children. There was little time for that. "The master, I think, does not often trouble himself with the government of these juvenile communities," observed a doctor from Kentucky. "He is not, therefore, an object of dread among them."[99]

To a great extent, children learned to shape their behavior to the expectations of other slaves. A beginning lesson was to respect slave elders, particularly the aged. Tradition shaped this differential treatment.[100] The child was, moreover, at the bottom of the hierarchy of both blacks and whites, while old slaves were in a manner the domestics of the slave quarters. Their functions were not unlike those of the slaves who ordered the master's children about and instructed them in etiquette. In Georgia, planter Howell Cobb described slave influence of this latter kind as a "social evil of no small magnitude." This "imbibing by [white] children of the superstitions, fears, and habits, of the negroes, with whom they are necessarily, to some extent, reared"[101] should, he thought, be stopped.

The slave child's early experiences helped to hone him into readiness for but not acceptance of bondage. He might start his work life by picking up a few sticks that cluttered the slave yard, advance to carrying his youthful master's books to school, and eventually merge into the adolescent "slave gangs" that went about the plantation doing odd jobs mixed with "funning." Children repeatedly slowed down the daily operations of the plantation. They naturally wanted to go to the fields to be near parents and friends, who doled out stories of spirits and connivance interrupted by orders to run to the bucket to fetch some water or into the woods to examine opossum traps.

By the time a child was six he might be assigned by a planter "to gather Small Wood, & run with his umbrella & great Coat in case.he should be caught by rain in the field."[102] The assignment was typical of many, all part of an effort to develop top work hands. An article in the *Southern Agriculturist* suggested one means by which a master might utilize a child "to pay for its support." The author proposed that "every child might annually save manure enough from the roads, avenues, and fields, where it is not wanted. . . ."[103] Children took pride in performing their duties well, but bore pressure erratically and even ran away if treated too severely.

In the cotton country of the Deep South children played an important role in the cultivation of the crop. They were widely employed as weeders and also gathered bits of cotton which, in their haste, adult pickers had missed. In this way they contributed to the strength of the work force, observed the varied contributions they were to make on a larger scale in the future, and were awakened to the meaning of slavery for their lives. Around age twelve, sometimes sooner, children worked in trash gangs and performed such tasks as gathering fodder or clearing roadsides of debris under the supervision of older hands, usually women. Though many of these chores were relatively light, planters were not averse to assigning children heavier labors that occupied the entire working day and kept them away from the fields and out of contact with their parents. In contrast, there was the responsibility of one South Carolina slave who recalled, "When I got old enough I minded flies off the table while my master and mistus was eating."[104] In Chapel Hill, North Carolina, wrote Lucy Battle in a letter to her husband, Jim Hogan "threw an axe at a boy of Henry Thompsons intending that the handle should strike him—the boy fell & the axe went into his back—*deep*."[105] The boy recovered but was lame for life. There was no mention of any punishment of Hogan.

Working in large groups, children cleared rocks from plantation roads and cared for farm animals. But they also worked at difficult assignments side by side with adults in the tobacco and textile factories of the Upper South. "Young slaves," occasionally less than ten years old, "operated many Kentucky and Missouri hemp factories."[106] Children, to be sure, might perform an important share of the work on plantations wherever their numbers were sizeable.

Travelers often came across half-naked and ragged slave adolescents who were "burning stumps" and foraging small pieces of wood for the master's fireplace and the slave quarters.[107] For reasons of safety, many parents tried to get work assignments for their children paralleling their own duties. In this way they could assume some of the work load during a particularly difficult day and thereby shield children from abuse. They were not always successful in this, although when a child failed at his tasks or violated plantation rules masters usually left it to parents to administer the appropriate discipline. Mothers and fathers accepted the responsibility willingly, for they could give the child a well-intentioned talking to. Parental assumption of childhood discipline also strengthened the primary identification young slaves had with their parents as symbols of authority.[108]

Some parents also saw initial work responsibilities, if properly performed, as an opportunity for their sons and daughters to escape the rigors of field labor. They encouraged their children to learn a trade if possible. A skill meant an opportunity to obtain preferred duties in later life. Masters wanted at least a few trained hands, chiefly as carpenters, for they increased the efficiency of the plantation as well as their own monetary value. John Mc Donogh of New Orleans hired a slave brickmason and later recommended him to a neighbor, suggesting that he might teach bricklaying to "two or three of your black boys" and "with two boys of 10 or 12 years of age to work with him in laying brick he will do all your buildings."[109]

Occasionally, children's jobs required that they go through a prolonged or permanent separation from their families; but a determined parent was willing to accept this if it promised ultimately to provide an easier life for a son or daughter. The slave Julianna, age twelve, was the subject of a contract that engaged her services for six years. Her contractual master guaranteed "to teach her to sew, & bring her up to be a good seamstress, and a useful servant." The arrangement continued on a partially personal note; "In addition to the above I agree to allow the said girl Julianna to go to Shirley [Plantation] . . . once each year to see her relations, & remain with them one week each year. . . ."[110]

Bondsman Henry Bibb was especially aware of the shortened childhood of the slave. "I was taken away from my mother," he wrote, "and hired out to labor for various persons, eight or ten years in succession. . . ."[111] Other hired-out children were more fortunate than Bibb. Employed as families, as were "Great Jenny & her 3 youngest children," they partially escaped the emotional turmoil that accompanied separations.[112]

Beyond the duties children had as plantation "hands," parents urged them to assume a full role in family affairs by doing small chores during the day. A slave born in 1844 recalled, "My father had some very fine dogs; we hunted coons, rabbits and opossum."[113] Parents expected each child to contribute his share to the family's welfare. Some children spent part of their time fishing or checking the animal traps set by their fathers. Henry C. Bruce wrote, "We often brought home as much as five pounds of fish in a day."[114] They would bring the catch in and reap the reward of an extra helping at dinner and much affection. Parents seldom hesitated to brag about such accomplishments. During the sickly season, if both parents became ill, total responsibility for taking care of the family garden and checking traps fell to children. Thus, as soon as young ones came of age they confronted a variety of role alternatives. They saw their parents as providers, loved ones, and disciplinarians. Moses Grandy's claim of "no lasting ties to bind relations together"[115] seems questionable at this point.

Despite the potential of bondage to disrupt the slave family, its members—for example, brothers and sisters—often tried desperately to nurture familial affections. When no separation occurred they naturally spent much of their time together, playing and fighting. Parents told older ones to look after youngsters and to protect them from the bands of little ruffians who often roamed plantations. An ex-slave observed, "Some of us children that were too small to go to the field had to stay around and take care of the slave babies. This was my job at times. Whenever the babies got to crying too much I would go and call their mothers from the field to come and suckle them."[116] There was also occasion to shield brothers and sisters from the "tyranny" of the master's children.

When the terms of bondage necessitated the division of families, parents often sought the aid of masters to reunite them. Lucinda, who served as a washwoman for a planter "nearly twelve years," asked him to hire her daughter Mary Jane from a nearby planter. "To oblige her," wrote her owner to Mary Jane's master, "I will become responsible for the amount, if you will let her have her daughter for the sum of Thirty dollars," which Lucinda was apparently willing to repay by her earnings during the remainder of the year.[117] In another case, the slave George approached his master R. Carter about his daughter Betty—"7 years old, motherless, now at Colespoint-plantation—." In a letter to his overseer, Carter noted that "George wishes Betty live at Aires, with his Wife who lives there." As if not to appear overly accommodating to George's wishes Carter continued, "If Betty is not useful where She now lives—I desire to indulge George . . . you will accordingly permit him to take his daughter."[118] At other times, slaves acted on their own to reunite themselves with loved ones. One runaway was persistent in this way: "She has a husband, I think, at his [a neighbor's] house & tho' taken up by him the first time came straight back to his house. . . ."[119]

On weekends and holidays families spent many of their hours together, resting and joining in various festivities. Remembering that his father "could read a little," an ex-slave observed that his "custom on those Sabbaths when we remained at home, was to spend his time in instructing his children, or neighboring servants out of a New Testament. . . ."[120] Such activities enhanced his prestige in his son's eyes.

Parents also carted children along to slave gatherings dressed in their cleanest clothes, little girls adorned with bright ribbons in their hair. On these occasions parents warned them in advance to watch their manners so as not to embarrass the family. They were also to be especially careful that they were not rude to their elders.[121] Parents would rush them from group to group, making sure that slaves on other plantations saw how intelligent and wellbehaved they were. Adults told children to run races and throw rocks in competition with other boys and girls. Some of the old slaves would catch them by the ears and just hold them there "looking 'em over." Slaves paid much attention to presenting the family's best "side" wherever they appeared together. Often they seemed overly concerned that they not shame themselves in any way, for it reflected poorly on one's upbringing.

When a master abused or humiliated one member of a family, the rebuff reverberated throughout the slave household and beyond. An example appears in the opening pages of the fugitive blacksmith's narrative. Following the whipping of his father, J. W. C. Pennington remembered, "an open rupture" developed in his family [against their master]. Each member felt deeply offended by the deed, for they had always believed their conduct and faithfulness was exemplary. They talked of their humiliation in the "nightly gatherings, and showed it in . . . daily melancholy aspect."[122]

Planters' ill-handling of slaves was only one of many factors that brought out family consciousness. Bondsmen's misdeeds against other bondsmen sometimes marked families for harassment and shame. A serious offense, such as stealing another's hunting catches, might lead to brief periods of social isolation, with members of the offending family finding themselves excluded from slave gatherings or nightly ramblings. Bondsmen saw themselves as having their primary identification with a distinct family unit to which they had responsibility and which had responsibility to them.

However, the slave family was a unit with extensions. Quite frequently it seems to have consisted of more than just parents and their natural children.[123] It could include a number of blood or adopted relations—uncles, aunts, and cousins—who lived on the same plantation or on nearby estates. Adults "claimed" parentless children, and the slave community seldom neglected old slaves. Local bondsmen usually absorbed new arrivals on a plantation into a family setting and expected them to make a full contribution immediately. But can such a group really be called a family? Slaves considered it as such and treated adopted relatives with real affection.

The extended slave family frequently arose to augment or replace the regular family unit split up by slavery's misfortunes. There were deaths resulting from disease, accidents, and natural causes that left wives husbandless and children without parents. Then there were the family breakups caused by the slave trade. In an important, though not typical, exception, however, Robert Carter of Virginia agreed to sell his slaves to the Baltimore Company only ". . . if the Company will purchase men their wives & children [ten families]. . . ."[124]

Into the extended family too were taken black mothers with mulatto children. The white father of a black woman's offspring was often known only to herself, sometimes because she feared reprisals if she revealed his name.[125] Although planters publicly expressed an abhorrence for such unions, and their deepest fears about resistance included visions of slaves taking brides among their wives and daughters, it was their desires, not those of slaves, which were responsible for the rise in the mulatto population. Their own behavior thus seems the source of many of their fears. Traveler Sir Charles Lyell, curious about race mixing, wrote that if slaveholders so abhorred white-black unions, as they professed, "we should not meet with a numerous mixed breed springing up every where from the union of the races." But he did meet with such a breed. His remedy for this was "negro reservations or large territories set apart for free blacks where they might form independent states or communities."[126]

Though slaves had many black children in and out of "official" wedlock, slaveholders and slaves placed a far different interpretation upon having the master's child. Some females willingly mixed their blood with that of planters, and did not try to disguise the fact. But such behavior was greatly frowned upon in the slave quarters, where it was the topic of considerable conversation and malicious gossip. Yet often the offspring of master-slave relationships gained an elevated status—additional privileges in later life. The reverse, however, was just as likely to happen, with mother and child the objects of the planter's wrath. A number of the slave narrators, who had white fathers, write of times when they experienced the scorn of both masters and slaves.

When they were victims of additional mistreatment, these black mothers sometimes blamed their mulatto children for their woes and abused them. But usually they blamed the master. Certainly, mulatto children were taken into the extended family, where they primarily identified with bondsmen, though their light color did inflate some with false pride.[127] Many black mothers of mulatto children went on to have offspring by slave husbands, and usually treated all their sons and daughters, light and dark, similarly. However the intrusion of masters in such a direct way into the slave family—by mixing their blood in it—intensified animosities between the races. Male slaves resented such intermixture as much as white males did.

In 1800 the slave Ben shot and killed Joseph Gooding, a white man, for consorting with his wife. Ben's wife had been living on a plantation owned by a Mr. Bass, and Ben had "continued to live with her for two or three years when without having done anything to give offence he was ordered by Bass to discontinue coming to his plantation." Ben obeyed the order so as to avoid punishment, but a short time later "he heard that Joe Gooding . . . was very much in favor with Mr. and Mrs. Bass and had taken up with [Ben's] wife. . . ." Two years followed during which Ben was not allowed to visit his wife, and then Bass and Gooding had a falling out. Ben next asked Bass if he might visit his wife again, his love for her having remained strong. Bass agreed. During his trial Ben testified that he had several conversations in which Bass advised him to put Gooding "out of the way," intimating that Ben had justification—since Gooding had had sexual relations with Ben's wife—for killing him. Ben first tried to poison Gooding but accidentally killed his own wife instead. Tormented by "having poisoned the last person in the world he wished to injure," he determined to take his "master's gun out of the house where it generally stood loaded and to go in pursuit of Joe Gooding and shoot him, which he did."[128]

This tragic attempt to reestablish a relationship of husband and wife is a good example of how frantic the slave could become in trying to protect the intimate features of his life. A personal drama, similar to the preceding, in which a slave killed his overseer, occurred in 1859. The slave's lawyer tried to prove "that about nine or ten o'clock in the morning of the day in which the killing took place . . . Coleman, the overseer, had forced her [the slave's wife], the witness[,] to submit to sexual intercourse with him, and . . . she had communicated that fact to the prisoner before the killing took place."[129] The court, reflecting southern mores, ruled that an act of adultery with a slave was not just grounds for such drastic action. But in this type of instance, and in a broader sense as well, slaves might resort to violence when they desired to protect wives, husbands, and children—the family's sanctity.[130]

In slave families wives seldom possessed greater financial stability than husbands, a circumstance that often gives rise to psychological problems in men of minority households in our day. Both worked at tasks that the slave culture did not stigmatize as menial, so there was no need for the male to feel a lack of importance in his family on that score. The power of masters to disrupt families at any time weakened male slaves' sense of responsibility and dignity, but they did not invariably see this as a slight to their manhood. Yet for the slave who experienced the breakup of his household there remained that indelible hurt, as perhaps exemplified by Charles Ball's father, who "never recovered from the effects of the shock" of losing a portion of his family and became "gloomy and morose."[131] Whenever the slave family—natural or extended—was intact, however, and slave males were reliably performing their duties, they most likely did symbolize authority within the family structure.

Except for sales of its members, much of the time slaveholders left the slave family to its own devices. And though the slave trade drove blood relatives apart, bondsmen's common persecution brought many of them back together in extended family groupings which provided for many of the emotional needs whose satisfaction the regular family, had it remained untouched, might have rendered less vexatious. Under these conditions the personalities of bondsmen were certain to gain much strength.

10
This Property Is Condemned

The personality and life experience of the slave are too complex and colorful to be profiled here in a few summary paragraphs, though hopefully I can informatively restate and make some additional observations. The slave lived through what was, and especially for him, a very difficult period of American history, some of whose prejudices still linger in our day. Historians have been very painstaking in their researches into the war that finally led to his release, but somewhat less painstaking in their study of him and his perceptions of his bondage. Indeed, the slave's personality has been so neglected that, more often than not, he becomes a nonperson, having little importance in a society he helped mold. Even when some of his contributions are noted he remains largely invisible. Ralph Ellison's description in his 1952 novel is applicable to the slave experience:

> I am invisible, understand, simply because people refuse to see me. . . . it is as though I have been surrounded by mirrors of hard, distorting glass. When they approach me they see only my surroundings, themselves, or figments of their imagination—indeed, everything and anything except me.[1]

Yet it is clear from sources relating to the lives of both slaves and masters that the tendency to treat bondsmen as invisible greatly distorts the historical record.

The discussion of the African slave's character has been far ranging. "The Africans were thralls," observed one southern historian in 1929, "wanted only for their brawn, required to take things as they found them and do as they were told, coerced into self-obliterating humility, and encouraged to respond only to the teachings and preachings of their masters, and adapt themselves to the white men's ways."[2] Still the reality is different than what he portrayed. The lack of a visible role, however, other than the one assigned to them by slaveholders that African slaves were traditionally believed to have played, has had a compelling effect on some scholars. In their view slaves were mere ciphers in a society that rescued them from savagery and cultural oblivion in Africa. The proper response to their saviors should be gratitude, and almost accordingly the happy-go-lucky, childlike slave depicted in much of the scholarly and popular literature seemed a logical by-product.

Historians have, in fact, been somewhat confused about how to view slaves more "accurately," and often with good reason. In the 1830's the English traveler James S. Buckingham explained in part why he thought the slave remained in the shadows. He observed, with some puzzlement, that when masters "spoke of coercion employed towards the negroes, and endeavored to justify the necessity of it, they [slaves] were represented as 'indolent, worthless, and ungrateful race,' . . . and so ungrateful for favors received that the better they were treated the worse they behaved." But he also observed in contrast that when talk turned to uplifting slaves from this wretched state masters noted how "they were perfectly contented with their condition, and on the whole a much better race without education than with, as they were now faithful, kind-hearted, and attached to their masters, whereas education would destroy all their natural virtues, and make them as vicious as the lower orders in other countries."[3]

As the discussion about slaves and slavery changed through the years, the slave's character remained suspect.[4] For example, Sambo remained the most common description set forth in secondary schools and universities, even as new research appeared which largely undermined this conception.[5] But now, one thing is most striking from the available evidence. It would have been virtually impossible for the slave to have been as neatly package as such past stereotypes have suggested. The inflexibility of Sambo especially does not permit us to understand how bondsmen were largely able, as the present study has argued, to survive and even transcend the complex kinds of suppression facing them. The slave proved himself a personality to be reckoned with.

All around them slaves saw how their companions peformed the essential functions of the plantation community, from its unskilled to its most highly skilled tasks. From these observations they understood that they were capable of doing everything they were permitted to do and more: "Jerry Horn Driver and now principle overseer and director for his Master until the new Overseer understand and gets the run of the business so that he can plan and go ahead advantageously. . . .[6] Even so determined a proslavery spokesman as Edmund Ruffin wrote—ambivalently to be sure—to another determined spokesman, James Henry Hammond, that "I still have no overseer, (excepting my negro foreman) & have become much more inattentive to my work." He added almost as a matter of record that "Of course it is done worse & more lazily"; though he conceded, "still, my crops on the general average have not decreased. But I think they ought to have increased. . . ."[7]

Because of the uses made of slaves in the Old South, many accumulated a great deal of valuable knowledge about agricultural endeavors. They advised masters on matters concerning the cultivation and harvesting of crops, made and invented many useful agricultural tools, and bred and cared for livestock. Many slaveholders believed that in order to obtain the best plantation results it was necessary to seek the advice of at least a few of the most knowledgeable but not necessarily, in other ways, most obedient fieldhands. They sometimes rewarded such slaves with money, goods, or additional liberties. They depended as well on slave carpenters to make tools, repair farm housing and sometimes construct and design buildings, large and small. Slave blacksmiths served in similar roles. And black slave drivers, as we have seen, might possess the most minute kind of agricultural and managerial information. George Skipwith in Alabama, Moses in North Carolina, and others of differing temperaments ran very successful operations. Their personal motives for assuming such weighty and ambiguous responsibilities are not always as clear to us as we might like them to be, but other bondsmen under such men's immediate care often fared far better than they would have directly under the hand of a white overseer or master. And though this was not always the case it appears generally to have been so.

Most slaves, in fact, knew the varied roles they might play in differing situations.[8] When they were sick, in most instances they saw to one another's needs. A sense of community thus developed out of a very common human bond—suffering. Probably as one consequence of widespread illness a host of slave conjurers and folk doctors, known for their frequent "intrusions" into plantation affairs, sometimes operated with relative impunity in both black and white communities, their spells and cures filtering into the fabric of plantation life. Slave conjurers and folk doctors have left us with some very perceptive assessments about the quality of the slave's life. They also competed with slaveholders in such important areas as the slave's obedience.

Slaves in touch with the mysteries of conjuration were occasionally summoned by masters to attend the needs of both sick slaves and masters in lieu of a white physician's services or after a physician's remedies had proven unsuccessful. Some of the available evidence traces conjurers' activities in the area of health while lamenting health problems as a matter of persistent and serious concern. The conjurer had much work to occupy his or her time and skills. One slaveholder used the services of an "old negro man named Lewis," the slave of another man, for several years, permitting him, after no doubt paying a fee to his master, "to see my woman Eliza who has been sick for 12 months or more."[9]

Slaves' capabilities illustrate that field hands rank as the most important individuals in the entire discussion of plantation slavery. It was the field hand's destiny that was most intimately tied to the institution, and he unwillingly contributed to slavery in order to sustain his very existence. He could not have done otherwise in his struggle for survival. The slave found it necessary to take care of himself as much as he could, since he could not rely on so-called paternalistic masters to see to his needs; he could not have easily understood those interpretations that depict the total-care quality of the bondage he lived through.

The bondsman's labors and behavior as a field hand illustrate that he did not leave his welfare totally to the discretion of masters or anyone else, but tried to influence it in ways beneficial to himself and loved ones. Charles Ball observed that on Sunday, usually the slave's day of rest, "it is, in truth by the exercise of his liberty on this day, that he is enabled to provide himself and his family with many of the necessaries of life, that his master refuses to supply him with."[10] A good example of what he meant is diet. The slave's personal labors produced most of the food both he and masters consumed, and he often failed to understand the reasoning behind the way it was rationed out to him and his family;[11] its amount and quality were often not what he thought they should be. He turned his efforts to Sunday gardening, hunting, and "stealing" to fill in dietary deficiencies: "there is nothing in all butcherdom so delicious as a roasted 'possum."[12] He knew too that his activities in this regard were valuable models for his children and others in the slave community, and he learned quickly that many of slavery's regulations designed to restrict and subdue his behavior had to be violated in order to give added meaning to his private life. The lesson was an essential one, speedily assimilated in the face of so much general physical and psychological hostility to blacks whose every motive might be challenged. Frederick Douglass said it well:

The doctrine that submission to violence is the best cure for violence did not hold good as between slaves and overseers. He was whipped oftener who was whipped easiest. That slave who had the courage to stand up for himself against the overseer, although he might have many hard stripes at first, became while legally a slave virtually a freeman.[13]

Such evidence helps to illustrate, too, that the repressed personalities attributed to slaves by much of our secondary source historical literature cannot be found in the record. The conspicuous absence of such personalities is in part what makes the search for the slave's identity all the more revealing. What one finds instead is a wide range of personality types and behavioral patterns influenced and shaped by a vast number of good and bad circumstances that have been little explored.

Perhaps because of this behavioral variety among slaves, one of the first things that catches the researcher's attention is the restlessness of the master slave relationship.[14] There was continually activity afoot among slaves to shift and sometimes totally erode the bonds that held them so tightly. Masters' knowledge of these kinds of influences on their daily lives and the nature of slavery in general was second only to similar knowledge among slaves themselves. For slavery's participants this restlessness related directly to recurring forms of resistance in the ranks of the slave population and not to what interpreters have often labeled the isolated presence of a slave rebel.[15] The slave's resistance to incredible circumstances was one of bondage's most persistent and —for slaveholders—expected features. Charges like the one brought against overseer W. C. Gillespie of Louisiana addressed the reasons, always present in bondage, that occasionally underlay aspects of slave resistance. Haller Nutt wrote about his former employee Gillespie, "I think I can prove very clearly that Gillespie, hung one of my negroes—and was the direct cause of two more deaths—besides a great deal of cruelty & damage to the other negroes. . . ."[16] Bondsmen did not simply stand by as such things happened to them. Whenever the occasion arose they responded in kind. Nonetheless bondsmen knew that cruelty "was an incident to the course, but the real injury was the making of a human being an animal without hope. . . ."[17]

The cruelty around the slave, engulfing him more often than he sometimes even dared admit to himself, and scorching his most tender feelings, was commonly resisted. The collective resistance signs among slaves speak of a disgruntled and occasionally rebellious slave population that in the nineteenth century became the key embodiment of those disturbing issues leading to white and black resistance in the Civil War.

Slaves constantly talked of changing their lives, often by making life unbearable for those who controlled them. But they were especially aware, as well they had to be, of the additional suffering their acts might put themselves and loved ones through in certain moments. Such matters are, of course, not easy to understand, even when a vast array of motivations is analyzed. Slavery operated in delicate balances that frequently produced numerous uninvestigated disturbances caused by groups like "a band of negroes—formed in the South in imitation of the Murrel [sic] band —to murder—depredate, and Steal negroes."[18] Most slaveholders were aware of the delicate balances that separated acceptable and unacceptable slave behavior at all levels. For resistance, they learned, took many forms, as in this interesting account:

About four years ago a negro who gave the impression of being a good subject, and even wanting to appear religious, came to see me for about a month, making me fine promises and begging me, almost on his knees to free him by buying him from a bad position. I was foolish enough to agree to this . . . ; and, in all of this, I was duped by a first-class knavery, either on the part of those who sold him to me well guaranteed, while he had been fraudulently brought into the state, or by the negro himself who, far from realizing what he had promised me, did not give me even one hundred dollars, . . . and who finally by negligence or bad will on the part of Mr. Soulé my lawyer, succeeded in having himself recognized as free, while it would have been so easy to prove the opposite. Hence I lost the negro, and, besides, I was condemned to pay him twelve Hundred dollars for *His work*.[19]

Another slaveholder extended the balance into the sometimes intertwined worlds of health and resistance. "I would rather sell &

buy unacclimated hands," he explained, "than own negroes that are dissatisfied. I care not from what Cause."[20] Resistance was endemic to slave-master relationships. Realizing how desperate one's situation could become, many slaves sought to take advantage of whatever situation they confronted.

Frequently, slaves' and masters' observations coincided on both crucial and minor issues related to bonded life, although the emphasis often varied significantly. Few plantation records dismiss the slave's folklore, dancing, and musical forms as irrelevant. Harsh plantation and farm restrictions were conceived to keep slaves in their appointed social position and perspective, but many slaveholders openly attributed the origins and vitality of much of their own social life to the creative imaginations and energies of bondsmen. In this they were quick to note what they believed were African influences or at least non-Western characteristics. Slaveholders went down to the Quarters, into the fields, and elsewhere to observe slave activities in progress, not simply for purposes of behavioral control but often for sheer enjoyment of the inventiveness they might witness. They observed the bondsman's religious forms and heard his music and folktales. Some slaveholders, of course, mocked these forms or saw them as testimony to their own power over a "childlike" race. Far many more did not, realizing how vital and life-giving much of what they observed was to plantation operations and survival. The bondsman in turn seldom doubted his rather obvious talents in these areas. There was no reason for him to do so.

Slaves, in effect, were able to structure in positive ways many of the circumstances surrounding them. One familiar interpretation of their religious forms addresses its otherworldly orientation —the longing for release and escape from this life. These features remain important to understanding the slave's enormous religious world, but what is worth equal or even greater consideration is how much the slave focused his attention on this life's physical and emotional experiences. Important exponents of this perspective were black spiritual leaders. They spoke coaxingly to the needs of their followers and dealt persuasively with the physical and emotional realities confronting them. If they did not, they could not maintain a genuine following among their fellows, for other bondsmen were apt to run them off or ignore those insensitive to life's constant realities.

Slave spiritual leaders did, for instance, counsel caution in dealing with whites, but they usually and wisely avoided counseling against retaliatory kinds of behavior they knew were bound to occur against masters. Many were quite selective about those masters who would have a pleasant life after death.[21] The figure was not very high, for from the beginning, slaves could see the hypocrisy of a society that justified their own severe oppression.

> Heaven will be no heaven to him [the bondsman], if he is not to be avenged of his enemies. I know from experience, that these are the fundamental rules of his religious creed; because I learned them, in the religious meetings of the slaves themselves.[22]

Even more traditionally oriented black Christian preachers among slaves knew the truth of these statements and realized also that to capture a following they had to compete with very skillful manipulators of the world of conjuration, a world very much concerned with structuring the events of one's present life.

This structuring was often intensely focused within the slave community. Slaves tried to influence the behavior of their fellows probably as often as they focused on restructuring that of masters. They naturally had to develop ways to function most comfortably with other bondsmen while braving the larger world of slavery. The influences they tried to exercise tended to address all levels of behavior. Indeed, bondsmen saw themselves in very complex terms. They directed their attention to romance, health, vengeance, family life, masters—to name a few of the most common concerns—and often addressed themselves delicately to having "better" relationships with husbands, wives, and children. At least in the world of conjuration bondsmen set behavioral norms, and these norms—as one index of behavior among slaves—indicate how varied they thought one another to be.

When bondsmen focused their primary attention on masters, their efforts indicate how clearly they saw what about their overlords needed to be changed in order to make life bearable. They directed their spells toward ending whippings and other kinds of punishments, and they tried extensively to modify overseers' behavior. Conjuring slaves were perceptive critics of slavery's operations and operators. They saw how the plantation regime used controlled and uncontrolled violence to enforce its will, and they tried to chip away at these features.

In the slave community, slave religious and spiritual forms were nearly all-pervasive.[23] Naturally, all bondsmen did not adhere to or practice conjuration or the often "curious" kinds of Christianity that slaves developed, but they could not escape direct influences of these worlds. While openly denouncing the ills of hoodoo for themselves and others, both Nat Turner and Denmark Vesey tried to put it to good use in their struggles. The slave's spiritualism, highly infused with the modes of an African past, is a very important key to his worldview. Some historians have seen its presence as further proof of the slave's accommodation to his bondage, one more demonstration of how masters molded Africans into exactly what they wanted them to be. But slaves were very eclectic in their approach to living, and they did not accept the conceptions of a slaveholding society that oppressed them and tried to prevent them from sharing especially in the psychological benefits that freedom affords even those who are denied many of life's other advantages. Slaves viewed many of the whites they dealt with as masters or in other capacities too frequently as unworthy persons; bondsmen did not permit themselves to fit the molds that slavery sought to pour them into.

To aid them in finding alternatives to the demands placed on them by masters, slaves cultivated varied private lives in the Quarters and family settings. The Quarters, whether it existed as a physical setting or not, was the center of much cultural and family activity. It was a collection of extensive experiences replete with singing, story telling, praying, conjuring, and suffering. For example, the words and rhythms of slave songs speak sensitively to persecution in this life leading to almost certain redemption later. This sensitivity rarely failed to persuade bondsmen that in spite of the many tribulations they endured on earth there would be just rewards for them. Most bondsmen believed that they were entitled to a certain kind of justice for all that they had suffered, but they were not simultaneously persuaded that one's situation on earth had to be fully endured for justice to be certain.[24] Their songs and folklore, two important indicators of their states of mind, seldom suggest otherwise. In cultural terms the closely related songs and folklore engulfed the bondsman from childhood, through work days in the field, in joy, sickness, old age, and death. And the Quarters, sometimes partially, sometimes entirely, and often mysteriously, encompassed and breathed its own special vitality into these experiences, frequently assuring that bondage did not snuff out the many-sided existence slaves created for themselves.

For many reasons the slave family served as the foundation for most of the slave's existence. The legal limitations placed on marriage and family relationships were never able to undermine the "sense" of family organization that most Africans possessed. Slave masters' manipulation of certain roles slave family members played need not be denied, but this manipulation was not successful in shaping the African's feeling for family life which the evidence so strongly supports. The slave family was split up repeatedly by sympathetic and unsympathetic slaveholders who saw that economic and personal needs required such splits, whatever hardships they worked on the slave population. What remained as the family unit has generally been and will continue to be the subject of very broad debate.

While the evidence needs further careful examinations, still, we know that all of the members of the slave family played roles structured largely by themselves to meet the family's survival needs. Charles Ball commented, on part of this relationship, that as "poor as the slave is, and dependent at all times upon the arbitrary will of his master, or yet more fickle caprice of the overseer, his children look up to him, in his little cabin, as their protector and supporter."[25] The slave community respected persons for the contributions they were able to make to the slave's communal life. We learn this in the narratives as well as plantation records and diaries. Slaveholders saw the family as the natural work and social unit, and this is generally where the visions of slaves and masters came together. But the slave knew that his family was the most important contributor to, and could not be easily separated from, the agonizing survival of North American slavery.

The consequences of the relationships set up by classifying men as property were nowhere so evident as in the privacy of the slave family. The emotional pressures produced by seeing blood relatives and friends sold away could not be eased. The good will of a sympathetic master could not be depended on in light of these possibilities. Many slaves with hopes so placed had them dashed against the rocks of money, profit, and racism. The slave knew that although he was "claimed" as a part of what masters commonly called their own extended black and white families, his half of the family was treated badly and capriciously. How often had he heard such familiar words as ". . . I am very desirous of keeping that family (the negroes) together." But "I have a note in [the] Bank for $600.00 for security of which I have made over to my endorser a negro boy [14 years old] contingently . . . son of a woman, & brother of some children. . . ."[26]

Slavery, in truth, had little room in its functioning for the real perpetual child or the happy-go-lucky slave. Such figures could serve no useful purpose in the slave community. It was necessary to grow up quickly in more ways than just as a master's field hand. However, in an age becoming increasingly conscious of the dilemmas slavery posed for egalitarian principles, it was a useful justification of bondage for society to spread the rumor of slave incompetence—a rumor which beyond a basic assumption of innate black inferiority broke down in daily master-slave contacts. It cannot in fact withstand the test of the evidence utilized in the preparation of this study.

In the Old South, Africans, whom we sometimes too easily call slaves, led thriving, though experientially sobered lives, in full awareness of the harsh circumstances they had to deal with in order to survive as men and women. They were never convinced by arguments concerning their own deep-seated inferiority. They knew, better than anyone else, the price one's humanity had to pay in an age that saw them as "this species of property." And they never permitted those who oppressed them so severely to live easy with their oppression.

Manuscript Sources

Two kinds of sources were most helpful in preparing this study—plantation records and slave narratives. Plantation records, which occasionally reveal such valuable items as slave letters, give the researcher a perspective on the total institution of slavery which cannot be gained any other way. These records have been explored by a few scholars but not as exhaustively as many now believe. Until recently slave narratives have not been utilized as much as they should have been. Besides disclosing many valuable insights, when they are used in tandem with manuscript sources and psychological research it can be shown that these narratives are generally more reliable than previously thought and that many are undeserving of the scorn formerly heaped upon them. They deserve further illuminating readings. In sum, each of the sources when used in relationship to the others helps the student of slavery to fit the slave's story together in a manner that I hope readers have found informative.

University of California Library, Riverside (UCR)
   Skinner Collection

Duke University Library (DU)
    Fletcher Harris Archer Letters and Papers
    Peter Barksdale Letters
    Alexander Robinson Boteler Diary
    Neill Brown Papers
    John Buford Papers
    John C. Calhoun Papers
    David Campbell Papers
    Robert Carter Plantation Records and Letterbooks
    Clement Comer Clay Papers
    Eaton Cobb Papers
    Francis Porteus Corbin Letters and Papers
    E. A. Crudup Plantation Diary
    Dismal Swamp Land Company Letters and Papers
    Samuel Smith Downey Papers
    Stirling F. Edmonds Papers
    J. Milton Emerson Journal
    William Ephriam Papers
    Chas. J. Faulkner Papers
    John Fox Letters and Papers
    William Haney Hatchett Papers
    Edward Hooker Letters and Papers
    James Hutcheson Papers
    David Flavel Jamison Papers
    George Noble Jones Papers
    Joseph Long Papers
    Duncan G. M'Call Plantation Journal and Diary
    Thomas M. McIntosh Papers
    Duncan McLaurin Papers and Letters
    Sarah Magill Papers
    Louis Manigault Papers
    Peter Minor Accounts of Estate, 1816-1835
    Haller Nutt Journal of Araby Plantation
    John Parker Manuscript Autobiography
    Lalla Pelot Papers
    Ebenezer Pettigrew Family Papers
    James W. Pierce Papers
    Charles Cotesworth Pinckney Letters
    Robert Potter Papers

Rankin-Parker Collection
William W. Renwick Papers
Richard H. Riddick Letters and Papers
William C. Ritzhugh Powell Papers
James Sheppard Letters and Papers
William Alexander Smith Papers
Benjamin T. Towner Papers
United States Census Bureau, Manuscript Census Returns for
 1860, Schedule II for Georgia, Kentucky, Louisiana, and Ten-
 nessee
David Garland Waller Papers
Henry Watson, Jr. Papers
James Moore Wayne Papers
Floyd L. Whitehead Papers
Henry J. William Papers
Levin Winder Papers
Samuel O. Wood Letters and Papers

Georgia State Archives (GSA)
 Thomas Reade R. Cobb Letters
 William Few Collection
 Richmond Oakgrove, Savannah unit, WPA

University of Georgia Library (UG)
 Baber-Blackshear Papers
 Colonel David Crenshow Barrow Papers
 Carr Collection
 John Carter Daybook
 Margaret Branch Sexton Collection
 F. O. Tichnor Papers

Henry Huntington Library, San Moreno, California (HU)
 Cabell Family Papers
 Joseph Clay Stiles Correspondence

Department of Archives, Louisiana State University (LSU)
 Michel Thomassin Andry and Family Papers
 Ashland Plantation Record Book
 John H. Bills and Family Papers
 Priscilla "Mittie" Munnikhuysen Bond Diary
 Louis A. Bringier Papers and Journal

William McAlister Britton Papers
Burgess (West) Agreement, 1804
John C. Burruss and Family Papers
Anna and Sarah Butler Correspondence
Thomas Butler and Family Papers
E. J. Capell, Pleasant Hill Plantation Record Books and Diaries
Samuel A. Cartwright and Family Papers and Diaries
Daniel Cato Statement
Rowland Chambers Diaries
Lemuel P. Conner and Family Papers
Emily Caroline Douglas Papers
Stephen and Stephen, Jr., Duncan Papers, Journals Diaries
Ellis-Farrar Papers
Edward Gary and Family Papers and Diaries
James A. Gillespie Papers and Diaries
William S. Hamilton Papers
Philip Hicky and Family Papers
Mrs. Isaac H. Hilliard Diary
Elizabeth Jefferson Reminiscences
John C. Jenkins and Family Papers
Kenner Family Papers
St. John R. Moses Liddell and Family Collection
Robert M. Livingston Letter
Samuel McCutchon Papers and Plantation Diary
John Mc Donogh Papers
R. F. McGuire Diary
Eliza L. Magruder Diary
Henry Marston and Family Papers
Charles L. Mathews and Family Papers
John Mills Letters
William J. Minor and Family Papers
James Monett Day Book and Diary (Louisiana Room)
William T. Palfrey Papers
Samuel J. Peters, Jr. Diary
Joseph X. Delfau De Pontalba Letters
Pre Aux Cleres Plantation Record Books
Alexander F. Pugh and Family Collection
Henry Remy Collection
Joseph Toole Robinson Papers

Robert H. Tyland Journals
H. M. Seale Diary
Merritt M. Shilg Memorial Collection
Slavery Collection
Alonzo Snyder Papers
Lewis Stirling and Family Papers
Calvin Taylor and Family Papers and Diaries
William Terry and Family Papers
John C. Tibbetts Correspondence
Clarissa E. Leavitt Town Diary
J. U. La Villebeuvre and Family Papers
Joseph Watson Correspondence
David Weeks and Family Collection

Maryland Historical Society, Baltimore (MHS)
Baltimore Town Account Book, 1742
Dr. John H. Bayne Papers
Grundy-Gibson Papers
Lloyd Papers
Jacob Michael Papers
Alfred J. O'Ferral Collection
William Patterson Diaries
William P. Preston Scrapbook
Mark Pringle Letterbooks
Richardson Papers
Charles Redgely Account Books
Virdin Papers
Susanna Warfield Diary

North Carolina Department of Archives and History, Raleigh (RNC)
Alexander Brevard Papers
James F. Jordan Paper
John Menan Patrick Diaries and Letter Books
David S. Reid Papers
Slavery Papers
Martin Van Buren Papers

University of North Carolina, Southern Historical Collection (UNC)
Samuel A. Agnew Diary
John D. Ashmore Plantation Journal

James B. Bailey Papers
Everard Green Baker Diaries and Plantation Notes
R. R. Barrow Journal
Battle Family Papers
Bayside Plantation Records
John Houston Bills Diary
Brashear Family Papers
Hamilton Brown Papers
John W. Brown Diary
Bumpas Journals
Burgwyn Family Papers
Burton-Young Papers
Cameron Family Papers
Mary Eliza Eve Carmichael Diary
Cocke Papers
Cole-Taylor Papers and Books
George Colmer Diary
Hardy Bryan Croom Papers
Davidson Family Papers
Dr. Louis M. De Saussure Plantation Book
Francis A. Dickins Papers
William Ethelbert Ervin Journal
Flat River Primitive Baptist Church Records
Fripp Journals
David Gavin Diary
Gayle-Crawford Papers and Books
Globe Baptist Church Records
William P. Graham Papers
James Hervey Greenlee Papers
John Berkley Grimball Diary
Peter Wilson Hairston Papers
Harding-Jackson Papers
William Hargrove General Account Book and Slave Record
Gustavus A. Henry Papers
William P. Hill Diary
Hubard Family Papers
Franklin A. Hudson Diaries
Kollock Plantation Books
Alexander J. Lawton Plantation Diary

Francis Terry Leak Diary
Lenoir Family Papers
Andrew McCollam Papers
William Parsons McCorkle Papers
Louis Manigault Plantation Records
A. W. Mangum Papers
Nicholas B. Massenburg Farm Journal
James S. Milling Papers
Columbus Morrison Journal and Accounts
John Nevitt Journal
Newstead Plantation Diary
Stephen Andrews Norfleet Diaries
William Page Papers
John Parhill Papers
Pettigrew Family Papers
P. H. Pitts Diary and Account Book
Potter and Platt Family Papers
Prudhome Papers
General John A. Quitman Papers
Mahala B. H. Roach Diary
John Rogers Books
Edmund Ruffin, Jr. Diary
Siler Slave Records
James Marion Sims Papers
Josiah Smith, Jr., Lettercopy Book
Mary R. Smith Journals
Peter Evans Smith Papers
James R. Sparkman Books
Sparkman Family Papers
John Steele Papers
Lewis Thompson Papers
A. and A. T. Walker Account Book
John Walker Diary
Zion Church and Frierson Settlement in Maury County Tennessee

University of South Carolina, South Caroliniana Library (SC)
Iverson L. Brookes Papers
Pierce Mason Butler Papers
Cantey Family Papers

Charles Family Papers
Caleb Coker Plantation Book
Bonds Conway Papers
Andrew Flinn Plantation Book
Michael Gramling Plantation Journal
James H. Hammond Plantation Book and Journal
Williams-Chestnut-Manning Papers
William Martin Catechism and Journal
William Moultri Papers
William Gilmore Simms Plantation Book
Dr. James Stuart Journal

South Carolina State Historical Commission, Columbia (SCHC)
Slavery Collection

Tulane University Library (Tul)
Burruss Family Papers
Everett Family Papers
Benjamin Farrar Papers
Joseph Jones Collection
Samuel Rankin Latta Papers and Journals
McGuire Papers
St. Martin Family Papers
William Newton Mercer Papers

Alderman Library, University of Virginia, Charlottesville (UVa.)
John Allen Letterbook
Baldwin-Lloyd Collection
Ada P. Bankhead Papers
Brown-Hunter Manuscripts
Cocke Papers
Dr. Thomas H. Clagett Papers
Edward Coles Letters
Grinnan Papers
Harris-Brady Collection
Mrs. William Houston Papers
Hunter-Garrett Journal
Jarrett and Bynum Family
Sigismunda Kimball Diary
James Monroe Papers
Letters from Liberia, Cocke Papers (typescripts)

Police Guard Manuscript Daybook, 1834-43
Public Record Office-Colonial Office (microfilm)
Register of Free Negroes, Washington County
W. M. Seward Farm Journal and Papers
David Shaver Item
Harry M. Sherman Family
Tayloe Family Papers

Virginia Historical Society (VHS)
Robert Henderson Allen Diary
Linnaeus Bolling Diary
James Powell Cocke Diary
Charles William Dabney Diary
John Tayloe Letterbook and Papers
William Macon Waller Papers
Bickerton L. Winston Slave Book

Virginia State Library (VSL)
William Cabell Diaries
Carter Family Papers (Shirley Plantation Records) (microfilm)
Jerdone Family Papers, Slave Book and Journal
William Massie Slave Book and Farm Journals

Washington, Library of Congress (LC)
Charles Bruce Family Papers
Richard R. Crawford Diary
Stephen D. Doar Plantation Records
Franklin H. Elmore Papers
Gregory Journal
James H. Hammond Papers
Daniel W. Lord Journal
James Monette Day Book and Diary
William B. Randolph Correspondence
Turner Reavis Account Book
Edmund Ruffin Diary
David W. Scott Diary
Shirley Farm Journals
Slavery Papers
Stephens Papers
Thomas Magruder Wade Family Papers
Sophie S. Wilson Diary

Notes

INTRODUCTION

1. Richard K. Cralle, ed., *Reports and Publications of John C. Calhoun* (6 vols.; New York: D. Appleton and Company, 1851-56), V, 461.
2. As quoted in Robert W. Wood, *Memorial of Edward Jarvis, Read at the Annual Meeting of the American Statistical Association,* January 16, 1885 (Boston, 1885), p. 11. See also Albert Deutsch, "The First U.S. Census of the Insane and Its Use as Pro-Slavery Propaganda," *Bulletin of the History of Medicine,* XV (1944), 469-82. For further information on views of the slave as an inferior being see Winthrop D. Jordan, *White Over Black: American Attitudes Toward the Negro, 1550-1812* (Chapel Hill: University of North Carolina Press, 1968); William Stanton, *The Leopard's Spots: Scientific Attitudes Toward Race in America, 1815-1859* (Chicago: The University of Chicago Press, Phoenix Books, 1966); and George M. Fredrickson, *The Black Image in the White Mind: The Debate on Afro-American Character and Destiny, 1817-1914* (New York: Harper and Row, 1971).
3. Cralle, ed., *John C. Calhoun,* V, 460. For a critique of the census see Edward Jarvis, *Insanity Among the Coloured Population of the Free States* (Philadelphia: T. K. & P. G. Collins, printers, 1844).
4. James G. Randall, *The Civil War and Reconstruction* (New York: D. C. Heath and Company, 1937), p. 48.
5. Stanley M. Elkins, *Slavery: A Problem in American Institutional and Intellectual Life* (2d paperback ed.; Chicago: University of Chicago Press, 1968 [1959]), p. 82. Elkins' argument for a slave type is similar in wording

to the claim advanced by Ulrich Bonnell Phillips, *American Negro Slavery* (1st paperback ed.; Baton Rouge: Louisiana State University Press, 1966), p. 291. Phillips stated that "the negroes, though with many variants, became standardized into the predominant plantation type." Three recent studies have assailed this view in important ways. See Eugene D. Genovese's recent study, *Roll, Jordan, Roll: The World the Slaves Made* (New York: Pantheon Books, 1974); John W. Blassingame, *The Slave Community: Plantation Life in the Antebellum South* (New York: Oxford University Press, 1972); George P. Rawick, *From Sundown to Sunup: The Making of the Black Community* (Westport, Conn.: Greenwood Publishing Company, 1972). All three examine the slave's view of his bondage. Consult as well the interesting but seriously flawed findings in Robert Fogel and Stanley Engerman, *Time on the Cross* (Boston: Little, Brown, 1974).

6. See note 5.

7. Elkins, *Slavery*, p. 82.

8. Kenneth M. Stampp, "The Historian and Southern Negro Slavery," *American Historical Review*, LVII (April, 1952), 617. Stampp, *The Peculiar Institution: Slavery in the Ante-bellum South* (New York: Vintage Books, 1956), makes the case for extensive role-playing in his chapter "A Troublesome Property"; Elkins, *Slavery*, pp. 80-86, argues that slaves who played roles such as the docile bondsman ultimately became the role they played. In a much later response to this, Stampp, "Rebels and Sambos: The Search for the Negro's Personality in Slavery," *Journal of Southern History*, XXXVII (August, 1971), 373, 389, recognizes that some slaves became the personality type known as Sambo, but argues against Sambo as a dominant figure. Blassingame, *The Slave Community*, p. 200, writes too that "Some slaves were compelled to shape their behavior so completely to the white man's moods that they became Sambos."

9. Among the most important studies to consult for an understanding of the slavery controversy are, in addition to those previously mentioned, Ann J. Lane, ed., *The Debate Over Slavery: Stanley Elkins and His Critics* (Urbana: University of Illinois Press, 1971); the 1966 edition of Phillips' *American Negro Slavery* which has a revealing foreword by Eugene Genovese entitled "Ulrich Bonnell Phillips and His Critics"; John Hope Franklin, *From Slavery to Freedom* (3d ed.; New York: Vintage Books, 1967); Frank Tannenbaum, *Slave and Citizen: The Negro in the Americas* (New York: Vintage Books, 1946); Chapter XIII, "The Lot of the Bondsman," in Allan Nevins, *Ordeal of the Union, I: Fruits of Manifest Destiny, 1847-1852* (New York: Charles Scribner's Sons, 1947); Chapter V, "Slavery in a World Setting," in Nevins, *The Emergence of Lincoln, II: Prologue to Civil War, 1859-1861* (New York: Charles Scribner's Sons, 1950) makes significant use of Tannenbaum's pioneering study—a usage antedating Elkins; Robert S. Starobin, *Industrial Slavery in the Old South* (New York: Oxford University Press, 1970); Carl

N. Degler, *Neither Black nor White: Slavery and Race Relations in Brazil and the United States* (New York: The Macmillan Company, 1971).

10. Susanna Warfield Diary, entry for February 5, 1849, MHS.

11. Fredrickson, *The Black Image in the White Mind*, Chapter II.

1. DRAWING THE COLOR LINE

1. See the beautifully descriptive but not always reliable account in Wilbur J. Cash, *The Mind of the South* (New York: Alfred A. Knopf, 1941), Chapters I, II.

2. See Stampp, *The Peculiar Institution*, Chapter I.

3. See, for example, Carl Bridenbaugh, *Myths and Realities: Societies of the Colonial South* (Baton Rouge: Louisiana State University Press, 1952).

4. See Arthur Zilversmit, *The First Emancipation: The Abolition of Slavery in the North* (Chicago: The University of Chicago Press, 1967), p. 220, for an extended discussion of the debate bringing about the end of slavery in northern states, primarily New England.

5. *Ibid.*, p. 222.

6. The statistics in this brief survey come from the returns of the U.S. Bureau of the Census covering the period 1790 to 1860. See also another bureau publication, *A Century of Population Growth: From the First Census of the United States to the Twelfth*, 1790-1900 (New York, 1964); Richard Wade, *Slavery in the Cities: The South*, 1820-1860 (New York: Oxford University Press, 1964), of which Chapter I and the Appendix have a good survey of the numbers and geographical dispersement of slaves in urban areas; and Robert S. Starobin, *Industrial Slavery in the Old South* (New York: Oxford University Press, 1970), pp. 11-12, for a rundown of slaves employed in southern industry.

7. See note 6 of *A Century of Population Growth*.

8. Everett C. Hughes, "Good People and Dirty Work," *Social Problems*, X (Summer, 1962), 3-11, has an interesting discussion of how the general populace tends to support the action and mores of a vocal and ruling minority against outcast groups. See further Eric Foner, *Free Soil, Free Labor, Free Men: The Ideology of the Republican Party Before the Civil War* (New York: Oxford University Press, 1970), p. 261.

9. Thomas Jefferson, *Notes on the State of Virginia*, ed. Adrienne Koch (New York: Random House, 1944), p. 256.

10. *Ibid.*, p. 262.

11. Quoted in Silvio A. Bedini, *The Life of Benjamin Banneker* (New York: Charles Scribner's Sons, 1972), p. 152.

12. Jordan, *White Over Black*, p. 6.

13. The New English Bible Standard Edition (Oxford University Press and Cambridge University Press, 1970).

14. Lamentations 4:7, 8. This is not singularly a biblical phenomenon. See non-biblical antecedents in Frank Snowden, *Blacks in Antiquity* (Cambridge, Mass.: Harvard University Press, 1970).

15. See Edward K. Trefz, "Satan as the Prince of Evil: The Preaching of New England Puritans," *The Boston Public Quarterly*, VII (January, 1955), 3-22; Trefz, "Satan in Puritan Preaching," *Ibid.*, VIII (April, 1956), 71-84; Trefz, "Satan in Puritan Preaching," *Ibid.*, VIII (July, 1956), 148-59.

16. "The Epistle of Barnabas, *The Apostolic Fathers*. Trans. Kirsopp Lake (2 vols.; New York: G. P. Putnam's Sons, 1919), I, 407; see also Adolphe Didron, *Christian Iconography: The History of Christian Art in the Middle Ages* (2 vols.; New York: Frederick Unger, 1965). Originally published in 1851. See Vol. II, "Iconography of Devils," 109-52; in Vol. I, 467, Didron notes that "in the History of the Devil a great number of texts will be given in which Satan is called an Ethiopian, black, smoky, dark, while angels and good genii are white. . . ."

17. Quoted in Walter L. Wakefield and Austin P. Evans, eds., *Heresies of the High Middle Ages* (New York: Columbia University Press, 1969), p. 75.

18. *St. Bernard's Sermons on the Canticle of Canticles* (Dublin: Browne and Nolan, 1920), p. 272.

19. The ambivalence about color expressed in St. Bernard's sermons is a recurring theme in Western European thought. See the origins of this ambivalence in Snowden, *Blacks in Antiquity*.

20. Olaudah Equiano, *The Interesting Narrative of Olaudah Equiano, or Gustavus Vasa, the African* (London: Stationers Hall, 1789), p. 8.

21. Alvin to ———, Summer, 1863, Skinner Collection, UCR.

22. *The Anti-Slavery Papers of James Russell Lowell* (2 vols.; Boston: Houghton Mifflin and Co., 1902), I, pp. 16, 20.

23. John Franklin Beard, ed., *The Letters and Journals of James Fenimore Cooper* (6 vols.; Cambridge, Mass.: Harvard University Press, 1960), I, 189-98. See also Robert E. Spiller, "Fenimore Cooper's Defense of Slave-Owning America," *American Historical Review*, XXV (April, 1930), 575-582.

24. *Southern Literary Messenger*, V (1839), 678.

25. Frederick Law Olmsted, *A Journey in the Seaboard Slave States in the Years 1853-1854* (2 vols.; New York: G. P. Putnam's Sons, 1904), II, 243.

26. R. Q. Mallard, *Plantation Life Before Emancipation* (Richmond, Va.: Whittet & Shepperson, 1892), p. 60.

27. Samuel A. Cartwright, "Natural History of the Prognathous Species of Mankind," *Annual Catalogue of the Medical Department of the University of the State of Missouri: Session of 1847-1848* (St. Louis, 1848), p. 709. Cartwright comments that "the lighter shades of color, when not derived

from admixture with Mongolian or Caucasian blood, indicate degeneration in the prognathous species."

28. *The Emancipator* (April 30, 1820).

29. D. W. Mitchell, *Ten Years in the United States: Being an Englishman's Views of Men and Things in the North and South* (London: Smith, Elder, and Co., 1862), pp. 241-42. In many regions of the Old South a high percentage of free blacks were mulattoes. For example, in Washington County, Virginia, in the twenty-three years before the Civil War, approximately 80 per cent of the free blacks living in the county were officially designated mulattoes. See the manuscript Register of Free Blacks, Washington County, Virginia, UVa.

30. Francis Fedric, *Slave Life in Virginia and Kentucky* (London: Wertheim, Mcintosh, and Hunt, 1863), p. 45.

31. For testimony on the Vesey conspiracy see Lionel H. Kennedy and Thomas Parker, *An Official Report of the Trial of Sundry Negroes Charged with an Attempt to Raise an Insurrection in the State of South Carolina* (Charleston: 1822).

32. Frances Ann Kemble, *Journal of a Residence on a Georgia Plantation in 1838-1839*, ed. John A. Scott (New York: Alfred A. Knopf, 1961), p. 234.

33. William Wells Brown, *Narrative of William Wells Brown, A Fugitive* (Boston: Anti-Slavery Office, 1847), p. 21.

34. Mallard, *Plantation Life*, p. 60.

35. Timothy Alden, *A Collection of American Epitaphs* (5 vols.; New York: Whiting and Watson, 1814), III, 60-61.

36. F. O. Ticknor to his sister, sometime after 1844, F. O. Ticknor Papers, UG; *De Bow's Review*, XI (1850), 335.

37. Edwin Adams Davis and William Ransom Hogan, *The Barber of Natchez* (Baton Rouge: Louisiana State University Press, 1954), p. 16.

38. Helen T. Catterall, ed., *Judicial Cases Concerning American Slavery and the Negro* (5 vols.; Washington, D.C.: Carnegie Institution, 1926-37), II, 119.

39. *Ibid.*, II, 109.

40. *Ibid.*, II, 103.

41. Louis A. Bringier to Monde, July 8, 1859, Louis A. Bringier Papers and Journal, LSU.

42. John C. Hurd, *The Law of Freedom and Bondage in the United States* (2 vols.; Boston: Little, Brown, 1858), II, 4, 19, 86, 90, 340.

43. Ebenezer Davies, *American Scenes, and Christian Slavery: A Recent Tour of Four Thousand Miles in the United States* (London: John Snow, 1849), p. 196.

44. Hurd, *The Law of Freedom and Bondage*, I, 43.

45. Statement of Jacob Bieller, Snyder Family Papers, LSU.

46. James Steer to John Minor, February 23, 1818, William J. Minor and Family Papers, LSU.

47. Seymour B. Treadwell, *American Liberties and American Slavery* (Boston: Welks, Jordan and Co., 1838), pp. 209-10.

48. Catterall, *Judicial Cases*, II, 530.

49. George Washington to General Alex. Spotswood, November 23, 1794, *A Documentary History of American Industrial Society: Plantation and Frontier*, ed. U. B. Phillips (2 vols.; Cleveland: The Arthur H. Clark Company, 1910), II, 56.

50. For extensive information on field slaves and other matters relating to bondsmen the slave narratives are invaluable. See especially the W.P.A. testimony of ex-slaves, much of which has been made generally available in George P. Rawick, ed., *The American Slave: A Composite Autobiography* (19 vols.; Westport, Conn.: Greenwood Publishing Company, 1972). On the sounding of the bell or horn see Vol. XVIII, Fisk University, *Unwritten History of Slavery*, p. 216. These volumes shall otherwise be cited as Rawick with the particular state narrative or Fisk University for the last two volumes.

51. Austin Steward, *Twenty-Two Years a Slave, and Forty Years a Freeman* (Rochester, N.Y.: William Alling, 1857), p. 15.

52. J. R. Brock to John Manning, June 16, 1840, Williams-Chestnut-Manning Papers, SC. On work hours see *Dr. Daniel Drake's Letters on Slavery to John C. Warren of Boston* (reprinted from the National Intelligencer, Washington, April 3, 5 and 7, 1851), p. 15.

53. On this point see Snowden, *Blacks in Antiquity*.

2. INTO THE FIELDS—LIFE, DISEASE, AND LABOR IN THE OLD SOUTH

1. P. Hairston to his father, December 4, 1821, Peter Wilson Hairston Papers, UNC.

2. Henry Tayloe to ———, July 15, 1835, Tayloe Family Papers, UVa.

3. See the reliable description in John Brown, *Slave Life in Georgia: A Narrative of the Life, Suffering, and Escape of John Brown, A Fugitive Slave, Now in England* (London: W. M. Watts, 1855), pp. 171-72.

4. Frederick Douglass, *Life and Times of Frederick Douglass* (New York: Collier Books, 1962 [1892]), p. 124.

5. Landon Carter Diary, entry for February 9, 1772, Carter Family Papers, VSL.

6. Charles Manigault to Louis Manigault, November 22, 1856, Louis Manigault Papers, DU.

7. Basil Hall, *Travels in North America in the Years 1827 and 1828* (2 vols.; Philadelphia: Carey, Lea and Carey, 1829), II, 222-23.

8. Elizabeth W. Pringle, *Chronicles of Chicora Wood* (New York: Charles Scribner's Sons, 1922), p. 67.

9. Haller Nutt Journal, entry for December 8, 1843, DU.

10. See Solomon Northup, *Twelve Years a Slave* (Baton Rouge: Louisiana State University Press, 1970 [1853]), pp. 159-63.

11. W. P. Gordon to E. J. Tayloe, June 30, 1856, Tayloe Family Papers, UVa.

12. *Ibid.*

13. Franklin, *From Slavery to Freedom*, p. 194.

14. *De Bow's Review*, X (1851), 326.

15. *Ibid.*, XXXIV (1858), 323.

16. Overseer to General John A. Quitman, October 28, 1853, Quitman Papers, UNC.

17. Charles C. Jones, *The Religious Instruction of the Negroes* (Savannah: Thomas Purse, 1842), p. 209.

18. William C. Emerson, *Stories and Spirituals of the Negro Slave* (Boston: R. G. Badger and Gorham Press, 1930), p 35.

19. Mr. Hicks to S. S. Downey, July 14, 1836, Samuel Smith Downey Papers, DU; William B. Lenoir to General William Lenoir, December 27, 1834, Lenoir Family Papers, UNC. See also the Shirley Plantation Records, entry for January 19, 1857, VSL, where we read about "the most dreadful snow storm I ever knew, drifting up even with the fences in many places, & filling up all the shelters . . . driving into the negro quarters through the shingles. . . ."

20. Haller Nutt Journal, entry for June 17, 1846, DU.

21. James H. Hammond to Lewis Tappan, September 6, 1850, James H. Hammond Papers, LC.

22. S. Palfrey to William T. Palfrey, December 5, 1836, William T. Palfrey Papers, LSU.

23. *De Bow's Review*, IX (1850), 325.

24. H. W. H. to William N. Mercer, March 22, 1837, William Newton Mercer Papers, TUL.

25. Thomas Affleck, "On the Hygiene of Cotton Plantations and the Management of Negro Slaves," *Southern Medical Reports* II (1850), 433. See Leland Langridge, "Asiatic Cholera in Louisiana, 1832-1873" (unpublished M.A. thesis, Louisiana State University, 1955).

26. James Brown to J. H. Bills, February 21, 1846, John H. Bills and Family Papers, LSU.

27. See Eugene Genovese, "The Medical and Insurance Costs of Slaveholding in the Cotton Belt," *Journal of Negro History*, XLV (July, 1960),

141; Robert S. Starobin, *Industrial Slavery in the Old South* (New York: Oxford University Press, 1970), p. 71.

28. Policy of slaves dated January 5, 1847, William McAlister Britton Papers, LSU.

29. James Drewry to Captain Paschal Buford, December 13, 1853, John Buford Papers, LSU.

30. C. T. Wills to John Buford, February 25, 1854, *ibid.*

31. James F. ———— to W. T. B. Haysworth, March 21, 1851, James F. Jordan Paper, RNC. Genovese calculates that slave premiums ran from two to three per cent of the slave's value. See note 27.

32. J. D. B. De Bow, *Industrial Resources* (2 vols.; New York: D. Appleton & Co., 1854), II, 298-99.

33. Alexander J. Lawton Plantation Diary, I, April 23, 1817, UNC.

34. Charles Ball, *Slavery in the United States: A Narrative of the Life and Adventures of Charles Ball* (New York: John S. Taylor, 1837), p. 60.

35. Landon Carter Diary, entry for September, 1771, Carter Family Papers, VSL. Joe Gray Taylor, *Negro Slavery in Louisiana* (Baton Rouge: Louisiana Historical Association, 1963), p. 152.

36. Henry Turner to General John A. Quitman, June 11, 1842, Quitman Papers, UNC.

37. Some masters did worry about how their bondsmen viewed them, though there was still an enormous amount of neglect where slaves were concerned. More important were masters' fears of resistance if they did not at least make the effort to accommodate some of these personal needs.

38. Everard Green Baker Diary, I, April, 1852, UNC.

39. Samuel A. Agnew Diary, III, entry for June 6, 1854, UNC.

40. See U. B. Phillips, *Life and Labor in the Old South* (Boston: Little, Brown, 1963 [1929]), Chapters X and XI.

41. Ino. E. Schley to Ann Tower, July 1, 1841, Benjamin T. Towner Papers, DU.

42. Allen Brown to Hamilton Brown, December 7, 1834, Hamilton Brown Papers, UNC.

43. Margaret Brashear to Frances Brashear, January 30, 1833, Brashear Family Papers, UNC.

44. John Berkley Grimball Diary, entry for August 9, 1832, UNC; see further Doris Yvonne Bacon, "The Health of Slaves on Louisiana Plantations, 1840-1860" (unpublished M.A. thesis, Louisiana State University, 1958).

45. Francis Terry Leak Diary, entry for June 24, 1855, UNC.

46. N. P. S. Hamilton to Charles L. Mathews, August 14, 1861, Charles L. Mathews and Family Papers, LSU.

47. John Mc Donogh letter, November 18, 1822, John Mc Donogh Papers, LSU; see also Martha Mitchell, "Health and the Medical Profession in the Lower South, 1845-1860," *Journal of Southern History*, X (November,

1944), 424-46. In 1858 James Henry Hammond theorized that "all persons brought up in Charleston have the yellow fever once. . . . Nearly all have it very young" (Hammond to William Gilmore Simms, September 21, 1858, James H. Hammond Papers, LC). See also Dr. Kenneth Clarke to L. Thompson, October 14, 1853, Lewis Thompson Papers, UNC: "Our whole country is impregnated with partial yellow fever miasma and our country towns from the Gulph to Natches on the Mississippi and to Shreveport on Red River Louisiana are almost depopulated many falling victims to the malady, the other flying to the country."

48. R. F. McGuire Diary, entry for Dec. 23, 1818, to March 13, 1819, LSU.

49. Yellow fever also infects rodents, opossums, and other animals that some Southerners, especially slaves, ate to supplement their diets.

50. See William Dosite Postell, *The Health of Slaves on Southern Plantations* (Baton Rouge: Louisiana State University Press, 1951), p. 8, who explores southern physicians' fixation with a miasma as the single cause of most diseases. See also James Hammond to William Gilmore Simms, September 21, 1858, James H. Hammond Papers, LC.

51. The swarms of mosquitoes were often so great that they could be clearly heard for more than a quarter of a mile; some planters left portions of their lands wooded or uncultivated because they were so infested with mosquitoes as to be uninhabitable even by workers. See Ball, *Narrative*, p. 197.

52. Henry to Sarah Tyler, April 27, 1849, Quitman Papers, UNC; see further Robert H. Crede, "The Physician, Emotions and Medical Illness," *Psychosomatics*, IX (January-February, 1968), 1-3. He writes, "At any point in time, the patient's state of health is affected by multiple factors: genetic endowment, environmental experiences and external influences, e.g., bacterial, physical, social."

53. Quoted in Felice Swados, "Negro Health on the Antebellum Plantations," *Bulletin of the History of Medicine*, X (October, 1941), 465.

54. *Annual Catalogue of the Medical Department of the University of the State of Missouri (Session of 1847-48)*, p. 702; Kenneth Stampp, *The Peculiar Institution*, p. 303. For a discussion of the particularities of slave susceptibility to disease see J. H. Lewis, *Biology of the Negro* (Chicago: The University of Chicago Press, 1942). About yellow fever he writes, "One of the best-established facts in the epidemiology of yellow fever is that the Negro shows a resistance to the disease not shown by any other race" (p. 210). In contrast, "Negroes seem to be much more susceptible to whooping cough than white people" (p. 216). In Africa many natives developed a sickle-cell blood characteristic which was helpful in fighting off some strains of malaria. One may suppose that some brought the trait with them to America, which helps explain their partial resistance in areas of the South heavy with malaria. In modern times the sickle-cell characteristic, no longer of benefit,

exists in one out of every 600 blacks, creating an anemic quality accompanied by much fatigue, painful periods of crisis and sometimes paralysis. The life span of its victims, though not necessarily its carriers, is comparatively short.

55. Haller Nutt Journal, section entitled "Directions in Treatment of the Sick." DU.

56. Genovese, "The Medical and Insurance Costs of Slaveholding in the Cotton Belt," p. 147.

57. Robert Henderson Allen Diary, entry for March 7, 1859, VHS.

58. Rosa H. ——— to Sarah Magill, July 25, 1850, Sarah Magill Papers, DU; see also Richard Shryock, "Medical Practice in the Old South," *South Atlantic Quarterly*, XXIX (April, 1930), 160-78.

59. *New Orleans Monthly Medical Register*, I (August 1, 1852), 129.

60. Rawle to Francis P. Corbin, August 7, 1833, Francis Porteus Corbin Letters and Papers, DU.

61. Isaac Avery to Thomas Lenoir, June 24, 1824, Lenoir Papers, UNC.

62. Mallard, *Plantation Life Before Emancipation*, p. 34.

63. Josiah Henson, *An Autobiography of the Reverend Josiah Henson* (London: "Christian Age" Office, 1877), p. 39.

64. Haller Nutt Journal, entry for February 10, 1843, DU.

65. James Hammond to William Gilmore Simms, July 17, 1861, James H. Hammond Papers, LC.

66. See Shryock, "Medical Practice in the Old South," and the *Annual Catalogue . . . Missouri*.

67. William Wells Brown, *Narrative of William Wells Brown, A Fugitive Slave* (Boston: Anti-Slavery Office, 1847), p. 25.

68. Louis Hughes, *Thirty Years a Slave* (Milwaukee: South Side Printing Company, 1897), p. 22.

69. John Q. Anderson, "Folklore in the Writings of the Louisiana Swamp Doctor," *Southern Folklore Quarterly* (December, 1955), XIX, 243-51.

70. Robert Carter to Bennett Real, September 15, 1781, Robert Carter Plantations Records and Letterbooks, DU.

71. John Walker Diary, II, entry for July 19, 1833, UNC.

72. *De Bow's Review*, XXIV (1858), 322.

73. See Fedric, *Slave Life in Virginia and Kentucky*, p. 25. The practice was widespread.

74. Adam Hodgson, *Letters from North America, Written During a Tour in the United States and Canada* (2 vols.; London: Hurst Robinson & Co., 1824), I, 45.

75. See Charles S. Sydnor, *Slavery in Mississippi* (paperback ed.; Baton Rouge: Louisiana State University Press, 1966), p. 49.

76. Thomas Affleck, "On the Hygiene of Cotton Plantations and the Management of Negro Slaves," *Southern Medical Reports*, II (1850), 435.

77. Rawick, ed., *Florida Narratives*, p. 174.

78. Gilbert Osofsky speaks directly to this point in his edited work, *Puttin' On Old Massa* (New York: Harper Torch Books, 1969), p. 38; in surveying the slave narratives he writes, "Elkins suggests that slaves found models of behavior and authority, 'significant others,' in the master caste. The narrators say the models were more likely to be other slaves." Osofsky's point seems to be substantiated fully by the manuscript sources.

79. Haller Nutt Journal, entry for February 10, 1843, DU.

80. John Houston Bills Diary, entry for January 16, 1846, UNC.

81. Samuel A. Cartwright Diary, entry for May 2, 1832, Samuel A. Cartwright Papers, LSU.

82. Joseph Hicks to S. S. Downey, February 27, 1836, Samuel Smith Downey Papers, DU.

83. Miller to James Sheppard, July 16, 1859, James Sheppard Letters and Papers, DU.

84. Francis Wyse, *America: Its Realities and Resources* (2 vols.; London: T. C. Newby, 1846), II, 68. He wrote, "The average term of life of a slave, in the Southern States, from the time that he is put to work, is variously estimated from five to six, or at furthest eight years." Charles S. Sydnor, "Life Span of Mississippi Slaves," *American Historical Review*, XXXV (April, 1930), 566-74, assails Wyse's claim, arguing that the notion that slaves "were generally worked to death in about seven years is certainly untrue. . . ." Census returns reveal that bondsmen had a lower average age than whites at the time of death but not markedly lower. The discussion of the average length of the slave's life continues to produce conflicting results. See Fogel and Engerman, *Time on the Cross*, pp. 125-26, who set the average at 36 years as compared to 40 years for whites in 1850. Consult as well Robert Evans, Jr., "The Economics of American Negro Slavery," in Universities–National Committee for Economic Research, *Aspects of Labor Economics* (Princeton: Princeton University Press, 1962), pp. 185-243. More interesting is the fact that although slaves were thought to be exceptional breeders, their numbers, percentage-wise, increased slightly less proportionally than the white population at large. See A Century of Population Growth, p. 80.

85. E. G. W. Butler to Thomas Butler, February 7, 1830, Thomas Butler and Family Papers, LSU.

86. Moses Liddell to John Liddell, November 13, 1838, St. John R. Moses Liddell and Family Papers, LSU. Northrup, *Twelve Years A Slave*, pp. 116-17.

87. Moses Liddell to John Liddell, November 13, 1838.

88. F. L. Olmsted, *A Journey in the Back Country in the Winter of 1853-54* (2 vols.; New York: G. P. Putnam's Sons, 1907), I, 83.

89. Northrup, *Twelve Years a Slave*, p. 117: "They plough, drag, drive team, clear wild lands, work on the highways, and so forth."

90. John B. Cade, "Out of the Mouths of Ex-Slaves," *Journal of Negro History*, XX (July, 1935), 309.

91. Andrew Flinn Plantation Book, 1840, Rule 15, SC. Also see Swados, "Negro Health on the Antebellum Plantations."

92. See Stampp, *The Peculiar Institution*, p. 316; Sydnor, *Slavery in Mississippi*, p. 64.

93. Louis Manigault to Charles Manigault, April 19, 1853, Louis Manigault Papers, DU.

94. Sydnor, *Slavery in Mississippi*, p. 49.

95. Affleck, "On the Hygiene of Cotton Plantations," 435.

96. R. F. McGuire Diary, entry for July, 1829, LSU.

97. Landon Carter Farm Journal, entry for March 12, 1772, Carter Family Papers, VSL.

98. Fedric, *Slave Life in Virginia and Kentucky*, p. 6; John Spencer Bassett, *The Southern Plantation Overseer as Revealed in His Letters* (Northampton, Mass.: Southworth Press, 1925), p. 21.

99. Henry Bibb, *Narrative of the Life and Adventures in Puttin' On Ole Massa*, p. 116. Shryock, "Medical Practices in the Old South," p. 175, writes, "The Negro children who survived were often suckled by hurried or overheated mothers from the fields, were more or less filthy, and were commonly infected with intestinal parasites of one sort or another."

100. See the George Colmer Diary, UNC. Colmer was the physician in attendance during the polio epidemic.

101. Ebenezer Pettigrew to James C. Johnston, September 23, 1821, Pettigrew Papers, UNC.

102. Ball, *Narrative*, p. 265. See also *De Bow's Review*, XXIV (1858), 323.

103. Sophia Watson to Henry Watson, June 26, 1848, Henry Watson, Jr., Papers, DU. Francis Terry Leak Diary, III, entry for February 5, 1853, UNC: "There has been great mortality among my little negroes during the last nine months" was a typical diary notation. In this instance fourteen died, and "but one of the above children was as old as four years."

104. Fedric, *Slave Life in Virginia and Kentucky*, pp. 7-8.

105. Compare E. E. Evans-Pritchard, *Witchcraft, Oracles and Magic Among the Azande* (Oxford: Clarendon Press, 1937).

106. James Mclvin to Mr. Audlel Clark Britton, September 29, 1862, William McAlister Britton Papers, LSU.

107. Richard R. Crawford Diary, entry for a Sunday in 1845, LC; see also Landon Carter Farm Journal, entry for April 4, 1772, Carter Family Papers, VSL.

108. *De Bow's Review*, XXXI (1861), 98.

109. *Ibid.*, XXV (1858), 42; Robert H. Crede, "The Physician, Emotions and Medical Illness," *Psychosomatics*, IX (1968), 1-3.

110. William Dosite Postell, "Mental Health Among the Slave Population on Southern Plantations," *The American Journal of Psychiatry*, CX (July, 1953), 52-54.

111. Clement Eaton, *The Growth of Southern Civilization, 1790-1860* (New York: Harper & Row, 1961), p. 64.

112. Robert Carter to Dr. Geo. Steptoe, January 28, 1779, Carter Family Papers, VSL.

113. William Pettigrew to his sister, January-February, 1857, Pettigrew Family Papers, UNC.

114. *Ibid.*, June 15, 1857.

115. Deutsch, "The First U.S. Census of the Insane and Its Use as Pro-Slavery Propaganda," p. 480.

116. See John C. Jenkins and Family Papers, LSU; Floyd L. Whitehead Papers, court order, July, 1832, DU.

117. Talbot Sweeney to Hill Carter, September 24, 1858, Carter Family Papers, VSL. This sum was more than the total yearly medical bill for most plantations.

118. Marc Fried, "Social Differences in Mental Health," in *Black Conflict with White America: A Reader in Social and Political Analysis*, ed. Jack R. Van Der Slik (Columbus, Ohio: Charles E. Merrill Co., 1970), p. 113.

119. Floyd L. Whitehead Papers, court order, July, 1832, DU.

120. *New Orleans Medical and Surgical Journal*, X, 244.

121. Starobin, *Industrial Slavery in the Old South*, p. 154; Kathleen Bruce, *Virginia Iron Manufacture in the Slave Era* (New York: The Century Co., 1931).

122. Daniel W. Lord Journal, entry for May 20, 1824, LC.

123. John Cabell to Richard Cralle, July 7, 1833, Cabell Family Papers, HU.

124. Bruce, *Virginia Iron Manufacture in the Slave Era*, p. 248.

125. Caroline Gilman, *Recollections of a Southern Matron* (New York: Harper & Brothers, 1838), p. 80.

126. Sydnor, *Slavery in Mississippi*, p. 66.

127. *Narrative of the Life of Moses Grandy* (London: C. Gilpin, 1843), pp. 51-52.

128. Mary Woodson to the mayor of Alexandria, June 21, 1813, Slavery Papers, LC.

129. M. W. Jackson to Thomas H. Clagett, December 20, 1841, Thomas H. Clagett Papers, UVa.

130. Phillips, *American Negro Slavery*, makes this case for planters in an attempt to stress the paternal features of slavery.

131. William Pettigrew to Charles Pettigrew, September 28, 1844, Pettigrew Family Papers, UNC.

132. Articles in the newspapers of the time frequently commented on such

practices. See, for example, issues of the Raleigh *Standard* during the 1840's and 1850's.

3. *BLACKSTRAP MOLASSES AND CORNBREAD—DIET AND ITS IMPACT ON BEHAVIOR*

1. The most thorough investigation of southern agriculture is Lewis C. Gray, *History of Agriculture in the Southern United States to 1860* (2 vols.; Washington, D.C.: The Carnegie Institute, 1933). See also the more recent discussion in Fogel and Engerman, *Time on the Cross*.

2. See Eugene D. Genovese, *The Political Economy of Slavery* (New York: Vintage Books, 1965), p. 45; John Hebron Moore, *Agriculture in Ante-Bellum Mississippi* (New York: Bookman Associates, 1958), p. 61.

3. James H. Hammond Plantation Book, SC. Also see Franklin, *From Slavery to Freedom*, p. 193, for a reliable capsulization of weekly food rations, and Fogel and Engerman, *Time on the Cross*, pp. 107-57, "The Anatomy of Exploitation."

4. Hammond Plantation Book.

5. De Bow, *The Industrial Resources*, II, 336.

6. This did not hold true throughout the Old South, but citations of this practice do appear often enough to support this statement.

7. Carter Family Papers, entry for January 12, 1858, VSL.

8. De Bow, *The Industrial Resources*, II, 319.

9. David Gavin Diary, I, entry for June 29, 1862, UNC.

10. Joseph Hicks to S. S. Downey, May 14, 1836, Samuel Smith Downey Papers, DU.

11. Bibb, *Narrative*, p. 99. See also Rawick, ed., *The American Slave*, XVIV, Fisk University, *God Struck Me Dead*, p. 163.

12. John Mills to Gilbert Jackson, May 19, 1807, John Mills Letters, LSU.

13. Thomas Affleck, "On the Hygiene of Cotton Plantations and the Management of Negro Slaves," *Southern Medical Reports*, II (1850), 429-36.

14. Charles C. Jones, *The Religious Instruction of the Negro* (Princeton: O'Harte and Company, 1842), p. 241.

15. Henry Turner to John Quitman, September 5, 1845, Quitman Papers, UNC.

16. Mark Pringle Letterbooks, II, 67, MHS.

17. John W. Brown Diary, entry for February 4, 1855, UNC.

18. Charles Elliott, *Sinfulness of American Slavery* (2 vols.; Cincinnati: L. Swormstedt & A. Poe, 1857), I, 207.

19. Genovese, *The Political Economy of Slavery*, p. 44. See the counter-

argument in Fogel and Engerman, *Time on the Cross*, p. 109: "The belief that the typical slave was poorly fed is without foundation in fact."

20. See Corinne Hogden, *Basic Nutrition and Diet Therapy* (London: Collier-Macmillan Co., 1970), for an informative discussion.

21. Herbert Anthony Kellar, ed., *Solon Robinson, Pioneer and Agriculturist* (2 vols.; Indianapolis: Indiana Historical Bureau, 1936), II, 161.

22. *De Bow's Review*, X (1851), 326. Fat is of course a valuable source of calories.

23. Benjamin Botkin, ed., *Lay My Burden Down: A Folk History of Slavery* (Chicago: The University of Chicago Press, 1945), p. 84.

24. Kemble, *Journal of a Residence on a Georgian Plantation in 1838-1839*, p. 145.

25. De Bow, *The Industrial Resources*, II, 336.

26. Lewis Clarke, *Narrative of the Sufferings of Lewis Clarke, during a Captivity of More than Twenty-five Years Among the Algerines of Kentucky* (Boston: D. H. Eli, 1845), p. 24.

27. Isaac D. Williams, *Sunshine and Shadow of Slave Life* (East Saginaw, Mich.: Evening News Printing and Binding House, 1885), pp. 58-59.

28. These figures are taken from standard calorie charts. Calorie intake in this discussion stands far below the estimates arrived at in Fogel and Engerman, *Time on the Cross*, p. 112, but were computed by the present author before that work appeared.

29. Compare Hogden, *Basic Nutrition and Diet Therapy*; Emanuel Cheraskin, *Diet and Disease* (Emmaus, Pa.: Rodale Books, 1968); Marie B. Krause, *Food, Nutrition and Diet Therapy* (Philadelphia: Saunders, 1966).

30. R. A. McCance and Elsie M. Widdowson, eds., *Calorie Deficiencies and Protein Deficiencies: Proceedings of a Colloquium held in Cambridge, April 1967* (Boston: Little, Brown, 1968), pp. 175-89, 319-28.

31. *Ibid.*, pp. 229, 249, 250; Ball, *Narrative*, p. 43.

32. Robert Hutchison, *Food and the Principles of Dietetics* (London: Edward Arnold, Ltd., 1956), p. 153; Kellar, ed., *Solon Robinson*, II, 381, notes that in parts of the Old South, but specifically on Edisto Isle, the primary sea-cotton island off the coast of South Carolina, "the diet is almost exclusively vegetable. . . ."

33. Samuel Cartwright, *The Pathology and Treatment of Cholera* (New Orleans: n.p., 1849), p. 394. Genovese, *The Political Economy of Slavery*, pp. 44-45, has a few thoughts relating to these matters which are concise but informative.

34. See G. E. W. Wolstenholme and Maeve O'Connor, eds., *Nutrition and Infection* (Boston: Little, Brown, 1967).

35. *Dr. Daniel Drake's Letters on Slavery to Dr. John C. Warren, of Boston*, Let. I (1851), p. 11.

36. Affleck, "On the Hygiene of Cotton Plantations . . . ," p. 431.

37. Isaac Avery to Colonel Thomas Lenoir, March 29, 1821, Lenoir Papers, UNC.

38. Her daughter to Mrs. Louis Lenoir, June 13, 1835, *ibid.*

39. Donat Ebert to John Mc Donogh, July 21, 1812, John Mc Donogh Papers, LSU.

40. Her daughter to Mrs. Louis Lenoir, June 13, 1835, Lenoir Papers, UNC.

41. De Bow, *The Industrial Resources*, II, 319.

42. Donat Ebert to John Mc Donogh, July 21, 1812, John Mc Donogh Papers, LSU.

43. Moses Liddell to Mary Liddell, December 7, 1851, St. John R. Moses Liddell and Family Collection, LSU. It is somewhat difficult to convey the extent of the problems of diet and health which plagued slave labor without seeming to overstress certain points. But these were clearly things with which bondsmen and planters had to live continually, with little letup, during most of the year.

44. John Mills to Gilbert Jackson, May 19, 1807, John Mills Letters, LSU.

45. Harold S. Diehl, *Healthful Living: A Textbook of Personal and Community Health* (7th ed.; New York: McGraw-Hill Book Company, 1960), p. 101.

46. Milton Terris, ed., *Goldberger on Pellagra* (Baton Rouge: Louisiana State University Press, 1964), p. 375. Physician Goldberger wrote, "It is probable that in each year for every death attributed to the disease there are fully 20 persons with clearly recognizable attacks and probably as many more with debility from the same cause but not definitely marked as such."

47. See Milton Terris, ed., *Ibid.* The term pellagra comes from the Italian words *pelle agra*, which mean "rough skin." See also R. Q. Mallard, *Plantation Life Before Emancipation*, p. 31. He writes, "The food was mainly maize. . . . This weekly fare the year round was with us supplemented, in the season when the work was unusually heavy, by rations of molasses, or bacon, or salt fish; and an occasional beef."

48. *Annual Catalogue of the Medical Department . . . Missouri*, p. 701.

49. Many of Cartwright's views were mouthed by pro-slavery politicians in what has become known as the politics of race. See Rudolph Matas, *History of Medicine in Louisiana*, ed. John Duffy (2 vols.; Baton Rouge: Louisiana State University Press, 1962), which, though it has surprisingly little on slave care, does address itself briefly to Cartwright's political influence.

50. Louis Manigault Plantation Records, IV, entry for the summer of 1862, UNC.

51. *Ibid.* See Henry C. Sherman, *The Nutritional Improvement of Life* (New York: Columbia University Press, 1957).

52. Diehl, *Healthful Living*, p. 101: "the results of a deficiency may in-

clude nervous irritability, impairment of the appetite, digestive disturbances, growth failure, weakness, multiple neuritis, and eventually beriberi."

53. Philo Tower, *Slavery Unmasked: Being a Truthful Narrative of a Three Years' Residence and Journey in Eleven Southern States* (Rochester, N.Y.: Darrow & Brother, 1856), p. 191.

54. Postell, *The Health of Slaves*, p. 32; Northrup, *Twelve Years a Slave*, pp. 152-53.

55. Charles William Dabney Diary, entry for July 10, 1834, VHS.

56. *Ibid.*

57. See Bennett H. Wall, "Ebenezer Pettigrew, An Economic Study of an Ante-bellum Planter" (unpublished Ph.D. dissertation, University of North Carolina, Chapel Hill, 1946).

58. Robert C. Reinders, "Dr. James G. Carson's Canebrake: A View of an Ante-bellum Louisiana Planter," *Louisiana Historical Quarterly*, XXXIII (October, 1950), p. 359.

59. De Bow, *The Industrial Resources*, II, p. 325; see also David Dickson, *A Practical Treatise on Agriculture*, ed. J. Dickson Smith (Macon, Ga.: J. W. Burke and Co., 1970).

60. Swados, "Negro Health on the Ante-Bellum Plantations," p. 467.

61. M. C. Shaffer to Misters Preston and Manning, January 30, 1844, William R. Preston Scrapbook, MHS.

62. See Robert Twyman, "The Clay Eater: A New Look at an Old Southern Enigma," *Journal of Southern History*, XXXVII (August, 1971), 439-48, for an informative discussion of the dirt-eating phenomenon.

63. *Southern Medical Reports*, I (1849), 190 ff.

64. *New Orleans Medical and Surgical Journal*, I (1884), 146 ff.

65. Twyman, "The Clay Eater," p. 447, writes, "Although it is considered possible that clay eating will on rare occasions cause hookworm, no hard evidence has ever been produced that hookworm causes clay eating; and contrary to the assumptions of some historians, the practice does not necessarily arise from an insufficient diet or a vitamin or mineral deficiency. Clay eating has been known to exist among persons whose nutritional intake was adequate even by modern standards. The question, however, is still being studied."

66. Swados, "Negro Health on the Ante-Bellum Plantations," p. 467.

67. *Ibid.*

68. *Ibid.*, p. 468.

69. Mitchell, "Health and the Medical Profession in the Lower South, 1845-1860," p. 425.

70. C. Claiborne Clay to C. Comer Clay, April 19, 1846, C. C. Clay Papers, DU.

71. Michael Gramling Plantation Journal, entry for April 25, 1850, SC.

72. William Ethelbert Ervin Journal, entry for June 6, 1855, UNC.
73. H. H. Gurley to John Mc Donogh, May 6, 1829, John Mc Donogh Papers, LSU.
74. J. Maynard to Mrs. H. Mathews, October 1, 1855, Charles L. Mathews and Family Papers, LSU.
75. Fisk University, *God Struck Me Dead*, p. 109.
76. See Harry H. Johnston, *The Negro in the New World* (London: Methuen & Co. Ltd., 1910), p. 375.
77. Everard Green Baker Diary, I, entry for April 22, 1850, UNC.
78. John Walker Diary, II, entry for June 18, 1836, UNC.
79. James H. Hammond Journal, entry for October 22, 1843, SC.
80. Sidney A. Palfrey to William T. Palfrey, December 5, 1836, William T. Palfrey Papers, LSU.
81. Kellar, ed., *Solon Robinson*, II, 381.
82. Hall, *Travels in North America*, II, 232.
83. J. Milton Emerson Journal, entry for May 25, 1842, DU.
84. Shirley Plantation Journal, entry for October 24, 1824, VSL.
85. Daniel W. Lord Journal, entry for March 17, 1824, LC.
86. Rachel O'Connor to David Weeks, January 11, 1832, David Weeks and Family Collection, LSU.
87. See Monroe Lerner, "Social Differences in Physical Health," in *Poverty and Health*, ed. John Kosa (Cambridge, Mass.: Harvard University Press, 1969), pp. 69-112; Josue de Castro, *The Geography of Hunger* (Boston: Little, Brown, 1952); Nevin S. Scrimshaw and John E. Gordon, eds., *Malnutrition, Learning, and Behavior* (Cambridge, Mass.: The M.I.T. Press, 1968); Ruth M. Leverton, *Food Becomes You* (3d ed.; Ames, Iowa: Iowa State University Press, 1965; *Nutrition, Health and Disease* (New York: Milbank Memorial Fund, 1950).

4. THE LOGIC OF RESISTANCE

1. Mrs. Isaac H. Hilliard Diary, entry for June 19, 1850, LSU. Henry Turner to General John Quitman, October 12, 1843, Quitman Papers, UNC, commented that "it is impossible to manage any set of negroes without resorting to the whip at times."
2. Bibb, *Narrative*, p. 64.
3. Joseph S. Roncek, "The Sociology of Violence," *Journal of Human Relations*, V (Spring, 1957), 18.
4. J. J. Pettigrew to Ebenezer Pettigrew, February 7, 1848, Pettigrew Papers, UNC.
5. E. B. Reuter, *Handbook of Sociology* (New York: The Dryden Press,

1948), p. 80, notes that "the social pattern that accommodation always takes is the subordination of a person or group to another person or group"; see also Elkins, *Slavery*.

6. James L. Smith, *Autobiography of James L. Smith* (New York: Negro University Press, 1969 [1881]), pp. 25-26.

7. See the interesting discussion in William W. Freehling, *Prelude to Civil War: The Nullification Controversy in South Carolina, 1816-1836* (New York: Harper & Row, Publishers, 1966), Chapter 3, "A Disturbing Institution."

8. This was a popular claim of the period. Its meaning extended beyond the mere dominance of an overseer over a field of slaves. P. Church to Reverend I. L. Brookes, March 27, 1860, Iverson L. Brookes Papers, SC. See also Herbert Aptheker, *American Negro Slave Revolts* (New York: Columbia University Press, 1943), *passim*.

9. Bassett, *The Southern Plantation Overseer*; William K. Scarborough, *The Overseer: Plantation Management in the Old South* (Baton Rouge: Louisiana State University Press, 1966).

10. Stampp, *The Peculiar Institution*, p. 378; Rawick, ed., *The American Slave*. All nineteen volumes have much useful information on this point.

11. Ball, *Narrative*, pp. 348-351, 361.

12. De Bow, *The Industrial Resources*, II, 337.

13. John C. Calhoun to A. Burt, September 1, 1831, John C. Calhoun Papers, DU.

14. George M. Fredrickson and Christopher Lasch, "Resistance to Slavery," *Civil War History*, XIII (December, 1967) make the prison analogy, and Elkins, *Slavery*, compares plantations to concentration camps. Erving Goffman, *Asylums: Essays on the Social Situation of Mental Patients and Other Inmates* (Chicago: Aldine Publishing Company, 1962), p. xiii, describes a total institution as "a place of residence and work where a large number of like-situated individuals, cut off from the wider society for an appreciable period of time, together lead an enclosed, formally administered round of life."

15. Rawick, ed., *The American Slave*, *passim*.

16. Letter to William S. Hamilton, July 29, 1851, William S. Hamilton Papers, LSU. In a recent article, "Rebels and Sambos: The Search for the Negro's Personality in Slavery," *Journal of Southern History*, XXXVII (August, 1971), 381, Kenneth Stampp, in partial agreement with Elkins, *Slavery*, p. 86, finds slavery "a closed system."

17. John Parker Manuscript, p. 30, DU. Compare George Jackson, *Soledad Brother: The Prison Letters of George Jackson* (New York: Bantam Books, 1970).

18. H. M. Henry, *The Police Control of the Slave in South Carolina* (Emory, Va.: Emory and Henry College, 1914).

19. John Parker Manuscript, p. 39, DU.

20. Henry A. Tayloe to his brother, February 16, 1835, Tayloe Family Papers, UVa.

21. Benjamin Drew, *The Refugee: or The Narratives of Fugitive Slaves in Canada* (Boston: John P. Jewett and Company, 1856), pp. 156-57; Rawick, ed., *Maryland Narratives*, pp. 49-50, 32.

22. Drew, *The Refugee*, pp. 156-57.

23. *Ibid.*, p. 157.

24. Police Guard Manuscript Daybook, 1834-43, entry for June 24, 1836, UVa.; also see the April 15, 1836 entry. In the June 24 notation the authorities indicated that a "$500 reward will be given for the apprehension of Manzu and the detection of the individual who furnished him with free papers."

25. See strong evidence on this point in nearly all of the generally available slave narrative accounts. See also Charles M. Harsh and H. G. Schrickel, *Personality: Development and Assessment* (New York: The Ronald Press Company, 1959), who make such feelings of kinship a general theme throughout their work. Some of the essays in Jack R. Van Der Slik, ed., *Black Conflict with White America: A Reader in Social and Political Analysis* (Columbus, Ohio: Charles E. Merrill Publishing Co., 1970), demonstrate this theme in a modern setting.

26. John Parker Manuscript, DU; Stanley Feldstein, *Once a Slave: The Slave's View of Slavery* (New York: William Morrow and Company, Inc., 1971), pp. 123-59.

27. It is difficult to estimate how many slaves were actually hired out in any given period. Plantation records indicate that two or three from an estate was not unusual.

28. Dismal Swamp Land Company Letters and Papers, Contract of Hire, January 1, 1835, DU.

29. Grandy, *Narrative*, p. 13.

30. Alfred to Mrs. Mary Steele, November 15, 1835, John Steele Papers, UNC.

31. John Parker Manuscript, p. 37, DU.

32. *Ibid.*

33. Adam Hodgson, *Letters From North America* (2 vols.; London: Hurst, Robinson & Co., 1824), I, 111. See Fogel and Engerman, *Time on the Cross*, conclusion 9, which states that "over the course of his lifetime, the typical slave field hand received 90 per cent of the income he produced." Few bondsmen would have agreed with this conclusion.

34. See the discussions by Raymond Bauer and Alice Bauer, "Day to Day Resistance to Slavery," *Journal of Negro History*, XXVII (October, 1942), 388-419; Roy Simon Bryce-Laporte, "Slaves as Inmates, Slaves as Men: A Sociological Discussion of Elkin's Thesis," in *The Debate over Slavery*, ed.

Ann J. Lane (Urbana: University of Illinois Press, 1971), pp. 269-92. Investigation of open slave resistance by bondsmen has generally proceeded along two lines: inquiries into day-to-day resistance to provoking circumstances, and inquiries into insurrectionary acts or threats.

35. John Mills to Gilbert Jackson, May 19, 1807, John Mills Letters, LSU.

36. See James Monroe to Major Wm. Noland, July 25, 1817, James Monroe Papers, UVa.

37. Linton Stephens to Alexander Stephens, January 22, 1862, Stephens Papers, LC. See also Richard Wright, *Native Son*, "How Bigger was Born," for some helpful thoughts relevant to the shaping of rebellious character.

38. G. F. Bristow to Alexander Stephens, January 22, 1862, Stephens Papers, LC.

39. For a geographical sampling see the Richmond *Enquirer*, the Charleston *Mercury*, and the Natchez *Mississippi Republican*.

40. Letter to William S. Hamilton, July 29, 1851, William S. Hamilton Papers, LSU.

41. *Ibid.*

42. *Ibid.*

43. Elliott, *Sinfulness of American Slavery*, I, 205.

44. *Ibid.*; see as well John B. Lamar to his sister Mrs. Howell Cobb, n.d., in U. B. Phillips, *A Documentary History*, II, 38.

45. Bruce, *The New Man*, p. 40; see also Aptheker, *American Negro Slave Revolts*, Chapter II.

46. Geo. Hamilton to his father William S. Hamilton, July 29, 1851, William S. Hamilton Papers, LSU.

47. Landon Carter Journal, entry for June 28, 1771, Carter Family Papers, VSL.

48. Fisk University, *God Struck Me Dead*, p. 194.

49. A. H. Pemberton to James H. Hammond, Dec. 21, 1846. James H. Hammond Papers, LC.

50. Henry Turner to General John Quitman, March 16, 1853, Quitman Papers, UNC; see also James Monroe to Major Wm. Noland, July 25, 1817, James Monroe Papers, UVa. Monroe wanted the major to tell his overseer, "I wish my people to work, but not to be cruelly treated."

51. A. Hodgson, *Letters from North America*, I, 102. See C. M. Conrad to Alfred Conrad, July 18, 1819, David Weeks Collection, LSU; Eliza L. Magruder Diary, entry for July 30, 1856, LSU; P. H. Pitts Diary and Account Book, entry for February 25, 1853, UNC. See, too, Carl D. Arfwedson, *The United States and Canada in 1832, 1833, and 1834* (2 vols.; London: R. Bentley, 1834), p. 342, who writes that "a disposition to disobedience and irritability among the slave-population towards the planters is too often manifested. . . ."

52. Everard Green Baker Diary, I, entry for March 15, 1849, UNC.

53. Eliza L. Magruder Diary, entry for January 31, 1857, LSU.

54. C. W. Knott to Mr. Weeaks, December 5, 1858, James Sheppard Letters and Papers, DU.

55. Andrew Flinn Plantation Book, SC, lists running away as the most punishable offense.

56. David Gavin Diary, I, entry for July 4, 1857, UNC.

57. M. Smelser to John Mc Donogh, December 31, 1815, John Mc Donogh Papers, LSU.

58. Landon Carter Journal, entry for September 22, 1773, Carter Family Papers, VSL.

59. E. Carter to Farish Carter, July 19, 1852, Carter Family Papers, VSL.

60. John L. Bourquin, Jr., to Joachin Hartstone, March 14, 1787, Slavery Papers, SCHC. Letter of Hugh L. Clay, June 25, 1854, Clement Comer Clay Papers, DU, gives an example in which a mistress persuaded two slaves to try to assassinate a white man who owed her money. See also Fisk University, *God Struck Me Dead*, p. 216, where the testimony of some ex-slaves reveals that some of their former masters encouraged them to steal from other plantations.

61. Landon Carter Journal, entry for September 22, 1773, Carter Family Papers, VSL.

62. *Columbian Herald* (Charleston), December 5, 1793.

63. Joseph Taper to Joseph Long, November 11, 1840, Joseph Long Papers, DU.

64. S. A. Cartwright to General Quitman, August 27, 1846, Samuel A. Cartwright Papers, LSU.

65. *De Bow's Review*, XI (1851), 332; Stampp, *The Peculiar Institution*, pp. 102, 109.

66. Quoted in Phillips, *American Negro Slavery*, p. 303.

67. See Ball, *Narrative*, p. 191; Fedric, *Slave Life in Virginia and Kentucky*, p. 100; Quitman Papers, UNC; Lenoir Family Papers, UNC: John Mc Donogh Papers, LSU; Susanna Warfield Diary, MHS.

68. John B. Ba—— to Farish Carter, February 15, 1846, Carter Family Papers, VSL.

69. Gordon W. Allport, *The Nature of Prejudice* (Garden City, N.Y.: Doubleday Anchor Books, 1958, [1954]), p. 461.

70. Ed Tayloe to his brother B. O. Tayloe, January 12, 1835, Tayloe Family Papers, UVa.

71. James P. Tary to S. O. Wood, July 18, 1854, Samuel O. Wood Papers, DU.

72. Joseph Thomas to John Mc Donogh, April 25, 1810, John Mc Donogh Papers, LSU.

73. Isabella Soustan to Master Manual, July 10, 1865, Edward Coles Letters (photostat), UVa.

74. Carter G. Woodson, ed., *The Mind of the Negro as Reflected, in Letters Written During the Crisis* (New York: Russell and Russell, 1969 [1926]), pp. 537-39.

75. Elizabeth Jefferson Reminiscences, LSU.

76. Fedric, *Slave Life in Virginia and Kentucky*, p. 100.

77. William Douglass to Georges [Jerdone], August 30, 1782, Jerdone Family Papers, VSL.

78. Compare Degler, *Neither Black nor White*, p. 48, and Stanley J. Stein, *Vassouras: A Brazilian Coffee County, 1850-1890* (New York: Atheneum, 1970 [1957]), pp. 145-50. Degler argues that slaves in Latin America did not usually take this approach; they did not attack the system as often.

79. Harriet Beecher Stowe, *Dred: A Tale of the Great Dismal Swamp* (2 vols.; Boston: Phillips, Sampson and Company, 1856), is an imaginative story of such hideaways; see also Herbert Aptheker, "Maroons within the Present Limits of the United States," *Journal of Negro History*, XXIV (April, 1939), 167-84, and his "Additional Data on American Maroons," *Ibid.*, XXXII (October, 1947), 452-560.

80. Charles MacKay, *Life and Liberty in America* (2 vols.; London: Smith, Elder and Co., 1859), I, 276.

81. J. Smith to George Austin, July 22, 1774, Josiah Smith, Jr., Letterbook, UNC.

82. Gabriel Manigault to Louis Manigault, January 21, 1861, Louis Manigault Papers, DU.

83. R. Carter to Tho' Sorrel, July 10, 1787, Robert Carter Journal, Carter Family Papers, VSL.

84. *Raleigh Standard* (North Carolina), July, 1838.

85. Grandy, *Narrative*, p. 8.

86. Overseer to William B. Randolph, September 14, 1833, William B. Randolph Correspondence, LC.

87. M. Pringle to Joseph Shirley, March 24, 1812, Mark Pringle Letterbooks, MHS.

88. A neighbor to John Mc Donogh, November 7, 1813. John Mc Donogh Papers, LSU.

89. *Ibid.*

90. M. Pringle to Joseph Shirley, March 27, 1812, Mark Pringle Letterbooks, MHS.

91. D. N. Moxley to George Noble Jones, October 8, 1854, in *Florida Plantation Records from the Papers of George Noble Jones*, ed. U. B. Phillips and James David Glunt (St. Louis: Missouri Historical Society, 1927), p. 107.

92. General Quitman to Eliza, November 18, 1842, Quitman Papers, UNC.

93. John W. Brown Diary, entry for January 24, 1854, UNC.

94. Susanna Warfield Diary, entry for September 30, 1845, MHS.

95. Thomas Butler to Ann, July 22, 1842, Thomas Butler and Family Papers, LSU.

96. Most overseers held their jobs for less than two years. The usual length of their contracts was six months to a year, a new one to be negotiated at the end of each period.

97. Often such checking of the overseer's authority was not an organized plot but a natural response to test his authority.

98. John J. Cabell to Richard Cralle, July 2, 1832, Cabell Papers, HU.

99. Bruce, *The New Man*, p. 41.

100. James H. Hammond to John Clark, August 26, 1831, Hammond Plantation Book, SC.

101. Garnett Andrews, *Reminiscences of an Old Georgia Lawyer* (Atlanta, Ga.: J. J. Toon, Publisher, 1870), pp. 45-46.

102. *Ibid.*; see also Chapter 5 in my text.

103. Gerhart Saenger, *The Psychology of Prejudice: Achieving Intercultural Understanding and Cooperation in a Democracy* (New York: Harper & Brothers Publishers, 1953), p. 29: "To preserve their self-esteem the minority group members may also identify with their oppressors," acting out their vengefulness on their companions. However, this rarely involves a loss of one's own identity. See also Seymour Parker and Robert J. Kleiner, *Mental Illness in the Urban Negro Community* (New York: The Free Press, 1966), p. 160, who write that "the psychiatrically healthy Negro is an individual with conflicts about his racial identification."

104. Mrs. Trollope, *Domestic Manners of the Americans* (London: Printed for Whitaker, Treacher, & Co., 1832), p. 199.

105. Bassett, *Slavery in the State of North Carolina* (Baltimore: The Johns Hopkins University Press, 1899), pp. 47-76.

106. The United States Census of 1840 reinforced this tendency to underestimate.

107. Ball, *Narrative*, p. 69. On pp. 69 ff. he writes, "Self-destruction is much more frequent among the slaves in the cotton region than is generally supposed. . . . Suicide amongst the slaves is regarded as a matter of dangerous example. . . . [by masters] slaves who commit suicide are always branded in reputation after death, as the worst of criminals. . . ."

108. Emile Durkheim, *Suicide: A Study in Sociology*, trans. John A. Spaulding and George Simpson (New York: The Free Press, 1951), p. 276. See also Herbert Hendin, *Black Suicide* (New York: Basic Books, Inc., 1969), p. 9, for an up-to-date discussion of the problem.

109. Rowland Chambers Diary, entry for June 11, 1860, LSU.

110. Anna M. Johnston to Sarah Butler, October 25, 1852, Anna and Sarah Butler Correspondence, LSU; in Fisk University, *God Struck Me Dead*, p. 182, a slave comments: "His master was such a man and worked his slaves so hard that most of them either ran off or killed themselves."

111. Everard Green Baker Diary, II, entry for June 15, 1861, UNC.

112. See the *Alexandria Gazette*, June 11, 1849, for some confirmation of this point.

113. Fisk University, *God Struck Me Dead*, p. 199.

114. Frank Ticknor to William A. Nelson, April 22, 1845, F. O. Ticknor Papers, UG.

115. Gary T. Marx, *Protest and Prejudice: A Study of Belief in the Black Community* (rev. ed., New York: Harper Torchbooks, 1969), p. 90.

116. J. Johnston to William Pettigrew, June 16, 1849, Pettigrew Papers, UNC.

117. Elkins, *Slavery*, p. 87; Harry Stack Sullivan, *Conceptions of Modern Psychiatry* (Washington, D.C.: William Alanson White Psychiatric Foundation, 1945).

118. Manale, Justice of the Peace, to John McDonogh[?], January 28, 1811, John McDonogh Papers, LSU.

119. There is some debate over whether a Denmark Vesey conspiracy existed at all. See Richard C. Wade, "The Vesey Plot: A Reconsideration," *Journal of Southern History*, XXX (May, 1964), 148-61. "Yet, in spite of the apparent agreement of most contemporaries and the consensus of subsequent historians, there is persuasive evidence that no conspiracy in fact existed or at most that it was a vague and unformulated plan in the minds or on the tongues of a few colored townsmen." Despite Wade's doubts it does seem clear that a conspiracy was indeed uncovered.

120. William P. Hill Diary, entry for April 9, 1849, UNC. On this point see Hannah Arendt, "Ideology and Terror: A Novel Form of Government," *Review of Politics*, XV (1953), 303-27; see Slavery Papers, Feb. 13, 1748, RNC, for an example of nailed and cut-off ears.

121. Rachael O'Connor to David Weeks, October 13, 1831, David Weeks and Family Collection, LSU.

122. *African Repository*, VII (October, 1831) 245.

123. Slave Autobiography Manuscript, Slavery Papers, LC.

124. *Ibid.*

125. See Jack R. Van Der Slik, ed., *Black Conflict with White America* (Columbus, Ohio: Charles E. Merrill Publishing Co., 1970), *passim*.

126. James C. Ballagh, *A History of Slavery in Virginia* (Baltimore: Johns Hopkins University Press, 1902), p. 99: "In the Southampton insurrection many armed their slaves for their defense, and in several instances the whites, especially women, escaped through the help of slaves."

127. Rachael O'Connor to her sister Mrs. Mary C. Weeks, January 11, 1830, David Weeks and Family Collection, LSU.

128. N. B. Powell to F. Carter, January 27, 1850, Carter Family Papers, VSL; William Pettigrew to J. Johnson, January 27, 1853, Pettigrew Papers, UNC.

129. John P. Runden, ed., *Melville's Benito Cereno* (Boston: D. C. Heath and Company, 1965), p. 7; compare to G. W. Hegel, *The Phenomenology of Mind*, trans. J. B. Baillie (5th ed.; London: George Allen and Unwin, 1961), pp. 228-40.

130. Eliza L. Magruder Diary, entry for December 2, 1850, LSU.

131. John L. Bourquin, Jr., to Joachin Hartstone, March 14, 1787, Slavery Papers, SCHC.

132. John Johnston to William Pettigrew, December 27, 1852, Pettigrew Papers, UNC.

133. *Ibid.*

134. For the latest argument for this point of view see Stanley M. Elkins, "Slavery and Ideology," *The Debate over Slavery: Stanley Elkins and His Critics*, ed. Ann J. Lane (Urbana: University of Illinois Press, 1971), 325-78.

135. Hayden, *Narrative*, p. 74.

136. Aptheker, *American Negro Slave Revolts*, p. 162, sets the number of slave revolts at 250, but he overlooks many disturbances because he makes use primarily of official printed source records and does not tap manuscript materials of planters who did not report such disturbances to the authorities. George M. Fredrickson and Christopher Lasch, "Resistance to Slavery," *Civil War History*, XIII (December, 1967), set no number on resistance movements but agree that "groups" of slaves were necessary. Marion D. de B. Kilson, "Towards Freedom: An Analysis of Slave Revolts in the United States," in *The Making of Black America*, eds. August Meier and Elliott Rudwick (2 vols.; New York: Atheneum, 1969), I, 165-78, labels revolts as Systematic or Rational, Unsystematic or Vandalistic, and Situational or Opportunistic. The quantitative statements in this article are based on Aptheker's findings.

137. Letter to John R. Liddell, August 18, 1860, St. John R. Moses Liddell and Family Collection, LSU.

138. R. Carter to Captain John Turberville, April 22, 1785, Robert Carter Journal, Carter Family Papers, VSL.

139. Affadavit, June 9, 1802, Slavery Papers, RNC.

140. Compare Degler, *Neither Black Nor White*, p. 65. Degler points out that women were scarce in many slave regions of Brazil. I believe that there is some likelihood that the presence in the American setting of relatively large groups of women—sometimes more than half the workers on a plantation after 1830—is an important factor in the two slave cultures' different

kinds of slave resistance. In some respects this factor perhaps made American slaves more careful, though no less persistent in their attacks upon bondage.

141. C. L. R. James, *The Black Jacobins: Toussaint L'Ouverture and the San Domingo Revolution* (2d ed. rev.; New York: Vintage Books, 1963), tells an interesting story of the problems with secrecy that the San Domingan rebels led by Toussaint L'Ouverture had in the 1790's.

142. R. F. McCuire Diary, entry for August 1837, LSU.

143. Letter dated December 30 (between 1852 and 1863), Lalla Pelot Papers, DU. See Genovese, *The World the Slaveholders Made,* for a discussion of the class question. During the Civil War one southern mistress relates that a Southerner who fought for the North and gained the rank of captain told her mockingly, "I was born near Richmond Va and am what you would call *poor White Trash.*" He had been sent to take her slaves away for use by the Union Army (Sigismunda Kimball Diary, entry for February 24, 1863, UVa).

144. Much of the problem surrounding docility is a definitional one. It is not a static concept, and only when we view it as such does the slave's behavior seem utterly perplexing. Docility has become one of those unfortunate stereotypes synonymous with "slave," and writing about bondsmen more often describes the relationship between master and stereotype than master and slave. See Allport, *The Nature of Prejudice,* especially the chapter "Stereotypes in Our Culture."

145. Susanna Warfield Diary, entry for May 31, 1849, MHS; see further Zephonia Kingsley, *A Treatise on the Patriarchal, or Co-operative System of Society . . . Under the Name of Slavery* (2d ed.; n.p., 1829), p. 12.

5. THE HOUSEHOLD SLAVE

1. See Herbert S. Klein, *Slavery in the Americas* (Chicago: The University of Chicago Press, 1967), p. 183, who writes that "only the house servants, who were associated closely with the white family's separate economic and social life, had the possibility of breaking out of the confined world of the plantation." He does not appear to be correct. See Genovese, *Roll, Jordan, Roll,* pp. 327-65, "Life in the Big House."

2. J. H. Cocke to ———, September 23, 1831, Cocke Papers, Cocke Deposit, UVa.

3. Blassingame, *The Slave Community,* p. 200, calls some of them Sambos, but his argument is not backed by strong evidence.

4. John H. Cocke to ———, September 23, 1831, Cocke Papers, Cocke Deposit, UVa.

5. See discussions of domestics in Stampp, *The Peculiar Institution*, pp. 151-52; Sydnor, *Slavery in Mississippi*, pp. 3-5; Genovese, "American Slaves and Their History," *The New York Review of Books* (December 3, 1970), 34-43; and Genovese's most recent and more detailed assessment in *Roll, Jordan, Roll*. For extended examinations of some of the personality implications, refer to Saenger, *The Social Psychology of Prejudice*, and Allport, *The Nature of Prejudice*.

6. Hall, *Travels in North America*, II, 216.

7. *Ibid.*

8. *Ibid.*

9. Fisk University, Vol. XVIII, *Unwritten History of Slavery*, p. 201.

10. G. Jarrett to his wife, December 21, 1836, Jarrett and Bynum Family Papers, UVa.

11. Richard Wright, *Black Boy: A Record of Childhood and Youth* (New York: Harper and Row, 1966), pp. 172-200, has a good description of this kind of relationship.

12. Hortense Powdermaker, *After Freedom: A Cultural Study in the Deep South* (New York: Atheneum, 1968 [1939]), pp. 119, 41.

13. Adam Hodgson, *Letters from North America*, I, 24.

14. Mrs. J. A. M. Howe to Louisa, November 4, 1838, Lenoir Family Papers, UNC.

15. Henry Watson to Julia Watson, November 7, 1847, Henry Watson Papers, Jr., DU.

16. Susanna Warfield Diary, entry for October 28, 1846, MHS.

17. *Ibid.*, entry for February 4, 1849.

18. *Ibid.*

19. *Ibid.* Mag appears to have been about eight to ten years of age.

20. Ed Tayloe to his sister, July 16, 1855, Tayloe Family Papers, UVa.

21. *Ibid.*

22. Lucilla Agnes (Gamble) McCorkle Diary, XIX, entry for 1850, William Parsons McCorkle Papers, UNC.

23. Henry Watson, Jr., to Sarah Carrington, January 28, 1861, Henry Watson, Jr., Papers, DU.

24. A brother to David Weeks, July 11, 1829, David Weeks and Family Collection, LSU.

25. Floyd L. Whitehead Papers, DU.

26. Mrs. M. B. Smith, *My Uncle's Family: or, Ten Months at the South* (Cincinnati: American Form Tract and Book Society, 1860), p. 38.

27. A sister to J. B. Bailey, March 24, 1856, James B. Bailey Papers, UNC.

28. Charles Manigault to Louis, January 20, 1860, Louis Manigault Papers, DU; see also the Louis Manigault Plantation Records, UNC.

29. F. F. Laforn to John McDonogh, May 31, 1830, John McDonogh Papers, LSU.

30. Powdermaker, *After Freedom*, p. 119, writes, "The servant is quite a different person Across the Tracks and is not as a rule communicative about the life she leads there."

31. The printed and manuscript sources used in this study do not dwell upon this kind of domestic behavior. Slave narrators do mention it, sometimes bitterly; but the literature would seem to support, in its broader outlines the view that domestics were not generally disloyal to other bondsmen.

32. Charles Manigault to Louis Manigault, January 19, 1860, Louis Manigault Papers, DU.

33. Historians continue to learn that during the Civil War domestic slaves apparently communicated information about Confederate troop movements to field hands who passed it on to Yankee officers. This is perhaps another indication of the close links some domestics had with other bondsmen. See Bell Wiley, *Southern Negroes, 1861-1865* (New York: Rinehart & Company, Inc., 1953).

34. Mrs. Andrew McCollam Diary, II, entry for April 20, 1847, UNC.

35. William Massie Slave Book, entry for September 24, 1847, VSL; see also the John H. Cocke Journal, 1863-64, p. 72, Campbell Deposit, UVa.

36. *Ibid.*

37. Robert Henderson Allen Diary, entry for July 1, 1841, VSL.

38. *Ibid.*

39. H. L. Clay to Virginia Caroline (Tunstall) Clay, March 11, 1846, Clement Comer Clay Papers, UNC.

40. Sophie S. Wilson Diary, entry for July 9, 1831, LC.

41. John W. Quarles to Cornelia Quarles, December 10, 1848, Peter Barksdale Letters, DU.

42. *Ibid.*

43. John H. Cocke Journal, 1863-64, p. 72, Campbell Deposit, UVa.

44. *Ibid.* See E. Franklin Frazier, *The Free Negro Family: A Study of Family Origins Before the Civil War* (Nashville: Fisk University Press, 1932), who has an entire chapter on the mammy. See also Sterling Stuckey, "Through the Prism of Folklore: The Black Ethos in Slavery," *The Massachusetts Review* (Summer, 1968), 417-537; and Robert Henderson Diary, entry for July 2, 1861, VHS.

45. M. E. Carmichael Diary, entry for July 27, 1845, UNC.

46. Frazier, *The Free Negro Family*, p. 39.

47. Adams, *A South-Side View of Slavery, or Three Months at South, in 1854* (Boston: T. R. Marvin and B. B. Mussey & Co., 1854), pp. 16-17.

48. Letter to John R. Liddell, August 18, 1860, St. John R. Moses Liddell and Family Papers, LSU.

49. John Parker Manuscript, p. 37, DU.

6. THE BLACK SLAVE DRIVER

1. Everard Green Baker Diaries, entry for July 1, 1858, UNC.
2. James H. Hammond Plantation Book, SC.
3. A. M. H. Christensen, *Afro-American Folklore: Told Round Cabin Fires on the Sea Islands of South Carolina* (Boston: J. G. Cupples Company, 1892), p. 3. On this ex-slave's allusion to Brer Rabbit, see the interesting analysis in Bernard Wolfe, "Uncle Remus and the Malevolent Rabbit," *Commentary* (July 1949), 31-41.
4. James H. Hammond Plantation Books, SC.
5. *Ibid.*
6. Dr. Stephen Duncan to Thomas Butler, October 4, 1831, Thomas Butler and Family Papers, LSU.
7. R. R. Barrow Journal, entry for April 24, 1858, UNC.
8. George Skipwith to John H. Cocke, July 8, 1847, Cocke Papers, Cocke Deposit, UVa.
9. A. M. Lobdell to L. Stirling, October 5, 1838, Lewis Stirling and Family Papers, LSU.
10. Fedric, *Slave Life in Virginia and Kentucky*, p. 6.
11. Drew, *The Refugee*, p. 73.
12. See Richard D. Powell to John Hartwell Cocke, August 14, 1857, Cocke Papers, UNC.
13. Peter Randolph, *From Slave Cabin to Pulpit* (Boston: James H. Earle, Publishers, 1893), pp. 212-14.
14. *Narrative of James Williams* (New York: The American Anti-Slavery Society, 1838), pp. 62, 43; see also Hannah Arendt, "Ideology and Terror: A Novel Form of Government," *Review of Politics*, XV (1953), 303-27; Kenneth B. Clark, *Dark Ghetto: Dilemmas of Social Power* (New York: Harper Torchbooks, 1967), especially his chapter "The Pathology of the Ghetto."
15. Quoted in Scarborough, *The Overseer*, p. 78. The author writes about white overseers that "it is doubtful whether many overseers had any humanitarian feeling for the slaves under their supervision," *ibid.*
16. William Gilmore Simms, "Caloya, or the Loves of the Driver," in *The Wigwam and the Cabin*, Second Series (New York: Wiley and Putnam, 1845), pp. 131, 139.
17. See the *North American Review*, LXIII (October, 1846). One critic called Mingo a "greasy, woolly-headed blubber-lipped negro driver. . . ." (p. 373).
18. Northup, *Twelve Years a Slave*, p. 172: "during my eight years' experience as a driver I learned to handle my whip with marvelous dexterity

and precision, throwing the lash within a hair's breath of the back, the ear, the nose, without, however, touching either of them."

19. John H. Cocke Journal, 1863-64, p. 72, Cocke Papers, Campbell Deposit, UVa.

20. Christensen, *Afro-American Folklore*, pp. 3-4.

21. Feldstein, *Once a Slave*, p. 118-21.

22. Walter S. Harris to Hiram M. Sherman, August 13, 1910, Sherman Family Papers, UVa.

23. John L. Bourquin to Joachin Hartstone, March 14, 1787, Slavery Papers, SCHC.

24. *Autobiography of James L. Smith*, p. 19.

25. Walter S. Harris to Hiram M. Sherman, August 13, 1910, Sherman Family Papers, UVa.

26. James H. Hammond Plantation Book, SC. See Douglass, *Life and Times*, pp. 112-13 for a discussion of slave breaking.

27. John Cocke Journal, p. 71, Cocke Papers, Campbell Deposit, UVa.

28. William Pettigrew to Moses, July 12, 1856, Pettigrew Family Papers, UNC.

29. John Cocke Journal, p. 77, Cocke Papers, Campbell Deposit, UVa.

30. William Pettigrew to James C. Johnston, December 31, 1845, Pettigrew Family Papers, UNC.

31. *Ibid*.

32. Charles Pettigrew to Mrs. Lunstall, June 22, 1803, Pettigrew Family Papers, UNC.

33. James C. Johnston to William Pettigrew, January 9, 1849, Pettigrew Family Papers, UNC.

34. William Pettigrew to James C. Johnston, December 7, 1848, Pettigrew Family Papers, UNC.

35. A. H. Pemberton to J. H. Hammond, December 21, 1846, James H. Hammond Papers, LC.

36. See Rawick, *From Sunup to Sundown*, p. 59. Blassingame, *The Slave Community*, pp. 161, 210.

37. George Skipwith to John Cocke, July 8, 1845, Cocke Papers, UVa.

38. Moses (written by Malicia White) to William Pettigrew, August 23, 1856, Pettigrew Family Papers, UNC.

39. J. Johnston to William Pettigrew, November 20, 1849, *ibid*.; see p. 274.

40. William Pettigrew to J. Johnston, December 24, 1849, *ibid*.

41. George Skipwith to John Cocke, August 12, 1847, Cocke Papers, Cocke Deposit, UVa.

42. George Skipwith to John Cocke, July 8, 1847, Cocke Papers, Cocke Deposit, UVa.

43. *Ibid.*

44. *Ibid.*

45. George Skipwith to John Cocke, November 18, 1847, Cocke Papers, Cocke Deposit, UVa.

46. George Skipwith to John Cocke, December 26, 1847.

47. George Skipwith to John Cocke, August 8, 1848.

48. George Skipwith to John Cocke, May 1, 1848.

49. *Ibid.*

50. George Skipwith to John Cocke, December 1, 1848.

51. Ed Tayloe to B. O. Tayloe, August 20, 1833, Tayloe Family Papers, UVa.

52. Simms, "The Loves of the Driver," p. 176.

53. Charles Cotesworth Pinckney Letter, 1803 listing of slaves, DU.

54. George Skipwith to John Cocke, December 1, 1848, Cocke Papers, Cocke Deposit, UVa.

55. *Ibid.*

56. George Skipwith to John Cocke, October 23, 1848, Cocke Papers, Cocke Deposit, UVa.

57. Haller Nutt to Alonzo Snyder, December 15, 1844, Alonzo Snyder Papers, LSU. Gillespie had apparently killed two or three other slaves as well.

58. Some of the slave narratives indicates that many drivers held their positions for life.

59. R. K. Cralle to Dr. John J. Cabell, September 11, 1831, Cabell Family, HU.

60. *Ibid.*

7. THE SHADOW OF THE SLAVE QUARTERS

1. Fisk University, *God Struck Me Dead*, p. 170. Also see the description on pp. 23-24 above.

2. *Narrative of James Williams*, p. 45.

3. James Curtis Ballagh, *A History of Slavery in Virginia* (Baltimore: John Hopkins University Press, 1902), p. 107.

4. Hall, *Travels in North America*, II, 216. See also Rawick, *From Sundown to Sunup*.

5. Robert Carter to Samuel Shoughan, July 6, 1787, The Carter Family Papers, VSL.

6. D. N. Moxley to G. N. Jones, October 21, 1854, in U. B. Phillips and James D. Glunt, *Florida Plantation Records from the Papers of George Noble Jones* (St. Louis: Missouri Historical Society, 1927).

7. Moxley to Jones, October 18, 1854, in Phillips and Glunt, *op. cit.*, p. 111.

8. Susanna Warfield Diary, entry for February 5, 1849, MHS.

9. Joseph Taper to Joseph Long, November 11, 1840. Joseph Long Papers, DU.

10. William Wells Brown, *My Southern Home; or, The South and Its People* (3rd ed.; Boston: A. G. Brown & Co., 1882), p. 70.

11. See Melville J. Herskovits, *The Myth of the Negro Past* (Boston: Beacon Press, 1958 [1941]), p. 238; Fisk University, *God Struck Me Dead*, p. 171.

12. Ball, *Narrative*, p. 201.

13. J. K[innard], Jr., "Who Are Our National Poets?" in Bruce Jackson, ed., *The Negro and his Folklore in Nineteenth Century Periodicals* (Austin: University of Texas Press, 1967), pp. 23-34.

14. Fisk University, *Unwritten History of Slavery*, pp. 216-17.

15. Katharine Jocher and Guy B. Johnson *et al.*, eds., *Folk, Region and Society: Selected Papers of Howard W. Odum* (Chapel Hill: University of North Carolina Press, 1964), p. 7.

16. We can perhaps uncover more of the details of the domestic slave trade by investigating the similar themes in slave folklore and how they were transported from region to region in the South.

17. Christensen, *Afro-American Folklore*, pp. 26-36.

18. *Ibid.*, p. 9.

19. J. Mason Brewer, *American Negro Folklore* (Chicago: Quadrangle Books, 1968), pp. 316, 320, 322.

20. *Ibid.*, pp. 314, 322.

21. *Ibid.*, p. 314.

22. John Parker Manuscript, DU.

23. Christensen, *Afro-American Folklore*, p. 3.

24. Richard M. Dorson, *American Folklore* (Chicago: The University of Chicago Press, 1971 [1959]), p. 186. See also Dorson, *American Negro Folktales* (Greenwich, Conn.: Fawcett Publications, Inc., 1967 [1956]). See parallels in Harry M. Hyatt, ed., *Hoodoo-Conjuration-Witchcraft-Rootwork* (2 vols.; Hannibal, Mo.: Western Publishing, 1970).

25. Christensen, *Afro-American Folklore*, p. 14.

26. Priscilla Bond Diary, entry for January 6, 1862, LSU.

27. *Ibid.*

28. His nephew to Tomas Davis, October 24, 1841, James A. Gillespie and Family Papers, LSU.

29. William B. Smith, "The Persimmon Tree and the Beer Dance," in Jackson, ed., *The Negro and His Folklore*, pp. 3-9.

30. Randolph, *From Slave Cabin to Pulpit*, p. 191.

31. See Richard Wade, *Slavery in the Cities: The South, 1820-1860* (New

York: Oxford University Press, 1964), pp. 59-60. The parallel with ghettoes seems difficult to escape.

32. *Ibid.*, p. 108.

33. Slavery Papers, James Mc Bride oath, November 7, 1795, SCHC.

34. Harriet Jacobs, *Incidents in the Life of a Slave Girl* (Boston: Published by the author, 1861), p. 109.

35. P. H. Pitts Diary and Account Book, entry for May 6, 1860, UNC.

36. Slave Autobiography Manuscript, p. 9, Slavery Papers, LC.

37. See Jordan, *White Over Black*, for a thorough discussion of these dilemmas.

38. John Cocke Journal, p. 72. UVa.

39. *Ibid.*, p. 74.

40. Joseph Jones to his parents, April 23, 1859, Joseph Jones Papers, Tul.

41. John Cocke Journal, p. 72. UVa.

42. William Martin Journal, entry for January 27, 1859, SC.

43. John Cocke Journal, pp. 72-73, UVa.

44. Rev. Richard Fuller and Rev. Francis Wayland, *Domestic Slavery Considered as a Scriptural Institution* (New York: Lewis Colby, 1845), p. 146.

45. See Donald G. Mathews, "The Methodist Mission to the Slaves," *Journal of American History*, LI (March 1965), 615-33.

46. Fedric, *Slave Life in Virginia and Kentucky*, p. 5.

47. Flat River Primitive Baptist Church Records, July, 1803, UNC.

48. Globe Baptist Church Records, UNC.

49. John Fort, Jr., to Hugh Brown, June 26, 1821, Neill Brown Papers, DU.

50. Kate Crosland to Nellie [her] sister, July 16, 1861, Thomas M. McIntosh Papers, DU.

51. Louis Hughes, *Thirty Years a Slave* (Milwaukee, Wis.: South Side Printing Company, 1897), p. 90.

52. W. M. Kenney to John Mc Donogh, March 10, 1835, John Mc Donogh Papers, LSU.

53. Degler, *Neither Black nor White*, pp. 33-39, argues that the Catholic cushion was not as substantial as previously believed.

54. Thomas Hamilton, *Men and Manners in America* (Philadelphia: Carey, Lea & Blanchard, 1833), p. 108. See also Joe Gray Taylor, *Negro Slavery in Louisiana* (Baton Rouge: Louisiana Historical Association, 1963).

55. John Cocke Journal, UVa. See James Hervey Greenlee Diary, I, entry for Dec. 31, 1848, UNC.

56. James Hervey Greenlee Diary, I, entry for July 2, 1848, UNC.

57. Zion Church and Frierson Settlement in Maury County, Tennessee, January meeting, 1850, UNC. That some slaves were Muslims is well known; the number that were cannot be estimated but does not appear to have been

very large. However, there is an occasional reference to them by slaves and masters. See Ball, *Narrative*, p. 165. Ball further writes about slaves at large that "Christianity cannot be, with propriety, called the religion of these peoples."

58. Olmsted, *A Journey in the Seaboard Slave States*, II, p. 81.

59. *De Bow's Review*, XXIX (1860), 364.

60. Flat River Primitive Baptist Church Records, July, 1820, UNC.

61. Samuel A. Agnew Diary, entry for September 9, 1854, UNC.

62. Ebenezer Davies, *American Scenes, and Christian Slavery* (London: John Snow, 1849), p. 198.

63. Rawick, ed., *Maryland Narratives*, p. 61.

64. Fisk University, *God Struck Me Dead*, p. 172.

65. Brown-Hunter Manuscript Diary, entry for December 17, 1843, UVa.

66. James L. Smith, *Autobiography of James L. Smith* (Norwich, Conn., 1881), p. 27.

67. This was a common practice in the Old South. See Clarissa E. Leavitt Town Diary, entry for March 27, 1853, LSU.

68. Fisk University, *God Struck Me Dead*, pp. 171-72.

69. Letter to General Harding, March 22, 1850, Harding-Jackson Papers, UNC.

70. Jones, *The Religious Instruction of the Negroes*, p. 128. See further Rawick, ed., *Maryland Narratives*, p. 33.

71. See Lionel H. Kennedy and Thomas Parker, *An Official Report of the Trials*. Vesey was a very influential "significant other" to many blacks who came in contact with him.

72. Zephonia Kingsley, *A Treatise on the Patriarchal, or Co-operative System of Society*, p. 15.

73. Rawick, ed., *Kentucky Narratives*, pp. 121-23, my italics.

74. Slave Autobiography Manuscript, Slavery Papers, LC. Marx, *Protest and Prejudice*, p. 97, emphasizes in contrast that the "quietistic consequences of religion are all too well known."

75. B. A. Botkin, "Folk and Folklore," in W. T. Couch, ed., *Culture in the South* (Chapel Hill: The University of North Carolina Press, 1935), pp. 570-93. See the familiar account in Frederick Douglass, *Life and Times*, pp. 137-39. See also Daniel Whitehurst to J. H. Hammond, June 4, 1830, Hammond Papers, LC. While on the Rio Nunez in West Africa, Whitehurst observed similarly, "Here, in this river, charms and incantations are supposed to produce good and evil, and it is rare indeed to find a negro, without something on his person, supposed capable of producing the desired benefit, [f]or removing the dreaded danger. . . ."

76. See the "Autobiography of Omar ibn Seid, Slave in North Carolina, 1831," *American Historical Review*, XXX (July, 1925), 791-95. Omar later became a Christian but still clung to many of his Muslim practices.

77. Feldstein, *Once A Slave*, pp. 67-80.

78. Penelope Hamilton to William S. Hamilton, July 19, 1851, William S. Hamilton Papers, LSU. John L. Manning to his wife, March 26, 1851, William-Chestnut-Manning Papers, SC, notes William and Maria, whose "air of mock submission and Christian resignation" merely served to mask a "fondness for liquer, pilfering, and palavering. . . ."

79. Henry Turner to General Quitman, October 26, 1843, Quitman Papers, UNC. See further Vincent Harding, "Religion and Resistance among Ante-bellum Negroes, 1800-1860" in *The Making of Black America*, ed. August Meier and Elliott Rudwick, I, 179-97. Harding sees religion as a prime stimulus to slave resistance.

80. Olmsted, *Back Country*, I, 188.

81. Caroline Gilman, *Recollections of a Southern Matron* (New York: Harper & Brothers, 1838), p. 81.

82. See Miles Mark Fisher, *Negro Slave Songs in the United States* (Ithaca, N.Y.: Cornell University Press, 1953), p. 83.

83. Gilman, *Recollections*, p. 81.

84. W. W. Mc Donogh to John Mc Donogh, December 28, 1845, John Mc Donogh Papers, LSU.

85. See Newbell Niles Puckett, *Folk Beliefs of the Southern Negro* (Chapel Hill: The University of North Carolina Press, 1926), p. 291.

86. Margaret Devereux, *Plantation Sketches* (Cambridge, Mass.: The Riverside Press, 1906), p. 32.

87. Charles Manigault to Louis Manigault, April 9, 1857, Louis Manigault Papers, DU.

88. See Sterling Stuckey, "Through the Prism of Folklore: The Black Ethos in Slavery," in *The Debate Over Slavery*, ed. Ann J. Lane, pp. 245-68.

8. THE RHYTHM OF CULTURE

1. Fisk University, *God Struck Me Dead*, p. 174.

2. Fisk University, *Unwritten History of Slavery*, p. 201. The first collection of slaves' songs was William Francis Allen *et al.*, eds., *Slave Songs of the United States* (New York: A. Simpson & Co., 1867). See also Bernard Katz, ed., *The Social Implications of Early Negro Music in the United States* (New York: Arno Press, 1969); Maud Cuney-Hare, *Negro Musicians and Their Music* (Washington, D.C.: The Associated Publishers, Inc., 1936); and Lydia Parrish, *Slave Songs of the Georgia Sea Islands* (Hatboro, Pa.: Folklore Associates, Inc., 1965 [1942]).

3. Albert Bushnell Hart, *Slavery and Abolition, 1831-1841* (New York: Harper & Brothers, 1906), p. 95.

4. De Bow, *The Industrial Resources*, II, 315.

5. John Berkley Grimball Diary, Vol. I, entry for August 2, 1835, UNC.

6. Eliza L. Magruder Diary, entry for December 18, 1849, LSU.

7. Andrews, *Reminiscences*, p. 74.

8. See Marvin Harris, "The Myth of the Friendly Master," in *The Debate Over Slavery*, ed. Ann Lane, pp. 191-209.

9. Andrews, *Reminiscences*, p. 76.

10. See Harold Courlander, *Negro Folk Music, U.S.A.* (New York: Columbia University Press, 1963), *Negro Songs From Alabama* (New York: published with the assistance of the Wenner-Gren Foundation for Anthropological Research, 1960), and *The Drum and the Hoe: Life and Lore of the Haitian People* (Berkeley: University of California Press, 1960).

11. Jeanette Robinson Murphy, *Southern Thoughts for Northern Thinkers* (New York: The Bandanna Publishing Company, 1904), p. 9.

12. See Harold Courlander, *The African* (New York: Crown Publishers, 1967).

13. The same is true of twentieth-century jazz, a highly individualistic art form, proclaimed to be America's only original contribution to the world of music. There is dispute over the exact stages of its development but not over its black origins. See Eileen Southern, *The Music of Black Americans: A History* (New York: W. W. Norton & Co., 1971), pp. 310-409.

14. Letter dated November 7, 1856, Williams-Chestnut-Manning Papers, SC.

15. Rawick, ed., *Maryland Narratives*, p. 33.

16. [Manning] letter dated November 7, 1856, Williams-Chestnut-Manning Papers, SC.

17. *Ibid.*

18. *Ibid.*

19. *Ibid.*

20. The minstrel tradition extends at least into medieval times when musicians traveled about singing and reciting poetry. Slaves in the American setting gave similar performances based in part on both their African and American heritages. In the first half of the nineteenth century Edwin P. Christy, a white man, sometimes known as the father of American minstrelsy, is said to have set up the first blackface minstrel group. This claim has come under some debate, for clearly slave minstrels performed in plantation neighborhoods even before Christy's time. Later well-known black-face performances by whites often mocked black life, and although some of the tunes Christy collected in *Christy's Plantation Melodies* (Philadelphia: Fisher & Brother, 1851) show black influence, we cannot however be certain if the specific songs were created by slaves.

21. Douglass, *Life and Times*, p. 55.

22. Kemble, *Journal of a Residence*, p. 164.

23. See the valuable collection of slave songs in William Francis Allen, *Slave Songs of the United States*.

24. Miles Mark Fisher, *Negro Slave Songs in the United States* (Ithaca, N.Y.: Cornell University Press, 1953), p. 80.

25. Sterling Brown, "Negro Folk Expression: Spirituals, Seculars, Ballads and Work Songs," *Phylon*, XIV (March, 1953), 47.

26. Antonín Dvořák, "Music in America," *Harper's New Monthly Magazine*, XC (February, 1895), 429-34.

27. *Ibid.*

28. Joseph Jones to [C. C. Jones], March 6, 1859, Joseph Jones Papers, Tul.

29. J. W. Work, *American Negro Songs and Spirituals* (New York: Crown Publishers, 1940), p. 189.

30. Edward Pollard, *Black Diamonds Gathered in the Darkey Homes of the South* (New York: Pudney & Russell, 1859), p. 36. Also noticeable in some of the slave's songs and in his regular manner of speaking was a distinctive speech pattern which appears to have had implications for his identity. It served to camouflage many of the slave's real feelings, but more than this seems to have underscored a fundamental pride in his blackness. Even today a black man can frequently pick out another black man—when he cannot see him—by the sound of his voice. A lack of education is no adequate explanation for the persistence of a slave (black) patois which was distinct from white modes of speech. One planter wrote, "he has never learned to talk plain." See Tom Lenoir to Thomas Lenoir, November 18, 1861, Lenoir Family Papers, UNC. The relationship of this patois to slave personality appears to have been close. See as well James Weldon Johnson, ed., *The Book of American Negro Spirituals* (New York: The Viking Press, 1925), for some of the songs and the experience they relate.

31. "Negro Spirituals," *The Atlantic Monthly*, XIX (June, 1867), 685.

32. *Ibid.*, 693. "These quaint religious songs were to men more than a source of relaxation; they were a stimulus to courage and a tie to heaven."

33. Fisk University, *God Struck Me Dead*, p. 172.

34. Henry Watson to Theodore Watson, November 7, 1834, Henry Watson, Jr., Papers, DU; *De Bow's Review*, XXIX (1860), 366: "As he weeds his row in the field, or follows the plough, the negro's voice may often be heard: 'I have some hopes up yonder!' "

35. Abigail Mott, *Biographical Sketches and Interesting Anecdotes of Persons of Color* (New York: Trustees of the Residing Estate of Lindly and Murray, 1839), p. 249.

36. M. B. Pettigrew to J. Johnston, June 19, 1845, Pettigrew Papers, UNC.

37. Henry Watson to Theodore Watson, November 7, 1834, Henry Watson, Jr., Papers, DU.

38. *Ibid.*

39. Martin R. Delany, *Blake: or The Huts of America* (Boston: Beacon Press, 1970 [1859]), p. 100. Mrs. Trollope, *Domestic Manners of the Americans* (London: printed for Whitaker, Treacher, and Co., 1832), p. 28, observed that "Negro boatmen regulate and beguile their labour on the river; it consists but of very few notes, but they are sweetly harmonious. . . ."

40. Lawrence Levine, "Slave Songs and Slave Consciousness: An Exploration in Neglected Sources," in *The National Temper*, eds. Lawrence Levine and Robert Middlekauff (2d ed.; 2 vols.; New York: Harcourt Brace Jovanovich, 1972), I, 186-200, makes a good case for this articulation. See as well Jesse Lemisch, "Listening to the 'Inarticulate': William Widger's Dream and the Loyalties of American Revolutionary Seamen in British Prisons," *Journal of Social History*, III (Fall, 1969).

41. Rawick, ed., *Maryland Narratives*, p. 33.

42. R. D. Laing, *Self and Others* (Baltimore: Penguin Books, 1971), p. 162, briefly discusses this matter.

43. M. C. Shaffer to Misters Preston and Manning, January 30, 1844, Williams-Chestnut-Manning Papers, SC.

44. See Gordon W. Allport, *Personality and Social Encounter* (Boston: Beacon Press, 1960), and R. S. Woodworth, *Dynamics of Behavior* (New York: Holt, 1958).

45. William C. Nell, *The Colored Patriots of the American Revolution* (Boston: Robert F. Wallcut, 1855), p. 249.

46. William Wells Brown, *Narrative*, p. 20.

47. Allport, *Personality and Social Encounter*, pp. 295-310.

48. Stuckey, "Through the Prism of Folklore," p. 263.

49. Allport, *Personality and Social Encounter*, p. 299.

50. Olmsted, *A Journey in the Seaboard Slave States*, II, 94.

51. Hall, *Travels*, II, 214. Captain Hall observed at the end of the 1820's that "all the blacksmiths' and carpenters' work, for example, was done by the slaves of each plantation; nor did it appear from all I could learn, that there was any deficiency of intellect in the negro, so far as these mechanical operations went."

52. C. G. Memminger to [Hammond], April 28, 1849, James H. Hammond Papers, LC.

53. Olmsted, *Back Country*, I, p. 80.

54. Kellar, ed., *Solon Robinson*, I, 461.

55. W. Pettigrew to J. J. Pettigrew, September 27, 1849, Pettigrew Family Papers, UNC.

56. Rawick, ed., *Maryland Narratives*, p. 20.

57. U. B. Phillips, *Documents*, I, John Lamar to Howell Calb, February 17, 1845, 171-72.

58. *Southern Literary Messenger*, III (1837) 646n.

59. W.P.A., *Alabama: A Guide to the Deep South* (New York: R. R. Smith, 1941), p. 149.

60. W.P.A., *Louisiana: A Guide to the State* (Boston: Houghton Mifflin Co., 1945), p. 176.

61. James Porter, *Modern Negro Art* (New York: The Dryden Press, 1943), p. 26.

62. J. W. C. Pennington, *The Fugitive Blacksmith* (London: Charles Gilpin, 1850), p. 8.

63. Hand & Co. to J. R. Liddell, September 11, 1856, John R. Moses Liddell and Family Papers, LSU.

64. John Parker Manuscript, p. 35, DU.

9. A FAMILY FOLK

1. See E. Franklin Frazier, *The Free Negro Family: A Study of Family Origins Before the Civil War* (Nashville: Fisk University Press, 1932); Jessie Bernard, *Marriage and Family Among Negroes* (Englewood Cliffs, N.J.: Prentice-Hall, 1966); Daniel P. Moynihan, "The Negro Family: The Case for National Action," in Peter I. Rose, ed., *Americans from Africa: Slavery and Its Aftermath* (Chicago: Aldine-Atherton, 1970), pp. 357-415; Lorenzo J. Greene, *The Negro in Colonial New England, 1620-1776* (New York: Columbia University Press, 1942).

2. Baudin to John McDonogh, December 19, 1820, John McDonogh Papers, LSU. See also Battle to Lucy, Dec. 18, 1859, Battle Family Papers, UNC.

3. Ulrich B. Phillips, "Racial Problems, Adjustments and Disturbances," in *The Slave Economy of the Old South: Selected Essays in Economic and Social History*, ed. Eugene D. Genovese (Baton Rouge: Louisiana State University Press, 1968), p. 43; see also letter to Lucy Battle, December 8, 1859, Battle Family Papers, UNC.

4. Botkin, ed., *Lay My Burden Down*, p. 156.

5. The trade continued illegally down to the Civil War. See Philip D. Curtin, *The Atlantic Slave Trade: A Census* (Madison: The University of Wisconsin Press, 1969), p. 234. Curtin estimates that the number of slaves imported from Africa after 1808 was under 55,000.

6. William B. Hamilton to William S. Hamilton, August 6, 1857, William S. Hamilton Papers, LSU.

7. William M. Waller to Jane H. Garland, February 17, 1848, David Garland Waller Papers, DU.

8. M. W. Jackson to Dr. Thomas H. Clagett, December 20, 1841, Thomas H. Clagett Papers, UVa.

9. George Tucker, *The Valley of Shenandoah* (2 vols.; Chapel Hill: University of North Carolina Press, 1970 [1824]), II, 206.

10. Lewis Stirling to Lewis Wakefield, June 10, 1843, William Terry and Family Papers, LSU.

11. See Frederic Bancroft, *Slave-Trading in the Old South* (Baltimore: J. H. Furst Company, 1931), Chapters I-III.

12. *Ibid.*, p. 208; George Lumpkin to Mr. Middleton Pope, January 23, 1844, R. R. Barrow Journal, UNC.

13. Pulliam and Slade of Richmond to James Brady, October 30, 1850, Harris-Brady Collection, UVa. Another item in this same collection, dated June 23, 1846, reads as follows: "No. 1 little girls 4 feet 5 to 7 inches high $275 to $300 very superior $325 to $350 and upwards according to make, countenance, intelligence & c All ungrown females in some ratio—Likely and well made boys 4 feet 9 and 10 inches $375 to $450. There will be this difference in the price of boys of same height owing to difference to countenance, make intelligence & c. . . . Likely women with either few or many children will sell as readily as any. . . ."

14. Drew, *The Refugee*, p. 187. Fogel and Engerman, *Time on the Cross*, pp. 44-52, argue that the domestic trade did not tear apart as many families as formerly thought, but the census evidence they use is not complete enough to support fully their argument.

15. Douglass, *Narrative of the Life of Frederick Douglass, An American Slave*, ed. Benjamin Quarles (Cambridge, Massachusetts: Harvard University Press, 1960), pp. 24-25.

16. "Negro speculation" was the standard expression used to describe investment in human property; see Hugh L. Clay to his sister Virginia C. (Tunstall) Clay, February 11, 1854, C. C. Clay Papers, DU.

17. W. A. L. [Wm. Lenoir] to his grandfather, Oct. 16, 1835, Lenoir Papers, UNC. Fogel and Engerman, *Time on the Cross*, pp. 78-86, argue that slave breeding was a myth, but their conclusion is not very convincing when viewed against such statements as this. See also Richard Sutch, "The Breeding of slaves for sale and the Westward Expansion of Slavery, 1850-1860," in *Race and Slavery in the Western Hemisphere: Quantitative Studies*, eds. Stanley L. Engerman and Eugene Genovese (Princeton, N.J.: Princeton University Press, 1975), 173-210.

18. Dr. James Marion Sims to his wife Theresa, December 29, 1859, James Marion Sims Papers, UNC.

19. Lysie to Sarah Lenoir, January 17, 1847, Lenoir Papers, UNC; William M. Waller to Sarah Waller, January 3, 1848, William Macon Waller Papers, VHS.

20. John W. Abraham to James Brady, July 20, 1852, Harris-Brady Collection, UVa.

21. Rawick, ed., *Missouri Narratives*, p. 294. The slave-holder Edwin

Torry stated, "it is my opinion that the best time for a southern man to purchase is in the winter after the traders have left." Torry to Samuel O. Wood, December 19, 1851, Samuel O. Wood Letters and Papers, DU.

22. James Redpath, *The Roving Editor: or, Talks with Slaves in the Southern States* (New York: A. B. Burdick, Publisher, 1859), p. 48.

23. J. H. Taylor to Franklin H. Elmore, January 30, 1836, Franklin H. Elmore Papers, LC.

24. John Parker Manuscript, DU.

25. Mortimer Thomson, *What Became of the Slaves on a Georgia Plantation?* (n.p., 1863), p. 7.

26. Ebenezer Davies, *American Scenes, and Christian Slavery: A Recent Tour of Four Thousand Miles in the United States* (London: John Snow, 1849), p. 54.

27. Hamilton, *Men and Manners in America*, p. 111.

28. Clement Eaton, *The Growth of Southern Civilization, 1790-1860* (New York: Harper & Row, 1961), p. 50.

29. Hall, *Travels in North America*, I, 210.

30. Samuel Rankin Latta Journal, entry for December 30, 1850, Tul.

31. This was a widespread attitude of the times.

32. John Parker Manuscript, DU.

33. *Narrative of William Hayden* (Cincinnati, Ohio: Published for the author, 1846), p. 79.

34. Edward S. Abdy, *Journal of a Residence and Tour of the United States of North America, from April, 1833 to October, 1834* (3 vols.; London: John Murray, 1835), III, 350.

35. Mary Boykin Chesnut, *A Diary From Dixie* (New York: D. Appleton and Company, 1905), p. 13.

36. Colin Bishop to Wyatt Bishop, January 1, 1822, Clement Comer Clay Papers, DU.

37. Hall, *Travels in North America*, II, 192-93.

38. Marshall Hall, *The Two-Fold Slavery of the United States* (London: Adam Scott, 1854), p. 146.

39. Northrup, *Twelve Years a Slave*, p. 78.

40. William M. Waller to David G. Waller, October 19, 1847, David Garland Waller Papers, DU.

41. The Harris-Brady Collection, UVa., has very good information on the mechanics of the trade, with discussions about the value of slaves in the upper and lower South and estimates of the number of slaves that might perish in transit. Several of its letters are of interest too because they give the researcher a good feeling for the chattel aspect of human property.

42. Robert Applegate, printed notice on a slave auction in 1857, Slavery Papers, LC.

43. Hall, *Travels in North America*, I, 207.

44. John Parker Manuscript, DU.

45. Phillips, "Racial Problems, Adjustments and Disturbances in the Ante-bellum South," p. 220.

46. Her husband to Elisa Gibson, April 9, 1810, Grundy-Gibson Papers, MHS.

47. Moynihan, "The Negro Family," p. 363, writes accurately in this instance that "the role of the family in shaping character and ability is so pervasive as to be easily overlooked. . . . By and large, adult conduct in society is learned as a child."

48. See Ball, *Slavery in the United States*, p. 124, for a discussion of how such relationships might develop.

49. *African Repository*, XXXI (April, 1855), 118; see also Bobby Frank Jones, "A Cultural Middle Passage: Slave Marriage and Family in the Ante-Bellum South" (unpublished Ph.D. dissertation, University of North Carolina, 1965).

50. According to the slave narrators many slaves took such matters quite seriously.

51. Rawick, ed., *Florida Narratives*, p. 128.

52. *Narrative of James Williams, An American Slave, Who Was for Several Years a Driver on a Cotton Plantation in Alabama* (New York: The American Anti-Slavery Society, 1838), p. 33. For a marriage by a planter see the Francis Terry Leak Diary, entry for January 24, 1857, UNC.

53. Clarissa E. Leavitt Town Diary, entry for February 5, 1853, LSU.

54. This was not a typical practice, but occasionally it did occur, especially on the South Carolina Sea Islands.

55. Joseph Embrees to Henry Marston, August 10, 1861, Henry Marston Papers, LSU.

56. *Narrative of William Wells Brown*, pp. 213-14. On the feelings side, see Mother to Mary E. Baber, May 7, 1836, Baber-Blackshear Papers, UG.

57. James S. Buckingham, *The Slave States of America* (2 vols.; London: Fisher Son & Co., 1842), I, 236.

58. Ann Firor Scott, *The Southern Lady: From Pedestal to Politics, 1830-1930* (Chicago: University of Chicago Press, 1970), presents the plantation mistress' portrait in the opening chapters of her book. See further Charles Pettigrew to his wife Caroline, June 4, 1856, Pettigrew Family Papers, UNC. Charles praises Caroline for her "progress towards being an obedient and submissive wife. . . ."

59. Lucilla McCorkle Diary, entry for 1850, William Parsons McCorkle Papers, UNC.

60. Herskovits, *The Myth of the Negro Past*, p. 139, rightly observes, "It is far from certain that undisturbed matings have not been lost sight of in the appeal of the more dramatic separations . . ." initiated by the slave trade.

61. Frazier, *The Free Negro Family*, p. 47. See recent support of the matriarchal theme in Moynihan, "The Negro Family."

62. See, for example, Jacob D. Wheeler, *A Practical Treatise on the Law of Slavery* (New York: Allan Pollack, Jr., 1837), p. 183; W. L. Hargrove to L. Thompson, May 7, 1855, Lewis Thompson Papers, UNC.

63. See Austin Steward, *Twenty-two Years a Slave and Forty Years a Freeman* (Rochester, N.Y.: William Alling, 1857), p. 14.

64. Bertram Wilbur Doyle, *The Etiquette of Race Relations in the South: A Study in Social Control* (Chicago: The University of Chicago Press, 1937).

65. Fisk University, *God Struck Me Dead*, p. 204.

66. Bibb, *Narrative*, p. 73; John Hamilton to William B. Hamilton, June 21, 1857, William S. Hamilton Papers, LSU.

67. Feldstein, *Once A Slave*, pp. 128-34. Many masters worked men and women side by side, perhaps to stimulate male labor. See the "Plantation work" ledger, January, 1837, Louis Manigault Papers, DU.

68. *Southern Literary Messenger*, III (1837), 647.

69. T. H. Jones, *The Experience of Thomas Jones Who Was a Slave for Forty-Three Years*, Written by a Friend (Boston: D. Laing, Jr., 1850), p. 31.

70. Robert Carter to John Pound, March 16, 1779, Carter Family Papers, VSL.

71. J. Wimbish to Colonel Elisha Barksdale, November 30, 1847, Peter Barksdale Letters, DU.

72. Fedric, *Slave Life in Virginia and Kentucky*, p. 25.

73. Noah Davis, *A Narrative of the Life of Rev. Noah Davis, a Colored Man* (Baltimore: John F. Weishampel, Jr., 1859), p. 31.

74. Louise Chadbourne to her father (Gen. Quitman?), January 6, 1857, Quitman Papers, UNC.

75. Charles S. Ridgely to General William H. Marriott, March 25, 1827, Lloyd Papers, MHS.

76. Frazier, *The Free Negro Family*, p. 37; a cousin to Sarah Lenoir, June 16, 1849, Lenoir Family Papers, UNC.

77. Grandy, *Narrative*, p. 18; see Charles M. Harsh and H. G. Shrickel, *Personality: Development and Assessment* (New York: Ronald Press, 1959), especially the section "Stimulation," pp. 57-59.

78. Harsh and Shrickel, *Personality: Development and Assessment*, p. 135.

79. Pennington, *The Fugitive Blacksmith*, p. 2.

80. William Ethelbert Ervin Journal, entry for 1847, UNC.

81. *Ibid.*

82. Ball, *Narrative*, pp. 275, 192.

83. *Ibid.*, pp. 262-63.

84. *Ibid.*, p. 263.

85. Pennington, *The Fugitive Blacksmith*, pp. 8-9; Doyle, *The Etiquette*

of *Race Relations in the South*, pp. 79ff.; Herskovits, *The Myth of the Negro Past*, p. 161.

86. See Chapter 7.

87. Slave Autobiography Manuscript, Slavery Papers, LC.

88. *Annual Catalogue of the Medical Department . . . Missouri Session of 1847-1848*, p. 708.

89. Thomas R. R. Cobb, *An Historical Sketch of Slavery from the Earliest Periods* (Philadelphia: T. & J. W. Johnson and Co., 1858), pp. 202, 212.

90. Devereux, *Plantation Sketches*, p. 155.

91. See Mary Ellen Goodman, *Race Awareness in Young Children* (New York: Collier Books, 1952), p. 25.

92. Jones, *The Religious Instruction of the Negroes*, pp. 113-14.

93. R. Carter to Charles Haynir, April 21, 1784, Carter Family Papers, VSL.

94. Lewis W. Paine, *Six Years in a Georgia Prison* (New York: Printed for the author, 1851), p. 122. Compare Phillips, *American Negro Slavery*, p. 313. Phillips writes, "The lives of the whites and the blacks were partly segregate, partly intertwined. If any special link were needed, the children supplied it."

95. Fisk University, *God Struck Me Dead*, p. 104.

96. Rawick, ed., *Maryland Narratives*, p. 5.

97. Sir Charles Lyell, *Travels in North America, in the Years 1841-2* (2 vols.; New York: Wiley and Putnam, 1845), I, 24-25.

98. *Narrative of James Williams*, p. 28; see also Walter S. Harris (ex-slave) to Hiram M. Sherman, February 4, 1909, Harry M. Sherman Family Papers, UVa. Harris wrote, "Oh! you and I and my brother John played under that tree just at the breaking out of that cruel war." He was 13 or 14 at the time.

99. Dr. Daniel Drake's *Letters on Slavery to Dr. John C. Warren, of Boston*, Let. I. He adds, "I am bound in truth and candor, to express the belief that the first eight or ten years of life are more joyous among the negroes of the south than among the people of the north."

100. See, for example, Douglass, *Life and Times of Frederick Douglass*; Benjamin Drew, ed., *North-Side View of Slavery: The Refugees, or Narratives of Fugitive Slaves in Canada* (Boston: J. P. Jewett and Co., 1856); also Doyle, *The Etiquette of Race Relations in the South*; Fisk University, *God Struck Me Dead*, p. 170.

101. Cobb, *An Historical Sketch of Slavery*, p. 220.

102. Charles Manigault to Louis Manigault, February 21, 1856, Louis Manigault Papers, DU.

103. *Southern Agriculturist*, IV (1831), p. 215.

104. William C. Emerson, *Stories and Spirituals of the Negro Slave* (Boston: The Gorham Press, 1930), p. 23; Rawick, ed., *Maryland Narratives*,

p. 29. Ex-slave Rev. Silas Jackson observed, "We all had task work to do—men, women and boys."

105. Lucy Battle to her husband, March 13, 1860, Battle Family Papers, UNC.

106. Starobin, *Industrial Slavery in the Old South*, p. 164; Farm Journal of Nicholas B. Massenburg, entry for February 14, 1842, UNC; Caleb Coker Plantation Book, entry for June 21, 1859, SC.

107. Alexander Robinson Boteler Diary, entry for August 29, 1845, DU.

108. See Harry Stack Sullivan, *Conceptions of Modern Psychiatry* (Washington: William Alanson White Psychiatric Foundation, 1947); see too Rachael O'Conner to Frances Weeks, October 2, 1840, David Weeks and Family Collection, DU.

109. John McDonogh to James Porter, September 3, 1829, John Mc Donogh Papers, LSU.

110. Contract, April 1, 1857, between M. C. Gary and Hill Carter, Carter Family Papers, VSL.

111. Bibb, *Narrative*, p. 65.

112. Contract, 1815, Cabell Family Papers, HL.

113. Rawick, ed., *Maryland Narratives*, p. 52.

114. Bruce, *The New Life*, p. 18.

115. Grandy, *Narrative*, p. 50; Mr. Haynes to Charles Manigault, October 25, 1847, Louis Manigault Papers, DU.

116. Fisk University, *God Struck Me Dead*, p. 171.

117. Tho. H. Ellis to Toles Hooke, February 28, 1849, Slavery Papers, LC.

118. R. Carter to Samuel Carter, March 10, 1781, Carter Family Papers, VSL.

119. Thomas Massie to William H. Hatchett, December 15, 1845, William H. Hatchett Papers, DU.

120. Davis, *Narrative*, p. 10.

121. See Doyle, *The Etiquette of Race Relations*, p. 16.

122. Pennington, *The Fugitive Blacksmith*, pp. 7-9. See also Walter S. Harris to Hiram M. Sherman, August 13, 1910, Sherman Family Papers, UVa.

123. Booker T. Washington, *Up From Slavery: An Autobiography* (Boston: Houghton Mifflin Company, 1901), p. 112, observed sixteen years after the Civil War (1881) that the pattern continued in Alabama: ". . . as a rule the whole family slept in one room, and that in addition to the immediate family there sometimes were relatives, or others not related to the family, who slept in the same room."

124. R. Carter to Clement Brooke, July 27, 1778, Carter Family Papers, VSL.

125. Wyse, *America: Its Realities and Resources*, p. 65, writes that "posi-

tive and unusual incentives are invariably presented to the white male by the [female] slave proprietary. . . ."

126. Lyell, *Travels in North America*, I, 169, 170.

127. See Rawick, ed., *The American Slave*.

128. Executive Papers, Archives of Virginia, Letters Received January 12, 1801, as quoted in James Hugh Johnston, *Race Relations in Virigina & Miscegenation in the South*, 1776-1860 (Amherst: University of Massachusetts Press, 1970), pp. 305-6. The planter Haller Nutt warned his overseer to avoid relations with "negro women." "It breeds . . . trouble and . . . neglect. . . ." Haller Nutt Journal, Rule 11, DU.

129. *Ibid.*, pp. 306-7.

130. See Hardy Hardison to William Pettigrew, February 11, 1858, Pettigrew Family Papers, UNC, for an account of a slave who helped kill a master who did not want him to take a wife off the plantation.

131. Ball *Narrative*, pp. 18-19.

10. *THIS PROPERTY IS CONDEMNED*

1. Ralph Ellison, *Invisible Man* (New York: Vintage Books, 1972 [1952]), p. 3.

2. Phillips, *Life and Labor in the Old South*, p. 194.

3. James S. Buckingham, *The Slave States of America* (2 vols.; London: Fisher Son & Co., 1842), I, 87-88. Cf. Charles W. Chesnutt, *The Marrow of Tradition* (Ann Arbor: The University of Michigan Press, 1969 [1901]), p. 142, for a literary treatment of a similar theme.

4. Key interpretations can be followed in Phillips, *American Negro Slavery*, Stampp, *The Peculiar Institution*, and Elkins, *Slavery*.

5. In the past few years Blassingame, *The Slave Community*, Rawick, *From Sundown to Sunup*, and Genovese, *Roll, Jordan, Roll*, have utilized valuable evidence supporting vastly different conceptions of slaves.

6. David Gavin Diary, I, entry for July 5, 1860, UNC.

7. Edmund Ruffin to James H. Hammond, December 8, 1853, James H. Hammond Papers, LC.

8. Elkins, *Slavery*, p. 117, argues that slaves primarily identified with masters. It is clear now that this argument cannot be substantiated. It tends to ignore too many of slavery's realities.

9. John Walker Diary, II, entries for June 5, 1833, and May 21, 1835, UNC.

10. Ball, *Slavery in the United States*, p. 235.

11. Northup, *Twelve Years a Slave*, p. 153.

12. *Ibid.*

13. Douglass, *Life and Times*, p. 52; see also Theodore Brantner Wilson, *The Black Codes of the South* (University, Ala.: University of Alabama Press, 1965), pp. 13-41.

14. Douglass, *Life and Times, passim.*

15. Elkins, "Slavery and Ideology," in *The Debate over Slavery*, ed. Ann Lane, p. 354.

16. Haller Nutt to Alonzo Snyder, April 30, 1844, Alonzo Snyder Papers, LSU.

17. John Parker Manuscript, DU.

18. Susanna Warfield Diary, entry for July 9, 1849, MHS.

19. Clotilde Bornet to John McDonogh, February 14, 1846, John Mc Donogh Papers, LSU.

20. Tho. O. Moore to Lewis Thompson, January 3, 1852, Lewis Thompson Papers, UNC. See my discussion of acclimation in Chapter 2.

21. Ball, *Slavery in the United States*, pp. 189-90; Douglass, *Life and Times*, p. 41.

22. Ball, *Slavery in the United States*, p. 190.

23. The slave narratives overwhelmingly make this point.

24. Henry Turner to Jno. A. Quitman, October 26, 1843, Quitman Papers, UNC.

25. Ball, *Slavery in the United States*, p. 235.

26. W. L. Hargrove to Lewis Thompson, May 7, 1855, Lewis Thompson Papers, UNC.

Index

OXFORD

"*This Species of Property* is a major work because of its unprecedented use of plantation records to augment ex-slave autobiographies and narratives. . . . [It] establishes Leslie Howard Owens as a major historian of Afro-American slavery."

Al-Tony Gilmore in **The New Republic**

"Owens . . . has very much deepened the study of the slave community. . . . This book breaks new ground. Owens is a very good writer who organizes his material skillfully and cleanly."

Freedomways

"In some areas of analysis *This Species of Property* provides a fuller description of slave life than can be found elsewhere. Both the second chapter—'Into the Fields: Life, Disease, and Labor in the Old South'—and the third—'Blackstrap Molasses and Cornbread: Diet and Its Impact on Behavior'—are significant expansions of existing knowledge on these topics."

Ronald M. Johnson in **The Journal of Southern History**

"Owens may be said to have accomplished his task with distinction. He has conveyed a mood, enhancing our understanding of slavery by citing evidence to correct some common misimpressions. The book is likely to become widely discussed by historians while serving as a valuable essay on the topic for the general reader."

Neil Thorburn in **History**

"A sensitive and useful study. Its appearance is another welcome indication that the slaves rather than their owners are now holding the center of the historiographical stage."

John Howard in **The Times Literary Supplement** (London)

Leslie Howard Owens is Director of the Africana Studies Program at the State University of New York at Stony Brook. He was formerly Associate Professor of History at the University of Michigan, Ann Arbor.

Oxford Paperbacks
Oxford University Press • New York
$9.95

ISBN 0-19-502245-9